The enduring memory

To the inhabitants of Minot whose patience
and trust enabled me to write this book

Françoise Zonabend

The enduring memory

Time and history in a French village

Translated by Anthony Forster

Manchester University Press

Copyright © Manchester University Press 1984

Published by
Manchester University Press
Oxford Road, Manchester, M13 9PL, U.K.
51 Washington Street, Dover, N.H. 03820, U.S.A.

First published in French by
Presses Universitaires de France, 1980

French edition © 1980 Presses Universitaires de France

This translation © Manchester University Press 1984

British Library cataloguing in publication data
Zonabend, Françoise
  The enduring memory.
  1. Villages – France – History – 20th century 2. France –
Social life and customs – 20th century
  I. Title II. La mémoire longue, *English*
944'.009'734   DC415

Library of Congress cataloging in publication data

ISBN 0–7190–1781–5

Filmset by J & L Composition Ltd,
Filey, North Yorkshire, England
Printed in Great Britain by
Butler & Tanner Ltd, Frome and London

Contents

Preface

Part I *The time of the community*   1

The enduring memory   2

The village: yesterday and today   5

1 *Daily living*   10

   A house to dwell in   10
   Gardens to tend   23
   Ways of living   36
   The art of exchange   46

2 *Time of life*   57

   The world of childhood   57
      The ceremonial of admittance   58
      In the old days   61
      At present   74
   The days of youth   80
   From dances to marriage   87
      Courting   87
      'Walking out'   93
      Hitches and disasters 95
      The marriage proposal 102
      Engagement   102
      Silence and noise   109
   Men and women   115
      Mothers-in-law/daughters-in-law   115
      Husband and wife   120
      The 'drinking party'   120
   Epilogue   132
      Life   132
      Death   135

3   *The link of time*   138

Part II   *The time of the family*   141

1   *A lifetime*   143
    'Talking family'   144
    The role of the maternal side   150
    At the *Maison-Dieu*   155
      Rules and practices   162
      The trip to Lourdes   165
      The golden wedding   167
2   *Breaks and continuities*   173
    A line of small drapers   173
    Craftsmen and shopkeepers   178
3   *Time remembered*   196

    Memories and identity   200
    Notes   204
    Books and articles on Minot   216
    Index *by Anthony Forster*   217

Illustrations

Figures

1 Parlour of a farm about 1900   12
2 Farmyard about 1900   13
3 The Chevenoz yard and garden   34
4 Nicolas Demonet's *chenevière* at Le Verger   50
5 Seating plan of relatives on the wedding photograph and
   round the table at the wedding meal   113
6 The Grivot genealogy   146
7 The transmission of land among the Grivot family   147
8 The Chevenoz family of drapers   175
9 The draper's rounds   184

Plates

Fourteen plates appear between pages 100–101

Preface

When memory goes out to pick up dead wood, it brings back the faggot that it likes. *Mossi proverb*.

The enduring memory of events in local history, the short memory of events outside the village, the teeming memory of the family – many are the faggots that make up recollection.

These fleeting memories, these varied accounts, were picked up in the village of Minot, which is situated on the south-east edge of the Langres plateau in that northern part of Burgundy which is called *le Châtillonnais*.[1] It is a typical village of that region of open fields, with the houses grouped in the centre of its territory and set in a network of gardens. Beyond it stretches the cultivated plain, hemmed in on the horizon by strips of the huge communal forest. This long study[2] (1968–75) was carried out, with much coming and going, by four researchers and has already given rise to several publications.[3] In fact our aim has been to build up an ethnology of this village in its many facets and try, as in a hall of mirrors, to catch the future of the community by looking at its present and its past.

In the course of this research we questioned and listened to the local inhabitants. Old inhabitants and newcomers, the young and the elderly, men and women, we met them all, or very nearly, and our interviews were long and varied. By eliciting information, by stirring up the past and sorting out memories ... we felt we were getting at the facts, but a verbal style gradually emerged – a vision of the world and an original way of expressing it. It is true that we did not grasp this style at first, probably because it used the same language as we did. It was only after some time that we recognised the villagers' own language and way of speaking it.

This language has a vocabulary marked by the village dialect,[4] which is still spoken by some old people, and it has certain peculiar traits of morphology and syntax. For instance, some prepositions have a local meaning that is different from the usual French meaning. It is a language that is coherent and well organised, whether it is treating of people or the world around them. This speech, which we wrote down or recorded, has been reproduced in this text with a few changes. We have cut it up for the sake of analysis and we have eliminated the 'spoken' element in reducing it to writing.

However, we have not eliminated the individuality of our subjects, reducing the experience of each one to the experience of the group and losing the statement of a single person in the generality.[5] By avoiding this, autobiography finds its own special place which enables one to watch the individual coping with institutions, and discover the social pressures that determine a life. Biography only yields its true meaning if it is placed in the social, economic and historical context from which it springs. In other words the isolated account of a life, not backed up by ethnographic enquiry, is like an empty shell. Once it is illuminated by other interviews and supported by the economic and social history of the group, biography becomes a means of getting to know society.

Careful attention to what the inhabitants had to say was accompanied by meticulously planned questions and reference to a mass of source material. For it was only by blending different views, by building up day-to-day detail and discovering the relevant fact that we were able to put the fragmented data, the incomplete memories and the garbled information given by our witnesses into some sort of logical framework.[6] Thus unexplained behaviour became clarified and odd changes were explained. A rural home today with its well-ordered and secluded courtyard can only be understood if you take the trouble to reconstitute its past state and retrace the gradual changes. But doing this involves repeated conversations and recourse to various sources of information.

In other words, when one works on the present in a society that exists in History and in its own history, one cannot capture it by a single method which would give one a comfortable distance from the subject, but only by a constant toing and froing between various kinds of witness — observation of the present, reconstitution of the past, memories handed down or actually lived, written records, a reading of the landscape, the topography and toponymy of the region, etc. Each of these memories requires its own deciphering, for they blend and interpenetrate one another. So we had constantly to ask ourselves whether we had recorded some written fact repeated to us or some ancient fact learnt by word of mouth.

We have also had to take account of our own presence, of our irruption into this reality, which has inevitably distorted the whole account. For the ethnologist in his own culture, as in all others, is never completely accepted or completely excluded. As a member of a different social class and the possessor of academic knowledge, the ethnologist remains a stranger and is excluded from the social group. At the same time the interest which he shows for the culture of that group, the care he takes to explain his research and the power he has to reveal the society he studies to the world outside, all lead to his eventual acceptance. This ambiguous status of the ethnologist, who remains inevitably on the fringe of a group, requires a certain vigilance, but above all it gives his relationships a distinct slant and distorts the information which he receives.

The duration of our research helped in part to sort out the complications of historical events and unconscious memory. The long time we spent in the village and our frequent return loosened up the contact between observers and observed so that, as the years went by, we were able to plumb the remotest depths of recollection, where the superficial details faded away. Time enables one to reach the profound significance of what seems trivial, and to decode what is unconscious or hardly visible.

Indeed it is Time that has imposed itself as central to our study and to this book. To all appearances the village lives in a time that is continuous and homogeneous, a chronological time that is broken up into days, months and years, and is fixed by the date which the village schoolmaster writes up each morning on the blackboard. This date is recorded by the children each day on the *tableau du temps*,[7] in which the weather is noted, together with other events that make up the village's time. Time in this tableau appears as differentiated, independent, punctuated by tasks and festivals peculiar to the community and broken up into the rhythm of the seasons and the years. Then in other conversations time seemed to us to be multifaceted and broken up into separate slices. So there rose up a 'time of daily living' and a 'time of life', made up of an 'in the old days' and a 'today', a 'before' and a 'now', that cyclically became the same, fused together in a 'time of the community' which plunged back into the origins of the group. There also appeared a 'time of the family', arising from

the family's genealogy, measured by the extent of family relationships and by the events that mark out a lifetime.

For time in a village breaks up and fragments, as it were, into a
series of parallel times that fuse with one another, so revealing
perhaps one of the basic dimensions of all social life.

Part I

The time of the community

The enduring memory

All stories and opinions about the life and behaviour of people 'nowadays' are spiced with a commentary on what used to happen 'in the old days'. Time lived has two sides to it, a present and a past, and the former only gains meaning when related to the latter. The present is always grasped through this logical antithesis – 'formerly / at present', 'before / now', a dichotomy which colours all recollection and illumines all comment. The dividing line between these two periods is to be found, according to the villagers, in the years which followed the Second World War. From then onwards everything toppled, all social life was turned upside down, and everything is now in a state of continual change. So the present is seen as a period of rapid and radical mutation, as opposed to a long past when all was static and changeless. It is a past without contours, going on serene and unending right up to the present day with all its agitations and interruptions. Indeed, as you listen to the stories that reveal this past, you see that the speaker passes straight from a description of his 'grandfather' to one of 'people long ago', from a time that dates back to the youth of the oldest villager, i.e. the last ten years of the nineteenth century, to another time that embraces the origins of the community, i.e. the neolithic age. There is no qualitative difference between memories of experience and recollections from hearsay, nor between the immemorial past and actual memories. The time is the same, the terms are identical and the references similar. 'People in the old days did it by tradition. ... Our grandfathers knew the custom. ... Tradition, custom', two terms which have the same value as reference and describe ways of speech and action which can as easily belong to a distant past as to a living person's life span. In this way all evocation of the past gives the impression of having actually been witnessed. It is immersed in the same time-flow and refers to one time, that of the community. It is a time that is outside history, outside events, which in fact boil down to a single one, the founding of the village. It is a village which, according to the locals, was founded a long time ago 'in the time of the Gauls' (i.e. around the Hallstatt period),[1] not far from the iron ore mines situated at what is called *les Cras de Maupt'iou* (Creux Maupertuis) in the communal forest. Mignae ... Mignot ... Minot, the village probably took its name[2] from these mines whose working evidently continued throughout the Middle Ages and was then abandoned. The gaping holes have remained in the depths of the forest ever since. However, people talk about this mining as if it had ceased yesterday. '*They* washed the loose stones there at the foot of the Cross, and *they* carried it in ox-carts as far as Cussey-les-Forges.' And of course they hope to see work resumed: 'It's good iron ore ... one could still mine it.'

No event since these distant origins enters the oral record, no fact of history backs up tradition. No war or invasion, although they were frequent in this border country, no history defines the collective memory. The time of the community shuns history, though the latter does appear in other connections, as we shall see. Between the account of the village's origins and the middle of this century nothing has caught the attention of the community, which considers itself to be outside history, outside chronological time, but existing in space. Doubtless the origins of the village are well remembered because they are marked out on the ground in the heart of the communal forest, in that wild public space that was so fiercely defended against 'encroachments and usurpations' of the squire and others. The fresh recollection comes from the evidence being on the ground. If the people of Minot are on such familiar terms with their origins, if they identify so easily with the 'ancients' who extracted iron ore at the Creux Maupertuis, it is because they have kept their home territory intact, their communal forest where for more than a thousand years, in the clearing, there has been the line of holes that were the mines – dark, open, never filled in.[3]

We must also remember that, at the turn of the century, writing came to revive the memories of the village's origins. Local scholars[4] about this time applied themselves to the history of the village. They deciphered the municipal and manorial archives and undertook archaeological excavations. Accounts of these researches were published in *l'Almanach paroissial* or in pamphlets that circulated among the village families. Those villagers who gave us their oral accounts had probably had these writings through their hands. But to tell their story these speakers concealed the written origin and favoured the spoken word. Never did anyone say to us that they knew something through having read it. They knew it 'from having heard it said', they knew it 'by word of mouth'. In fact everything happened as if the written word had only confirmed a tradition that was already known or a story that was common knowledge. The same process is at work today when archaeologists[5] are again digging on the village's ground. Each find, each new fact brought to light reveals nothing that was not known before, and it finds its place in an established history that is common knowledge. It is as if facts could only be transmitted orally, as if only the spoken word were a true guarantee of the facts put forward. In the same way the *assemblée communale* and later the *conseil municipal* down the centuries relied on 'custom', 'the memory of the oldest inhabitant' and 'usage from time immemorial'[6] to establish their rights. The squire and then the State put forward written proof to support their claims: the register of the squire's domain, the deliberations of his court duly noted down, the published law.

This oral tradition of the group was transmitted by a process that was well known: 'At the *veillée*, one approached the grandmothers and talked of past times. . . .' A mechanism which evokes a characteristic feature of that past – *la veillée*, or evening gathering – and shows the inward-looking closeness of the group. At the same time it gives rise to a moral judgment: 'In the old days we visited one another, and we listened to one another.' So the past takes on the hue of a golden age. By concealing the written and relying on the spoken word, the community invents a time without blemish or interruption, and adorns it with every virtue.

But is there really a break between yesterday and today? This present time, seen everywhere and always as a time of upheaval and crisis in moral values, is it really irremediably opposed to the past? Shouldn't a community, in order to survive, constantly link up with its history and find its lasting nature? An analysis of village life at the beginning of the century and today helps us to seize both the moments of change and the permanent currents.

The village: yesterday and today

At the turn of the century, 'in the old days', as they say, Minot was only slightly more populated than now. At the 1901 census there were 371 inhabitants; at the 1968 census there were 359. The decline of manufacturing activities and the crisis in agriculture, which hit the Châtillon region[1] from the mid-nineteenth century onwards, forced much of the population to leave the area. Minot did not escape the general trend. Between 1836 and 1901 the village lost nearly three-quarters of its inhabitants, and the decline intensified during the first two decades of this century.

However, Minot is remembered by those who lived there before the last war as a busy, lively world, a crossroads and a centre of attraction for the region. At the same time it is remembered as a closed community, turned in on itself, where one 'stayed at home and minded one's own business'. These views are borne out by the existence up to about 1950 of a great feast-day celebration and six fairs a year,[2] which were very well attended. Furthermore, the wide range of professional activities made the village look self-supporting up to about 1940. In the census of 1901, for instance, were listed forty heads of farming families, twenty craftsmen connected with agriculture, building or woodworking. A few women were dress-makers, milliners or laundresses. There were also seven merchants, fifteen woodcutters-cum-charcoal burners, forty-nine farmworkers and ten people living on private incomes.

However, the social reality of those days is not recollected in terms of separate professional activities. For the people of Minot the village was made up of two groups[3] who were distinguished from one another according to their connection with the soil and domestic animals. On the one hand there were those who had direct access to the *finage* or cultivated land and owned cows, sheep, etc. These were *les gens du finage*, who consisted of the farmers in the village and the outlying areas,[4] the artisans, shopkeepers and merchants who, apart from their own activities, owned a few blocks of land, one or two cows and ten sheep or so. . . . On the other hand there were all those who 'had no land or cows, but owned a goat, a pig, a few hens, and that was all'. They were *les gens du bois*, 'the hewers of wood' in the old days – woodcutters, charcoal burners, manual workers and day labourers.

These two groups, who seemed to differ so much in their work location and their way of life, in fact complemented one another. They came together at the busy farm season when the wood folk came to help out the land folk; and they all combined in the forest, when free firewood was collected by the whole village.[5] But it was above all the religious and secular ceremonies throughout the year which brought the land folk and the wood folk together. These common activities, connected with festivals or with work, were carried out in a 'spirit of goodwill', 'understanding all along the line', on equal terms, for 'in those days we were all poor, everyone was in the same boat, and the farmers were hardly better off than the woodcutters and the labourers'. All this gives a touch of lost paradise to their memories. This hard grind, this poverty shared by everybody, is accounted virtue. The time of penury was also the time of harmony and mutual help: 'Minot in the old days was one large family. Everyone got on; people visited and helped one another; there was still ready exchange between neighbours. Life was better than nowadays.' All these evocations hark back to a world of understanding and unity, because it was a world closed in on itself. Indeed the village has this appearance in photographs taken about 1900 – well tucked away in its hollow, its roofs pressed against one another, stone tiles alternating with ordinary tiles, all rising out of a jungle of greenery. The paved streets weave in and out between a massive oven, the pedestal of a cross, the sharp edge of a wall. . . . The houses follow closely on one another, enclosed by high walls and turning a blind gable to the street.

Now the village has a very different appearance. The streets have been tarred and straightened, the dwellings have been aligned. The big trees which shaded the front of the church have been cut down; so have those which marked the entrance to the château. Neglected trees are dying in the orchards. There is now no jumble of vegetation to mask the empty spaces, the huge corrugated-iron roofs of the new hangars or the sad frontages of the modern villas. The village has developed extensively along the north-south axis.[6] The old ruined houses have been razed to the ground and new houses have been built on the gardens and enclosures, which used to encircle the village with a narrow band of space. So the dwellings appear to be more spaced out and well separated from one another. The new villas reveal their wide expanse of frontage to the road; windows have been pierced in the gabled walls of the old farms; their high walls have been knocked down. Houses and courtyards open out on to the street, showing themselves to all and sundry. The village seems more spread out, more dispersed. The image of dispersion comes back in connection with the village community of today. 'People stay at home much more than before. They are turned in on themselves. Things are not as they were; there is no more need for neighbours.' These assertions are supported by the disappearance of the *veillées* and the festivals that brought most of the community together, and by the apparent isolation of individuals. It is unusual to see a group, or even two people, together in the street. Each person goes alone to the post office and the grocer, and young women take their babies out on their own. Changes in the economy, and the technical and social organisation of the village are blamed for this break-up and dispersion.

Among the most important milestones of economic change one should mention the appearance about 1930 of new means of communication, for example, the first private motor cars, the bus network and the introduction of radio. Then about 1950 – and this was the most important series of changes – the general ownership of motor cars, the mechanisation of farming, household gadgets, then finally (and above all) television, which has become the scapegoat for just about everything: 'There used to be a very active social life. We used to spend evenings in one anothers' houses. Men played at tarot, women made waffles. Television has spoilt everything. Wretched television; everyone complains about it, but no one dares turn it off!' In fact television has only confirmed and speeded up a trend which had already started between the two wars.[7] One should also take account of the adolescents' extended education, for most of them 'go to study', i.e. in town. Also the administrative reorganisation of the Church[8] has considerably weakened the sense of belonging to the parish.

The village is more spread out, its houses are more open to the public view; and accordingly the village has followed suit, looking outward on the region as a whole and, beyond that, on the world outside.

As for the inhabitants of the village, they have renewed themselves racially speaking and impoverished themselves professionally. Although Minot is far from the important highways, it has always known immigration, and this intensified after the First World War. Around 1920 refugees from the devastated areas bought farms outside the village. Then, about 1930, some Swiss started a cheese and dairy factory where men from the Jura came to work. In 1936–37 Poles, Yugoslavs, Italians, Portuguese and Spaniards came to join the last woodmen or be taken on as farm labourers. The population was renewed from outside and was at the same time transformed professionally. Technical change affected the craftsmen, who either had to shut up shop or change their activity. The traders mostly left the village for want of enough local custom, for the regular annual fairs came to an end. Activities linked to traditional forestry gradually came to an end, so the woodcutters and charcoal burners disappeared.

At present the inhabitants of the village are divided into two categories – 'the farmers' and 'the workers', or 'those who till the soil' and 'the rest'. The farmers are owners or tenants of properties varying between 170 and 370 acres. Well equipped and trained for modern methods of agriculture, these farmers are comfortably off.[9] The term 'worker' has a much vaguer connotation. It applies equally well to employers running small local businesses[10] and to their employees, and also to those who work at Valduc, the research and experimental centre run by the *Commissariat à l'Energie atomique* and situated in the forest twenty kilometres from the village. So there are two groups, named as of old according to their connection with the soil, still claiming social equality, but now prosperous. But this prosperity and easy living, which came late and are now general, have become a disruptive factor. 'Mentalities have changed; people have become rich and their characters have altered. They stay at home and jealousies spring up.' Such words betoken dispersion and isolation, as do the houses of the village that are now so far apart. So the more the groups making up the village take part in the world outside and lay themselves open to external influences, the more they become fragmented and turned in on themselves.

Yet, just as one finds dispersion, one also finds solidarity. 'Minot is a village where people get on well, and there are no cliques. People help one another and there is no friction between farmers and workers. There is still communication between neighbours.' In fact, at one and the same time, there exist solidarity of the community and isolation of family groups. There is talk of both division and unity, arising out of a necessity for 'agreement', 'mutual help', 'exchange', all values that were so highly esteemed in the old days and that endure today despite the demographic, economic and social changes. In practice, the village community, impelled by internal disruption and opening itself out on the world, has kept its old system of moral values and in some ways lives the present in a bygone style.

By an analysis of other levels of social reality we can grasp more exactly this confrontation of what changes and what remains, of what comes from the past and what belongs to the present. The house makes up one of these particularly sensitive levels; the relations between generations and between members of the same age group are another. By studying the house you penetrate *living time*. The study of social relations and their topography examines *the time of life*. The two facets of memory — 'in the old days' and 'today', — 'before' and 'now' — border and interpenetrate one another. These variations blend, as we shall see, into a stable time-span where we can find *the time of the community*.

1

Daily living

A house to dwell in

At Minot, the *house* consisted not only of the living quarters,[1] but also 'the farmyard with the barn, the stable, and nearby the kitchen garden ... then people often also had a plot nearby and a hemp-field at the entrance to the village'. We must now describe each of these places.

At the beginning of the century the farms, scattered throughout the village, made up a series of cells closed in on themselves. The buildings set around a yard were hemmed in by high stone walls, and their blind gables gave onto the street. All had the same architecture, bar a few details, the same plan and the same internal organisation.

The living quarters, roughcast in pink ochre, were to be found on the right as you entered the yard. They consisted of a ground floor with a cellar and a first-floor loft. On the ground floor was the parlour, which one entered directly from outside up two steps. It was lit by two windows on each side of the door, and out of it ran the *agöt*, a vaulted alcove with a stone sink which thrust into the yard its *geuliron*, i.e. a long stone channel through which the water flowed into a tub.

Shelves were carved out of the stone walls of the *agöt* and carried the kitchen utensils – cast-iron pans and stoneware jars, the copper basin for clean water, the metal can with a spout for oil. Wooden buckets, or *sapines*, on the floor collected the dirty water. On the whitewashed walls of the parlour hung a crucifix with a sprig of boxwood that was changed every Palm Sunday, a post office calendar and a religious picture on each side of the chimney. The grey-brown paving of the floor, pitted by constant washing, matched the dim reflection of the oak furniture. The long table with a chest underneath it was set under the window, surrounded by benches and straw-seated chairs. The cupboard with two doors and two interior drawers was placed in the opposite corner. In it were piled the household linen on one side, the crockery and perishable food on the other. The few family jewels were crammed in the first drawer near the family papers, a thick wad held together by black cotton braid and consisting of fifty or so private or legal documents, for example, leases, marriage contracts, wills, etc. In the second drawer the mourning shawl was carefully folded, together with two white sheets for the master of the house's shroud; and on top the family candle to be lit on the occasion of a death or to ward off lightning. Just near the cupboard stood the clock. Between these two pieces of furniture the children took refuge to hide their tears and their fears. There they no longer heard the rumble of thunder or the scolding of their parents. Next to the cupboard was the bread bin in which the large round loaves were kept.

Opposite the door was the high stone fireplace that had recently been filled in. The walls were still black with the smoke that used to be given out. A small wood-burning kitchen range with four rings, set on four legs, occupied the space in front of the chimney, its shiny black pipe crossing the space like a dark beam of light reflecting the sparkling brass of the oil lamps, the *luzettes*, and the line of candlesticks along the high shelf. On the ground near the range was a charcoal hotplate for slowly heating up *daubes* (stews). Albertine, who is seventy, recalls 'I never saw a fire lit in the hearth at the farm. But when I was a child, fires were lit in the chimneys of many houses. At my grandmother's they had both – the wood range and the fire in the hearth. In the winter one sat between the two, which was very cosy. Your back and your legs were warmed at the same time.'

The wicker armchair of the master of the house lorded it over the left of the range, with a cushion on which the cat, the only animal allowed in the parlour, slept. The watch-dog was tied up in the yard and the gun dogs remained in the stable. Opposite this male preserve, near the window giving onto the yard, there was another wicker chair, more modest in size, and this was the female area. Under the window was a treadle sewing machine with its wooden slab supported by cast-iron legs. This was where the housewife was to be found between her chores. As she sewed or knitted, she kept an eye on what went on outside, hiding discreetly behind the light foliage of an evergreen plant.

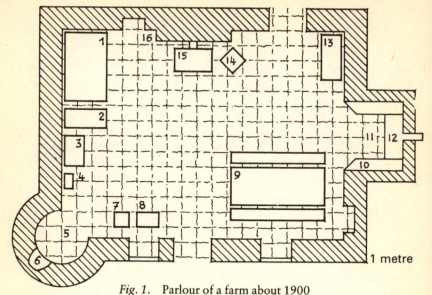

Fig. 1.   Parlour of a farm about 1900

1. Parents' bed. 2. Children's bed. 3. Wardrobe. 4. Clock. 5. Oven corner.
6. Oven. 7. Wife's armchair. 8. Sewing machine. 9. Table and benches.
10. Shelves. 11. *Agöt.* 12. Sink. 13. Bread bin. 14. Husband's armchair.
15. Cooker. 16. Fireplace.

The parlour also served as a bedroom. The bed was sometimes
sunk into an alcove, or it was simply pushed against the wall.
Ample curtains of calico, hanging from a *ciel de lit* (tester), assured
intimacy. The younger children also slept in the parlour, while the
older boys often went out to sleep with the labourers in the barn,
where there were box beds made of wood. The girls remained with
their parents or occupied a room on the first floor, if such a thing
existed, while the young servants slept under the staircase. The
wooden beds were made by the village carpenter and the mattresses
filled with straw from the farm. 'In the old days beds were a
hundred and ten centimetres wide. They were corner beds, not
jutting into the room like nowadays, but one managed to sleep two
in them. The under-mattress was made up of rye stuffed into a great
sack. It was changed once a year at threshing time. On top one put
a mattress or two; my grandmother had three. The higher the bed
the finer it was. At my grandmother's you needed a chair to climb
up. The mattress consisted of a sack made of ticking, which was

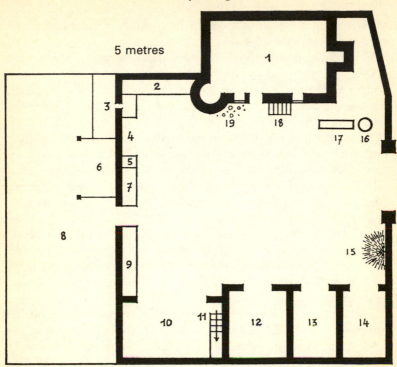

Fig. 2. Farmyard about 1900

1. Parlour. 2 & 9. Rabbit hutches. 3. Hen-house. 4. Wood. 5. W.C.
6. Wooden shed. 7. Pigsty. 8. Garden. 10. Wheat store (open). 11. Steps.
12. Stable. 13. Barn. 14. Cowshed. 15. Manure heap. 16. Wells. 17. Water
trough. 18. Steps down to the cellar. 19. Flowers.

thicker than mattress cloth and prevented the feathers from coming
through. The mattresses were filled with chicken or duck feathers,
which were dried in the bread-oven. Down was kept for making
eiderdowns. The feathers were stirred from time to time.'

Out of the parlour opened the oven chamber. Every week up to
the 1914 war the mother baked the household bread there. There
up to the turn of the century she did the washing twice a year in the
copper.[2] There the food for the poultry was prepared; and finally
the members of the household washed themselves there discreetly
every Sunday in a great wooden tub, and every day they gave
themselves a cursory clean in front of the only mirror in the house.
'It was all we had in the way of a mirror – we didn't look at

ourselves much.' In those days the body received the minimum of care and attention.

On the first floor opened out two bedrooms with whitewashed walls. One was used by the daughters of the house or the young couple who would inherit, so long as the parents lived at the farm. The second bedroom was furnished and ready to receive relations who passed through.

Facing the living quarters on the other side of the yard were the outbuildings[3] – fine structures of stone with arched entrances. They consisted of two stables, one for the cows and one for the horses, and two stores. There was a loft the length of the building. Sometimes a sheep-fold completed the whole. In the farmyard the hens pecked away, attracted by the pile of manure at the side of the stable. On the third side of the yard was the line of rabbit hutches, pigsties, and the sheds for firewood and the faggots for peas and beans. Under the window of the house were the drinking trough and the well where water was drawn in a bucket hung on a long branch with a hook at the end.

The craftsmen's houses lining the village street were organised internally in the same way. The yards, situated in front or at the side of the living quarters, were places for working and storing materials. In a photograph of a carpenter's yard taken in 1900, you can see planks of wood stacked up in a corner and acting as an improvised seat for the tired visitor. On the other side there is the high trestle of the pit sawyers with a pile of sawdust not far off.

The craftsmen's yards were extensions of their workshops, as the farmyards were of their holdings. They were the centre of activity where all the daily work was organised; they were the scene of all initiatives, all the comings and goings of man and beast. The visitor was bound to pass through the yard, and if he was a stranger he would go no further, for only people that were known could penetrate the parlour: 'However, they did not enter without being invited ... they knocked and waited outside the door ... then one let them in and asked them to sit down. ...' The yard was the place of transit between the village that was open to all and the closed world of the parlour.

The parlour was the family centre, the place where the private domestic life of the family took place. The meals prepared by the womenfolk simmered in the cooker. The family gathered round the oak table for the two main meals of the day. In winter they always sat round the fireplace to spend the evening in a warm and relaxed atmosphere, listening to a book or magazine serial story being read aloud. 'The evening gatherings were very intimate in the old days. It was delightful. There were oil lamps which didn't give much light, so that the parlour was full of patches of darkness. Father told stories or else there was reading aloud; he used to read, and then I did when I knew how. We subscribed to *L'Intrépide* and we followed the episodes in stories about the Comanches. We also read Hector Malot's *Sans famille*, René Bazin's *La Terre qui meurt*, and *Pécheurs d'Islande* and Mandrin, I can't remember the author's name. They were school books. Mother knitted or made lace.' The different generations slept side by side, separated by calico curtains. In the great wooden bed in the alcove the parents made love, the mother gave birth and the old people died. At times of death or birth the young children were removed while the other members of the family remained. There was even one story of a poor woman who got tired of watching over her husband's corpse and got in beside him, saying; 'You never harmed me in your lifetime: I'm sure you won't harm me now you're dead'; and she went peacefully off to sleep in the matrimonial bed. There was no separation between the living and the dead, between the healthy and the sick; and the generations were not isolated. Distance was abolished.

This was the very centre of the household, where all members lived round the same hearth, under the same light. They rubbed shoulders incessantly in the same room. Day and night they were under the scrutiny of the others. This constant proximity was controlled by the imposition of a strict discipline between generations. Each individual obeyed rules and conventions which, as we shall see,[4] brought back the distance that was indispensable in this collective existence. The children kept silent, the old people stayed in the background, only the adults spoke. . . . All this was behaviour designed to reduce the tensions caused by promiscuity. In other words what was lost in space was recovered in time, i.e. in the hierarchy of generations. Family relationships in the old days were above all forged in the narrow context of the parlour.

Other forms of conduct, other gestures and taboos, tended to protect the household from the outside world and keep neighbours at a distance. One should bear this in mind when noting the women's anxiety to hide all traces of their personal life in front of a visitor: 'The first thing that all women did on getting up was to make their beds. No one should come in and see the bed unmade. They set great store on their bed being smooth and flat. Nearby there was always a large stick, the *bâton de lit*, which was used to push the blankets up against the wall and flatten the surface well.' In the same way, washing out the house, which exposed the interior to outward view, was done very sparingly: 'The house was only washed out once a year. You shouldn't do it, said my mother-in-law, it brings on rheumatism. When old Demonet saw us washing the windows, he said, "You'll make them rot."' Any excuse was good enough to avoid opening the house and revealing it to outsiders. For the same reason one never let anything leave the parlour, not even the dust removed from the fire. 'Oh at the Ferlets' you couldn't do what you liked with the *ch'ni* (fire dust). No putting it out of doors. There was a hollow in the paving near the cooker. It was there, always in the same place, that you had to collect it up and throw it on the fire. At the Arnaults' it was the same. Sweepings had to be pushed towards the cooker and put on the fire.' By excluding the outside world as much as possible and concealing the family group you kept others at a distance. You claimed symbolically your living space, and the parlour remained a closed world which allowed the group to close in on itself. Everything happened and was contained there, altogether hidden and private.

Closed to the outside world, the parlour was also a place in which to display family possessions. It was a world in which everything was well ordered and catalogued. Here every object and every piece of furniture had a history which was carefully recounted: 'The table came from the Grivots of Velbret. It was Marguerite who told me. This table was at the house of my great-grandmother, who gave it to my grandmother. That's how I got it. The dresser came from my Vernet aunt, who was Mother's godmother. The clock came from my cousin's. ... I got the cupboard for my wedding, it belonged to Mother, and my son took another one that came from an aunt.' 'When my grandmother died, I inherited the small soup tureen, Nicolas had the big one. As for the two brass candlesticks, we took one each. The eldest boy got his grandfather's rosary. I inherited Mother's rosary and I gave it to my youngest nephew when he made his first communion.' A careful catalogue of things received, shared and handed on, a tangible record of family history by objects and furniture. The importance of lineage and the network of family relationships were at once evident in these houses. In this sombre, well-ordered space everything bore witness to the family's position in the clan by its possessions. It was these objects, these papers stuffed in the drawer of the cupboard, this furniture, this linen marked with the initials of the mistress of the house, that revealed the continuity of the family's history, and not the house itself, which changed its name with each occupant.[5]

Besides being a showroom the parlour was also a space that was marked out. It was divided distinctly into a masculine and a feminine area, man and woman each having their own place. At table the master and mistress sat on the long side facing the window and the front door, sometimes separated or rather united by the last-born child inserted between them. The whole space was evenly divided and seats equally distributed, the mirror of an egalitarian society where no one clan took precedence over another. So the parlour, the stage on which the household acted out its life, was divided up internally and protected from the outside world by a whole series of mechanisms, symbolic or practical. At the same time this one room existed in a village as part of the collective space and time.

Throughout the year the households were brought together by communal tasks and by festivals. In the village or in the fields men and women, young or old, found reasons for assembly and conviviality in the unfolding of the ceremonial calendar and the succession of seasonal labours. The streets were where the fairs were held, where the traders circulated, the flocks passed each other and the gatherings in summer were held: 'We met at the Jodelets, the Vilets, or at our place, Demonet's, at the gate of the yard. . . . We children were made to sing.'

The craftsmen's workshops were where the men gathered; the women collected at the washing-places, around which the different quarters of the village revolved: 'Everyone stayed in their sector for water.'

All these open-air spaces made up a collective geography of the village community. So the houses were at the same time closed in on themselves and linked to the rest by these periodic gatherings, by this network of communal meeting-places. The living space of the household was thus amplified and multiplied by these spaces outside. The old way of life combined the closing-in of the domestic group on itself with its opening-out on the community as a whole, intensity of family relationships with lively communal links, limited personal space with an abundance of public meeting-places.

Nowadays it is only the homes of retired people living in old craftsmen's dwellings, or the buildings still occupied by farms that keep traces of the old style of living. There one finds the parlour entered directly from outside, the little scullery and the floor of paving stones. In the houses of the oldest inhabitants stands the large wood-burning cooker of blue enamel in front of the blocked chimney. Everywhere else gas stoves[6] and electric cookers of an aseptic whiteness have replaced the sombre old equipment.

From 1930 onwards the walls of the parlours and bedrooms were covered in coloured wallpaper. This paper, which you still find in old people's houses, varies little from room to room. Coloured in tones of brown, red or deep blue, it has a design of stylised bouquets in parallel lines and gives the room a greenhouse, winter garden look that fits in well with the quiet existence of these old inhabitants. Only a crucifix, a post office calendar or a first communion photograph breaks the autumnal monotony of these walls.

Towards the nineteen-sixties most of the parlours were given a thorough whitewashing, and the sombre paper was replaced by another that was gayer and lighter, dominated by pseudo-rustic motifs of the *toile de Jouy* variety. In recent years we have also seen 'false stone' and 'false brick' papers. These hide the attractive stone of the old walls and the dark, warm centre of the old chimneys. These new papers change the light and general appearance of the parlours, but just like the old papers they suggest a nature that has been tamed, put in order and civilised. For the village people Nature can only intrude into the home in a form that is arranged and modified by *trompe l'oeil*.

The parlour has long since ceased to be used as a bedroom. The beds were taken out after the 1914 war. Parents and unmarried children then took to occupying one of the bedrooms of the house all together. The beds of the girls, the boys and their parents were simply separated from one another by curtains. This night cohabitation of parents and children lasted a long time: 'Up to my marriage I slept in my father's room, so did Nicolas, who stayed there till he married. ...' It was only after the Second World War that the generations were separated, each occupying a bedroom. This expansion of night occupancy brought about the disappearance of the guest bedroom, just as the custom of putting up relations ceased. Motor cars enabled family reunions to be shortened.

Having thus started to lose its family life, the parlour has in recent years undergone a final transformation; for the kitchen has been separated from it. In the old houses the kitchen has been accommodated in a large penthouse at the side of the house – well lit, tiled and equipped with every modern gadget – and it has become the centre of domestic life. The household meets there round a large table permanently covered in a flowered oilcloth to eat its meals, spend evenings in front of the television and entertain informally relations and neighbours in the village.

The parlour, now emptied of all life, has become a reception area with its central table, on which a bouquet of wheat made of spun glass has pride of place, and with the chairs pushed against the wall. It is a place of ceremony which one penetrates on tiptoe. One no longer now talks of 'the parlour' but of 'the drawing-room'.

The parlour used to be a space in which everything happened and everything was done. It symbolised a world turned in on itself, as were the village groups. The first break occurred when public life was separated from private life, the latter being hidden from those who did not belong to the household. The second break separated the room for formally receiving people from the room for simple socialising. At the same time the intimate life of the family was in its turn split between generations. The bourgeois model had decisively triumphed in the country.

Those interior transformations were not systematically carried out in most old houses, but one finds them complete in the modern villas which farmers and work hands, young and old alike, have had built in the village since 1950. These buildings follow the same pattern. They stand perched high above a basement garage and are approached by a staircase which opens up into a terrace before the front door. The interior plan is based on a central corridor out of which open rooms with a precise function: a drawing-room, a kitchen-dining-room, two or three bedrooms for the parents and the children. The large windows of the front which faces on the street enable the inhabitants of the house to watch the comings and goings of the village in comfort. The plans of these villas, just like the transformations of the old houses, seem to reflect a desire to contradict the chief characteristics of yesterday's houses. The latter were shady, turned in on themselves and showed a blank wall to the street; the new ones are light and airy, looking out on the street and the open air. The old houses were low, sunk into the ground, while the modern ones are tall and built high above street level, an exaggeration that doubtless implies social prestige.

The courtyards have also been involved in this vast transformation and opening-up. The farmyards have been gutted, their high walls and porches of wood and stone demolished, their *portes cochères* destroyed to allow enormous farm machines to enter freely. Wide open to the street, they are now totally visible to outsiders, and any signs of agricultural activity are carefully camouflaged. The dunghill has disappeared as the manure is now stacked mechanically behind the cowshed, the poultry is shut up in a run hidden behind a building, the animals enter their stalls direct from the fields. The new houses surround themselves with a partly lawned area, separated from the road by a light balustrade of wrought iron. The recently built villa of the building contractor, who is mayor of the village, is a typical and much admired example of the new-style layout. A mown lawn surrounds the house on three sides, crossed by paved paths which lead to the house, the garage, the back gate and the leisure area behind the house where there are tables, chairs and a barbecue. A few clumps of flowers and some cement containers filled with plants dot the lawn with splashes of colour, to which are added glittering fragments of rough glass spread at random to shine in the sun. This finished model of a villa garden tends to be imitated everywhere. Indeed nowadays in the village one notices very little difference, except in size, between the surroundings of a farm, a retired man's home and an ordinary worker's dwelling. They all present the same ordered, artificial space where no wild flower grows and where no utilitarian object is left lying about.

Now the forecourts are empty of all life and all equipment, either professional or domestic. Furthermore, an untidy forecourt, covered in weeds or littered with objects, attracts criticism, and the resulting comment often foreshadows the departure of the occupants. The social rank and economic status of a person are deduced from the appearance of his house and its surroundings. From being a centre of work and movement, the forecourt has become an area of display. For a show of plants and minerals is organised in these open gardens paved with cement, gravel and grass. Flowers and shrubs in lines, clumps and arcades make up the décor. The flowers are banked in borders edged with perennials or potted plants. There are flowers on the windowsills, on the walls, on the outside steps or on wooden tiers. Sometimes they are staked or guided along two strands of wire, and they blossom on a trellis along the fence or on arches on the front of the house. The shrubs are cropped and pruned to make lines, pyramids and spheres.

Nature in these gardens is always domesticated and sophisticated, like the wallpapers indoors. Even the flowers on display generally come from a seed merchant. The women (for it is they who are in charge of the flowers) rarely plant cuttings picked up in the woods or grown themselves. Bulbous begonias, red, yellow and bronze-coloured calceolarias, trailing geraniums, pink and blue petunias compete in the various gardens.

A baroque décor is sometimes added to this floral adornment. The garden becomes a theatre, with an old cartwheel hung on the wall (the sun?), a well coping made of tyres painted in *trompe-l'oeil* brick, pierced stones[7] *à la* Henry Moore piled up to make a pyramid, a grotto or a niche. Elsewhere rustic scenes, landscapes and imaginary worlds are evoked by plaster gnomes and stucco statuettes. It is as if man – for it is the male of the household who always initiates these fantasies – seeks to fight against the rigidity and insipidity of modern housing. The straight, geometric lines of the villa are counteracted by the writhings of pierced stones, the curliness of rubber baskets and the curves of the wrought-iron gates. A luxuriant décor now replaces the bustle that once filled the old yards, and enlivens the prevalent silence.

The general effect is sometimes heightened and emphasised by bright paint that contrasts with the whiteness of the new villas. This paint may be put on pots of flowers, tiers, stakes, containers or baskets, shutters or grilles; occasionally it extends right into the sitting-room. The illusion of continuity between sitting-room and forecourt thus becomes complete. Private quarters nowadays begin at the front gate. Indeed it is there that the visitor stops; he no longer goes as far as the door of the parlour as in former days.

In brief, the intimate life of the household is now carried on between a house divided into rooms and a forecourt that has been retrieved from the public. The old parlour has gone, its functions and characteristics having disappeared or been transferred to other places. For example, the forecourt has taken its place as the family's showcase. The order revealed there, the general neatness, the competition in horticultural embellishment between households, these are the merits displayed for all to see. In the old days, through the organisation of the parlour, families were set in the time of the lineage, in geneological time, now they estimate themselves in social space and define their hierarchical relationships.

The space has been expanded and the life of the household has been fragmented between these separate spaces. At the same time the rules for bringing up children within the family group have altered. The silence and the deference shown by the younger generation towards their parents are no longer to be found: 'We belong to the "shut up!" generation', said a woman of fifty. 'In the old days children were not allowed to speak and now it's the parents who have to keep quiet.' The change in parent-child relations has evolved simultaneously with the layout of the home. 'There is a correlation between the house as a building and the house as a social structure.'[8]

Parallel with these space changes in the family and its way of living, the village itself has become largely empty. The fairs have come to an end, the women have left the washhouses, the craftsmen have shut up shop, the places of assembly have disappeared. Most of the public celebrations and class ceremonies are nothing but memories recounted to attentive ethnologists.... The village space seems to have become a void, and the family group, having lost its place to circulate outside, has withdrawn within its own home.

It was at the time when gradually the fields were enclosed, when community activities came to an end, when the village celebrations ceased and the places of assembly were shut, that families enlarged their houses, opened them up and showed them off. Now each family quietly watches the others from its own home. 'I don't like passing through the lower village because they look at you from behind their shutters to criticise you. You are judged from top to toe. It upsets me; I don't like the lower village.' This watchfulness between neighbours, which still finds expression in the age-old opposition between the upper and the lower village, has always existed. However, in the old days it occurred among acquaintances, among members of households who saw each other and conversed every day. Now it survives in an apparently fragmented society where the places and opportunities for contact hardly exist. So supervision and curiosity quickly become resentment and a source of friction and disruption.

Change in the inhabited countryside has gone hand in hand with the changes in the social organisation of the village.

Nowadays, as of old, every house in the village extends to a garden to which are attached a field and an orchard. Most of the inhabitants of Minot enjoy this combination of outbuildings and land around their house. The whole constitutes the ancient *meix*[9] with its dependencies, which has hardly varied in its nature or size since the Middle Ages.[10] Ownership is enough, today as yesterday, to give rights of use in the communal woods and common lands.[11] So the house and its surroundings constitute a form of anchorage in the community. Through them a man's links with his space and his land are maintained, together with the sentiment of belonging to his village. Each household, in spite of private ownership of land for cultivation or pasture, and of fallow ground and forests, has the right to draw on the neighbouring countryside for part of its sustenance. The village territory remains a source of nourishment and a shared space for every household. This collective tenure of land and its communal management for the general good still preserve the feeling of belonging to the village: 'We are from Minot.' In spite of economic and architectural changes, in spite of demographic and social upheavals, the community still expresses its unity through a whole network of exchanges and mutual aid. It derives mainly from the resources of the surrounding land, but also from the produce of the *meix*. It is above all in its garden, its poultry run, its hemp-fields and its orchard that each household finds its nourishment, and it is from its own produce that the exchanges that put every household into contact with all the others are organised.

Gardens to tend

The kitchen garden is next to the forecourt, or it extends behind the house. 'Everyone has a garden. It would be a poor show if one didn't cultivate it.' Every adult woman, whether unmarried, married or widowed, should have a kitchen garden. Those who have not got one, for example, a few young married women recently arrived from town, and one or two wives of prosperous contractors, incur disapproval.

The garden lies half-hidden behind a hedge or a low stone wall with wire fencing along the top; and so one can see it from the road. Visible to everyone, it seems at first sight like a place for display. The skill of the gardener is on show, together with his knowledge and aesthetic sense, which can be judged by the layout of his crops and the fertility of his plants. The houses in the village are distinguished by the beauty of their gardens, and credit redounds to the man or woman who tends his or hers most skilfully. 'People came from miles around to admire my grandmother's garden. Oh, she was a clever gardener all right.' The passer-by looks at these gardens from afar, contemplates them over the hedge, and exchanges remarks with the owner from the other side of the fence. He will only penetrate them after a pressing invitation. The garden is forbidden territory which no stranger enters freely, a special area where everything is visible and displayed but which remains private and inaccessible. Half-way between the old parlour and the new forecourt, the garden has undergone no real change between the old days and now.

Averaging from half an acre to one acre in extent, the village gardens always have the same layout. Traced out *à la française*, they are divided into two or three areas separated by straight paths. The areas are subdivided into beds. Each bed is devoted to one crop, so that one reckons in beds: 'I have one bed of strawberries and two of carrots.' On the beds they trace out furrows and plant the seed.

Planting in the gardens is always and everywhere disposed in the same way. On the perimeter, along the walls and on the edge of the paths are planted the flowers. Only a few varieties are raised, and they are to be found in all gardens – white marguerites, dahlias, zinnias, phlox, white lilies and chrysanthemums. This monotony is, however, sometimes broken by the appearance of a species in one place and nowhere else – red poppies at the draper's wife's, *couronnes impériales* at a farmer's wife's, 'bleeding hearts' in the garden of the solicitor's granddaughter. So flowers become a mark of distinction, a sign of property and individuality.

Several considerations enter into the choice of flowers grown. First of all one enquires after their hardiness and their ease of upkeep. Too much time should not be spent on flowers. 'If it comes up, that's all right. Apart from that one shouldn't bother with flowers.' Their colour also comes into it. They must be bright – but yellow is ruled out, it brings bad luck. No attempt, however, is made to match colours or arrange harmonious groupings. You plant where there is room and disregard the tones of the flowers nearby. For the most part only plants with long stalks are grown because they make handsome borders, visible from far off; for flowers are the garden's only ornament and the kitchen section is entirely devoted to utilitarian crops. Furthermore, although the flowers seem to be planted only to beautify the gardens and make an effect, they do have their uses, as we shall see. And for all the assertions that too much time must not be spent on them, great care is taken in tending flowers, and those who know how to multiply them (or rather *knew*, because it is a dying skill) are much admired. 'Old Madame Pelletier, she knew how to make cuttings. . . . Take chrysanthemums, she always had her knife in her pocket and when she saw a fine bunch on a tomb, she quickly cut off a stalk. . . . Later she got flowers as big as plates.'

The central beds in the garden are taken up with vegetables for hot-pot and soups. One finds there the various cabbages according to season, for example, Savoy cabbage and the various late varieties that spend the winter out of doors; French beans picked green or dried; potatoes, peas, turnips and carrots to be eaten fresh or gathered in the autumn and kept in the cellar; spring leaks which spend the winter in the earth and finally the green salads sown together with other vegetables. 'Corn salad and lamb's lettuce are sown after potatoes if you want some in the spring. Lettuce sows itself; you let it run to seed and it spreads. Clémence has some among her leaks. Among my carrots I sow *Bon jardinier* lettuce because it makes good hearts.'

At the bottom of the garden one finds the asparagus ridges and the spinach bed, carefully tended and manured. In the parts facing south, well protected from wind and frost, they plant the vegetables that are to be eaten raw in a seasonable salad or taken with salt almost like a sweet; also rows of tomatoes with courgettes or cucumbers at their base, next to red or black radishes.

Then one comes across the 'seasonings', sometimes in beds dotted around the garden, or along the paths, for example, garlic, onions, sorrel, gherkins that will be pickled, parsley, tarragon and thyme. The 'little red fruits' complete the collection of produce. Introduced after the 1914 war (except for strawberries, that had long been known), these fruits – redcurrants, blackcurrants, raspberries – are spread here and there or assembled at the bottom of the garden.

The beds and the paths are kept immaculate, being constantly cleared and carefully weeded. Indeed, the neatness of the planting leads to the good reputation of the garden, for its beauty simply consists of its orderliness and perfect layout. However, a corner of the kitchen garden is allowed to go wild. There the rubbish is stacked to be burnt two or three times a year, there wild plants grow freely, destined to feed both man and beast. 'I find a nettle leaf there for my soup. I pick burdock which is a sovereign remedy for everything, and celandine which acts against warts. I leave golden rod there, it's a flower that bees like. I gather pigweed there too, for my rabbits.'

The garden is a meeting-place where order and disorder, the wild and the cultivated, coexist. There one plants out flowers picked in the forest: periwinkles, lily of the valley and scillas find a place along the paths or near the entrance. The garden is a crossroads where all species meet, where exchanges are made. The division of labour among the sexes is yet another proof of this.

At Minot gardening is essentially 'women's work'. The kitchen garden is the domain of the mistress of the house. It is she who, from one end of the process to the other, takes responsibility, chooses varieties, decides on qualities, sites the plants, traces out the furrows, sows and looks after the plants, picks them and decides on their future, i.e. immediate consumption or preservation in different forms. Furthermore, a good gardener is recognised not only by the fair appearance of her garden, but also by the skill she shows in planting in due season and in sufficient quantities to stagger crops, and therefore preserves.

The granddaughter starts gardening at the tender age of seven or eight. She never has a garden of her own nor even a plot in her mother's garden; but she learns by working at the side of her mother, or rather her grandmother, for the latter is more patient, less in a hurry and is more of a teacher than the mother of the family. Grandma teaches the child to recognise plants, pick out seeds and collect them, and mark out beds. She hands on the stock of plants that she has established empirically: 'For each plant my grandmother had selected the best variety, the one that grew best. For every flower there was a variety that she liked and stuck to. . . .'

This empirical knowledge, handed down from grandmother to granddaughter for generations, is based partly on varied experience; but books have played, and still play, a major role. The draper's wife always uses the *Guide Clause* (1910 edition) which her mother-in-law left her. Rural ladies at the beginning of the century derived all their knowledge from the same bible, *La maison rustique des dames* by Madame Millet-Robinet, a domestic and horticultural handbook which in 1888 was in its thirteenth edition.

The husband in the garden only carries out the heavy work, i.e. ploughing up the beds once a year with a cultivator and digging them over twice a year with a spade. He is apt to say that he 'knows nothing about gardening' or that 'he hasn't a clue, you must ask the womenfolk about that.' Once retired, however, the man takes a more active part in horticultural activities. Then a subtle division of tasks comes into force. Small seeds are the wife's department, large seeds the husband's; spreading manure and weeding are done by the father of the family, daily maintenance and picking by the lady of the house.

There are some exceptions to this feminine control of the garden. In the village there are two or three gardens tended by men, either with or without their wives' help. The craftsman in retirement or the worker with some free hours – formerly the jack of all trades or the well-to-do man with time on his hands – sometimes devote themselves to gardening. While the woman takes up horticulture as a matter of course, just like cooking or poultry, the man, on the contrary, gardens for pleasure and not by obligation. For a woman, 'doing the garden' is a job, for a man, it is a pastime. However, for a husband to be seen gardening does not incur ridicule as would other domestic jobs carried out by him. The garden is a place where roles can be exchanged.

These gardens run by men are cultivated on the same pattern as all the others, and they contain the same basic plants. However, they are distinguished by being places where experiments and new ideas are tried out. The husband, who is the partner who moves around and is in contact with the outside world, is more aware of what is being done elsewhere than is his stay-at-home wife. From his trips and his contacts with strangers he brings back new plants and new methods. And then men who garden are said to have the gift[12] for experimenting with new varieties and acclimatising new species. Their *savoir-faire* and the time at their disposal encourage their innate tendencies. It is in gardens run by men that exotic vegetables and new varieties are grown for the first time. If their efforts are successful or promising, the plants in question spread to other gardens in the village.

Thanks to the stimulus given by these male gardeners, this century has been marked by the arrival of vegetables and flowers first tried out by their imaginative efforts. At the turn of the century the imagination was usually to be found in the garden of the local bigwig. He was at that time the only person in the village to receive nursery catalogues and gardening reviews; he was the only one who could afford the luxury of experiment. The local solicitor's granddaughter, born in 1896, remembers: 'It was we who introduced asparagus when I was a child. Then after the 1914 war we had the first tomatoes.'

After the First World War, gardening catalogues and guides became available to everyone; so the good work was carried on by other men of skill and ingenuity: 'It was André Fleurot who started endive just after the last war. He raised it in his cellar. He took sand down there and it grew during the winter. Now it is grown in gardens, but it comes later.' At present, new species are first grown in the gardens of newcomers who bring their methods and their vegetables with them. So the postmaster, who comes from the south, plants beetroot in his garden: 'I've given some to Madame Louet and Madame Jeunet. They find it delicious and say they are going to grow some.' In the same way, around 1950, courgettes appeared in the kitchen garden of a Spanish immigrant, and they are now to be found in nearly all Minot gardens: 'Courgettes have only started recently, and not everyone does them. You've got to know them and like them. I don't care for them myself, but Madeleine makes her kind of *ratatouille niçoise* with courgettes. She adds an aubergine, which she buys, and some potatoes.' This Burgundy-style *ratatouille* completes the culinary marriage of north and south. Novelties that bring changes in diet come not through the fields but through the gardens, where the outside world and the village community meet. Technical change, on the other hand, does not come through the gardens, but through the open countryside where the crops grow.

People are wary of chemical fertilisers in kitchen gardens. They prefer to stick to natural methods: 'I put in ashes to enrich the garden all winter. I spill them in as soon as they leave the cooker. It's potassium. Of course there's always a bit of coal in it, that's not so good. However ashes lighten the soil when it's too compact. Take Madeleine for instance, she's got her garden going very well with ash. It was rotten soil to start with, and now she says, "Since I put in a lot of ash the soil is much looser and works much better. It's cleaner and healthier." But manure must be put in too. You dig it in during November. Sheep's dung is the best, but one can't find it any more. It's disappeared, like cow manure. It had to be well rotted. . . . Now we only have a little rabbit manure, but it's not very good – it makes the grass grow. Horse dung used to be used, especially for forcing beds and seedlings under glass. It warmed and pushed the seeds along. If one laid down half a cart of horse manure and some soil on top, the seeds came along very well. Cow manure is no good for forcing beds, it's too rotten; horse manure is less rotted and has more straw in it. The best fertiliser for flower cuttings is dung diluted with water. One starts watering with eighty grams to one litre, and after flowering one uses one litre of matter to four litres of water. . . .'

Treating with chemicals is avoided in gardens. People prefer to use natural methods, even if modern times do not favour them. 'Cabbages are full of greenfly. They should be treated, but I don't like doing it. In the old days there used to be the ground beetle which was called "the gardener". It ate up the insects, but it's completely disappeared. There were also ladybirds, which are coming back. ...'

Natural elements are always preferred to artificial products. 'Rainwater is best for plants. ... I collect it in a tub under the drainpipe and I water as required. The water from the cistern is too cold. ...' In the same way pests are disposed of by natural means. Hence a whole list of recipes and tricks that are passed from garden to garden. 'Take moles, for instance, Clémence has a lot in her garden, which have done much damage this year ... So she tries to kill them with a branch from a rosebush inserted in the galleries which the moles dig out. There is even a mole grass, Clémence has got some ... it has a strong taste and smell and it repels moles. It should be planted in gardens.' Insecticides and pesticides are left to the farmer and are not allowed into the garden.

The gardener counts on Nature to help him or her with the work and in no way tries to control her. 'Parsley – there's a plant that grows where it will, and you must let it come of its own accord. In some gardens you get no results at all, in others it grows everywhere. Cauliflowers don't come up here, but my mother-in-law used to say she had good ones in the garden opposite. Here it's not possible. Carrots are the same: this is not a garden for carrots. We have lovely potatoes, but not carrots. You have to sow them in the field. ...'

Planting in a garden obviously depends on the nature of the soil. Most of the gardens in Minot have the same soil as the whole cultivated plain, i.e. limestone and clay that is heavy and permeable. 'Cauliflowers need water. We can't grow them here, it's too dry. The earth is like a sieve, it doesn't hold water. Ditto broad beans, we never plant them. The soil is not dense enough, and it's too chalky.'

As for the cycle of tasks in the garden, it is dictated above all by the continental climate that prevails on this extreme south border of the Langres plateau – long hard winters and hot stormy summers. Gardeners fear the early frosts at the beginning of the autumn and the late ones at the end of the spring. They don't go into their kitchen gardens until the end of March or beginning of April, and they bear these meteorological tendencies in mind when they choose their varieties. 'French beans you must sow in May, but not before 18 May, or they get frozen. There are no more frosts after 18 May.

However in one year, 1949, everything froze. In these parts you must not buy early varieties. There's always bad weather in the spring, cold with sudden showers and frosts which may spoil everything. So you need semi-earlies, because if you get real earlies, you sometimes run into trouble and there's frost. You've got to be careful.'

Another weather consideration is wind. At Minot one is careful not to plant when the north and east winds are blowing, because they are dry and cold in winter and hot and withering in summer. 'André Marrolet, he's always careful about wind. I no longer bother about it. This year the north wind never stopped blowing, so what was to be done? You had to plant!' The west and south-west winds are kind because they bring rain. When they blow you sow the small seeds. Apart from these favourable and unfavourable winds you are wary of gales, the violent winds that come from any and every direction, parching the plants and the soil.

These gales occur in March or at the beginning of August, on Saint Lawrence's day, and they are associated with certain phases of the moon which, in its turn, also has influence on the garden programme. The March moon, which starts at the last new moon of the month, is cold and harmful like the dry, icy winds that accompany it. One has to be careful of this moon, as one does of the April moon. Once this first bad moon is over, you start spring sowing, only interrupted by the April moon, the last new moon of the month. These April moons are said to be sterile.[13] The August moon, on the other hand, which is linked with the Saint Lawrence gales, is beneficial and favourable to planting. Under this friendly moon autumn sowing is started. You hasten to cut back weeds and brambles, for they will not grow again.

Quite apart from these special moons, either disastrous or helpful, lunar phases continue to influence crops as the seasons advance. According to the type of plant, you sow or plant out with the new moon, i.e. as it waxes, or wanes. The former helps growth in height and the spread of everything that grows above ground, the latter helps life in the earth and the fruiting of ground plants. 'With a new moon everything seeds and flowers well, with an old moon everything becomes luxuriant. One plants anything that shoots upwards, all small seeds, as the moon waxes. Peas and French beans then pod better. ... Spinach, carrots and potatoes should be planted with the old moon, otherwise they'll flower all the year; lettuces and cabbages then form hearts and onions swell. .... If you plant onions with a new moon, they grow straight upwards and don't make bulbs.'

So the phases of the moon divide plants into two categories – those that grow up in the air, and those that grow under or along the ground. The saints of the religious calendar each protect their own plants: 'On Saint Agatha's day, 5 February, one sows spring salad; on Shrove Tuesday, parsley. On 3 May, Saint Cross day, one should plant French beans, and on Rogation day too, which produces an abundance. But they say that a thousand beans come up from one seed if you sow on Saint Petronella's day; on Saint Médard's day a billion, but on Saint Barnabas's day only a thousand. ...' So the gardening calendar is put in the form of proverbs and jingles, which act as a guide and jog the failing memories of our gardeners.

The old people of the village are the repositories of this planting lore, and people turn to them in moments of hesitation. At *le Mont* an able gardener holds the role of adviser: 'Monsieur Mulot knows it all and warns us when we ought to plant this or that.' At the centre of the village the former draper is the expert and acts as special guide for her neighbourhood: 'Take Marie Larmier, she's for ever coming to me for chicory, and every time she asks me when she must plant it out. "You have a Claude in your family", I tell her. "You could remember that way." It's the same with Madeleine who's always coming to ask me, "Can one plant this or that?" She adds, "You ought to write it all down. There are lots of things we shan't know once you're gone."' The written and the oral are both great supports for the memory in these rural societies, even if the latter is simply used to confirm the former.

Individual hard work and personal skill are indispensable for obtaining good results; but in addition it is wise to respect a certain number of principles which, in the form of rules and prohibitions, help a garden to prosper.

Gardens are under the influence of the moon and the protection of the saints, and they are blessed by the *curé* at Rogation time; but as a last precaution account is also taken of their geographical position. The seeds used always come from the north or east of France: they come from the cold to the less cold. 'We always buy seeds from merchants in the department of Moselle. That part of the world is at least as cold as it is here, so the plants acclimatise themselves better. If we take plants, even flowers, from the south, they are more fragile and don't prosper.' In fact the people of Minot merely follow the general trend, started in the nineteenth century, of getting their provisions of seeds from the great merchants of the north of France.[14] Just before the last war supplies were bought at the fair on 6 March, to which nursery gardeners came from the Langres plateau. There the women found seeds for onions, peas, French beans and flowers. The menfolk ordered the small seeds for field crops, for example, lucerne, sainfoin, clover and rape.

Yet only the necessary minimum was bought at the fair, for then normal practice was to provide one's own stock of seed: 'My grandmother obtained her own seeds for lettuce, parsley, onions and leeks – in fact anything that ran to seed. She wrapped the plants in newspapers and hung them in the loft. In February she said, "Children, we must go and get the seeds." Then we beat the dried plants on the newspaper. For potatoes she took the seedlings to the cellar, and we went a long time before changing them.' It was only concern to avoid plant degeneration that led to purchases of seed. Nowadays seeds and seedlings are no longer collected because the present varieties are so forced and improved that they have become too fragile. 'It's not worth planting out potato seedlings now; there's no result. Even packets of seeds can't be kept from one year to the next.'

In addition, some vegetables are disappearing. Parsnips, which were essential in the old days for making hot-pot, are no longer grown. 'As for kohlrabi, you can't get it any more. Formerly we had it by the cartload; we used to put it in the hot-pot or rabbit stew; there was so much of it that we gave it to the cows.' In the same way, just as the fairs have disappeared, the famous places for vegetables have gone. 'The Orret turnip was famous. Not it's finished, it's no longer grown.'

The garden does not escape the upheavals of the time and is seen as a place where the forces of nature and of history link up.

Every house has a fairly extensive poultry run, hidden behind a building or included in the garden. The mistress of the house takes full control of it, deciding on the number of fowls to rear and the hatchings to arrange. If she wishes, she can even trade in poultry. The farmers' wives nearly all do it because they have the time and space. Spending less time in the fields than before, they can spend more time on their birds. Some competent, hardworking workers' wives are tempted by this trading and go in for new, sought-after breeds such as pheasants and turkeys. The profit that results belongs to these women absolutely and they spend it as they like. Anyway these activities cannot be carried on to the detriment of family feeding; nor can they be pursued in partnership with other members of the village, and so they are marginal.

The garden of a house is too small to supply the total food needs of a family, and so recourse has to be had to the *chènevière*, or hemp-field.

These plots of land, originally planted with hemp, and later with hops,[15] now carry potatoes and fodder. However they still take the name of their original crop. The *chènevières* are to be found on the perimeter of the village. Inserted between the orchards and en-closures, they help to encircle the village with a thin band that comes just before the cultivated fields beyond.

These plots used to carry commercial crops and were well tended and enriched: 'It's good soil, the vegetables come up well; but it's a heavier soil than in the gardens.' The soil does not suit all vegetables. 'I don't plant my salads in the *chènevière*, the soil's not light enough.' This excessive richness of the soil means that no seedbeds can be laid down there; these are all confined to the garden. Once the plants are developed enough to stand the vital thrust of the soil, they are transplanted to the *chènevière*. For this reason, no fragile plants are put there. The only crops are 'soup vegetables', for example, cab-bage, French beans, carrots, turnips and onions; also fodder for the poultry run.

Fortunately this great vigour of the soil is moderated by the dampness and good ventilation of the area. Being situated in low-lying ground with underground springs, the soil always enjoys enough irrigation: 'You never have to water the *chènevière*.' As they are placed outside the village on the edge of open fields and are not enclosed – a simple stone marks the limits of the properties – the *chènevières* are well ventilated. 'In gardens the walls and trees afford shelter from frost, but they prevent air from circulating. In the *chènevières* everything grows better because the air gets at every-thing. The vegetables flourish, and the carrots and cabbages are less troubled by caterpillars.' Water and air are the two elements which tone down the strength of the soil. In the *chènevière* the water remains constantly fresh; the air circulates neither too much nor too little, just enough to repel harmful insects and refresh the plants. The happy balance of nature here leads to a good growth of plants, just as in a larder a good draught of air, not too hot or too cold, keeps the bacon fresh.

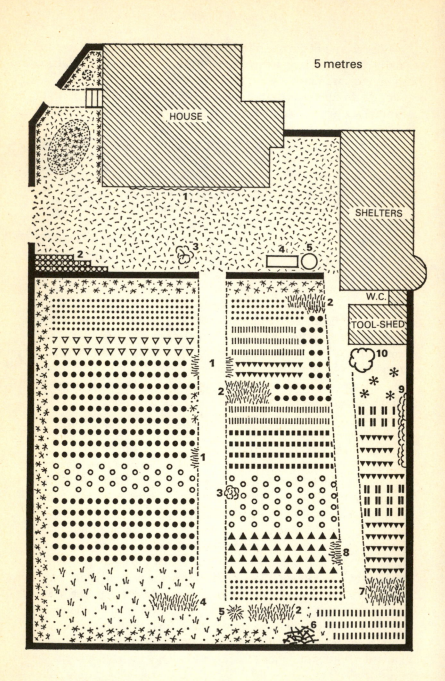

5 metres

HOUSE

SHELTERS

W.C.

TOOL-SHED

The *chènevière* shows a delicate, natural balance between meteorological and geological elements. Here 'good water, good soil, good
air' combine in harmony to make certain plants grow unimpeded.
Gardens and *chènevières* are complementary: you cannot imagine
one without the other.

The *chènevières* are long in shape, usually about a quarter of an
acre in extent. They are generally divided in two unequal parts, separated by a narrow band of earth. The smaller half is devoted to
growing fodder such as lucerne, maize and beetroot to feed poultry.
The other is subdivided into rows which are evenly spaced and
planted with vegetables. Each vegetable occupies two or three rows.
In the *chènevières* you count in rows: 'A row of cabbages amounts to
more than five hundred feet and fills two carts.'

The work cycle on the *chènevière* responds to the same meteorological, astrological and religious imperatives as the work in the
garden. However, there is only one crop a year there, whereas in the
garden there are two. The kitchen garden is sown between February
and June to obtain a harvest in June-September, and again between
June and September for a second harvest at the very beginning of the
following spring. In the *chènevière* sowing takes place between 1
May and 14 July; after that one lets things grow, and the crops are
picked around the time of the first frosts. In both gardens there is
rotation of crops; one does not put the same species in the same spot
two years running. 'You have to change for the soil to be renewed.'

The garden goes on for ever, the *chènevière* is temporary, lasting
about ten years. When the weeds multiply and the thistles abound,
the *chènevière* is ploughed in depth and planted with lucerne and
sainfoin for three to five years; then the cycle of garden crops is resumed.

Gardens and *chènevières* carry few fruit trees, or none at all. They
are only to be found in orchards situated below the gardens or

---

Fig. 3 (opposite).   The Chevenoz yard and garden

Yard: 1. Climbing clematis. 2. Pots of flowers. 3. Decorative shrub.
4. Trough. 5. Well and pump.
Garden: 1. Chives. 2. Parsley. 3. Redcurrant bush. 4. Chervil. 5. Tarragon.
6. Rubbish heap. 7. Sorrel. 8. Thyme. 9. Raspberry bush 10. Pear tree

salads	strawberries	spinach	asparagus
turnips	leeks	onions	pumpkins
potatoes	carrots	beans	flowers

interspersed amid the *chènevières*. Neither the soil nor the climate in
Minot lends itself to real fruit-growing: 'One gets fruit every two or
three years', also the orchards which required care and skill for poor
results have now been abandoned. The dead trees have not been
replaced. Only a few old people still know how to graft and renew
their orchard, and these do it more for pleasure than profit: 'Nicolas
still does good grafting. He finds wild stock in the woods and grafts
on cuttings which he takes off the trees in the garden. He either puts
them in his own garden or he leaves them in the woods. He had one
too many the other day, an apple shoot, so he put it in our garden
and grafted it on our pippin. You've got to graft to have fine fruit.
You do it either in August or in March, when the sap rises.'

In the old days the orchards were almost entirely planted with
apples, pears and plums, all in late, hardy varieties, whose fruit was
above all destined for stewing, for jam-making or drying: 'In our
orchard we used to have large pears called Cadillac which we used
for stewing or jam. Then there were Curé pears and above all, on a
very old tree, some small greenish pears which appeared in Decem-
ber; we used to call them "black pears" and I've never seen them
elsewhere. Two apple trees provided hardy apples for stewing;
another tree called "Grandmother's" yielded excellent grey apples in
September. Another one produced large red apples with white flesh,
and we also had several local pippins. There used to be cherry trees
but they didn't amount to much. There were quinces for jam,
medlars, walnuts, and above all plums – quetsches, Damascus blues
or white ones to make liqueur, and Damiselles for tarts.' But just as
the village has sold its walnut trees and has not renewed them, so
individuals have let their orchards die. Indeed most of them are used
as paddocks for fattening livestock.

Ways of living

In the old days the produce of the farm provided nearly all the food
needs of the household. Nowadays its place in the family diet tends
to be less. Anyway, before we consider how families feed themselves,
let us enquire into the size and organisation of the group which
shares this nourishment.

At Minot each married family sets up its own home. Father and
married son, father-in-law and son-in-law do not live together, or for
as short a time as possible. The household group consists generally of

parents and unmarried children. In practice the situation is less clear
cut. When parents hand over their farm or shop to their heir, they
retire to a small house, rented or bought, as near as they can find to
the workplace, in the same street if possible. Of course strict conditions, duly laid down in written form before a solicitor, govern the
inheritance, i.e. the shares allotted to brother and sister and the rights
to be exercised by the parents.[16] It is nevertheless true that mutual
help is the rule, and there are constant exchanges of food between the
young and the old generations. This goes so far that it is sometimes
difficult to determine who produces and who consumes, even when
the two houses are clearly separated. For instance it sometimes
happens that the two households grow things together and eat them
separately in their own homes: 'I'm the one who breeds the rabbits;
my daughter gives me hay and beet to feed them. And then when one
of them is ready to be killed, I cook it at her place, but I take away a
piece for us two to eat, my husband and I. I raise a few chickens
which my daughter gives me together wth the grain to feed them. As
for eggs, we each help ourselves.' One household can produce food
while the other gives material help, then each party eats it separately:
'When Grandfather retired he went down every day to work on the
farm. He took the cows to the fields and then took home with him
enough to eat.' In these two cases the two homes share the same 'pot',
but it is served at two different tables. But there are cases where
husbands' households produce separately and consume together. It
happens when a widower or widow continues to run a garden, but
comes twice a day to have meals with the children. The produce from
the two gardens contributes to the common table. The proximity of
the homes helps this sort of relationship, just as it helps mutual aid
and work in common. The father, so long as he has the strength, still
goes every day to the farm. He shares in the work of the fields, he
milks the cows and cleans out the cowshed. The old mother helps her
daughter or daughter-in-law every day with the cooking, the cleaning or in looking after the children. Generous presents or contributions are tokens of thanks given to all those who work in the
enterprise.

The household, considered as a unit of consumption, is sometimes
difficult to define and determine. It seems to be diffused in space and
differentiated in time. To put things simply, let us say that in most
cases the meal table consists of the parents and their unmarried
children, together with the father or mother of one of the couple, to

whom an unmarried brother or sister or an orphan niece sometimes attach themselves. In former times a farm hand or servant for the farmer, an apprentice or worker for the craftsman, used to be added to the family group. All eat at the same table: 'At our place the farm-hands eat at the same table and had the same food as we did. In well-to-do houses there were two tables in the same parlour, and there wasn't the same food for the master and servant. The latter got the rabbits' heads and paws. But ours was a good house. Indeed it was well known and we always got servants. The food was good and the wine was not watered down.'

Every day two main meals bring the household together – dinner about noon and supper served about half past six in winter and half past seven in summer. But according to the time and the season both children and adults come to the table for other rapid collations – breakfast, ten o'clock and four o'clock snacks, eaten in the fields when important work is on.

In former times the eating utensils were put straight on the oak table in the parlour. Mats and napkins were put away, folded and starched, in the cupboard and were only used on feast days. 'At meals we wiped our mouths with our aprons. Tante Virette took out a handkerchief to wipe hers. She always carried a hanky to blow her nose and one to wipe her mouth. My grandmother used to say that she had a lot of trouble with her handkerchiefs.'

Each person at table had a fork and a hollow plate with a slice of bread in it. Men, women and children took a knife out of their pockets: 'For one always had a knife with one. When you work on a farm you always have to cut something. With animals it was a harness that needed cutting quickly or a string to unfasten. . . . There were different kinds. There was the carter's knife, it was a stout one with a blade, a saw, a punch and even a pruning knife. It was used by those who went to work in the woods to strip bark. The Swiss knife had a corkscrew and was more delicate. One bought a knife for small boys when they were seven or eight. For women there were knives with horn or mother-of-pearl handles, less complicated than men's knives. But women always had knives just like men.' The mother served the whole table. As we know, she sat on the long side of the table next to her husband. Opposite sat the children, and at the two ends the hired hands and visiting relations.

Until after the 1940 war nearly all the food consumed was prepared at home. Bread was kneaded and baked at the farm. 'With us it was Grandmother who kneaded, she had the right touch. We kept the yeast from one baking to the next. She made the dough the night before, kneaded it at daybreak, and then put it in round baskets while the oven heated. Before putting the bread into the oven with the wooden shovel, one marked a cross on it because the dough had to be opened up. She used to make seven or eight loaves weighing about four pounds each, and then a smaller one that we ate at dinner on the first day. This fresh bread was a treat compared with the last loaf that was eight days old. With what remained of the dough we made *salée*, i.e. a bit of dough, some butter and cream, sprinkled with coarse salt, and the whole thing put in a baking tin. In autumn we put plums, wild pears and apples to dry in the warm oven to make them tender. The loaves were put away in the bread bin.' After the 1914 war people preferred to buy their bread from the baker.

The basis of cooking consisted of colza oil, melted butter and lard kept in earthenware pots. 'We used to make two sorts of cheese, fat and thin. Fat cheese was made as follows. Just after milking we put the milk in a pot and added a coffee-spoonful of rennet. Then we left the pot near the fireplace in winter and in a cool place above the sink in summer. When the cheese was "cooked" (in the sense of "fermented") we strained it and put it in the cheese strainer to dry. When it was dry, it was washed with salt or white wine, then we placed it back in the drainer to dry, with chaff around it. Thin cheese was made with milk from which the cream had been removed.'

Meat was provided by the pig and the small amount of poultry kept, though often, among poor folk, these were sold: 'When there was a bird or a rabbit, it was for selling; we didn't always eat it. We hadn't enough money to buy a few sous worth of tobacco. My father used to send me out to get some, and I said I would call later to pay. We found the money by selling a dozen eggs.' To this meat was added the bag resulting from shooting and poaching: 'My father shot a lot of rooks. . . . He used oxen for ploughing and he always had his gun on the plough. . . . Oxen are not frightened of gunfire. A horse would not have been the same, he would have bolted. . . . Rooks follow the furrow, so my father turned round and could kill seventeen at one shot. All birds that are black are like rooks . . . you can eat them. This wild loot brought some strange smells to the daily cooking. We skinned rooks, otherwise they tasted bitter. My Grandmother put them in a saucepan with potatoes. What I loved was a rook stew, or what they called a *fricassée*. And then wild birds have far more brains than domestic birds. You've no idea how big the rooks' brains are, they have large heads . . . and that's what I liked – rooks' brains. Then there were jays, which are still eaten; Jacky picks them up. You don't skin jays, you simply pluck them. We also eat *fricassée* of crow.'

Every household had its hives, and the honey gathered from them replaced sugar. At the four o'clock snack the mother spread it on bread; she also used it to make gingerbread and hydromel. 'Wine was a luxury', only the rich drank it every day, the rest only on feast days. On ordinary days people were content with *la pique* which was made of wild fruit: 'We gathered wild pears and wild apples. We put them in a barrel with some water and waited three weeks; then you could start drinking. When you were really thirsty, it rasped like lemonade. We drank it at evening gatherings and at meals. You added water as the level went down: and in the end it was nothing but water.' *Goutte* or *eau-de-vie* was made by the distiller 'who set himself up on the village square, and you brought your fruit along. You provided the wood and you fed the fellow.' *Goutte* was made from orchard plums to which, in bad years, were added the fruit of the service tree and the rowan, sloes and 'much else'.

Fruit and vegetables were provided by the garden and orchard, to which were added a mass of wild crops. Following the slow gait of the cows in the fields, grandmothers and children picked spring mushrooms, lamb's lettuce and dandelions and snails hidden in the grass. On summer evenings or autumn afternoons the same parties scattered along the footpaths and picked the pungent fruits of the underwood – 'medlars and *culs-de-singe*, you have to let them get really ripe or else they sour the mouth' – and the coloured berries of the hedgerows – 'we used to pick berberis and hawthorn and dog-berries to make jam.'

These sour fruits, these bitter-sweet vegetables and the gamey meat of shot birds were a sharp contrast in taste to the normal flavourless family food. This consisted largely of hot-pot made up of vegetables and pork. 'We made hot-pot every day. One put water in a cauldron, then various vegetables according to season, but always a cabbage and potatoes, then fat bacon. The hot-pot cooked on its own without bother. In the morning there was the soup from the hot-pot, then after the animals had been seen to, there was a bit of bacon and occasionally an egg. We ate the soup and vegetables at midday and the rest of the hot-pot liquid in the evening with a little cream. For the four o'clock snack a slice of hot-pot bacon on bread with chopped parsley and a drop of vinegar, sometimes a piece of cheese.' Only feast days and Sundays brought a little change to meals. On those days a poultry or game dish, an omelette or bread and milk, broke the culinary monotony of the week.

The fundamental principle in all these homes was to be self-sufficient. One only ate what one had produced, shot or picked up. What one did not produce oneself, one obtained by exchange. Money circulated as little as possible for the purchase of food, and barter remained the basis of exchange. Eggs, poultry and butter from the farm were the basic elements of barter, and at home they were consumed most sparingly. 'We never made an omelette entirely of eggs; too many would be needed. We added potatoes and the remains of rice and beans. We also made little pancakes, just omelettes with flour. You mixed flour with milk and eggs. It was a red-letter day when we ate an omelette made of nothing but eggs.' This farm produce was exchanged for sugar, rice, pasta, coffee and a bit of chocolate with the dealer who came once a week and sold it at Châtillon market. This was inevitable because the butcher would not barter: 'One hardly went to the butcher except for holidays, when one bought a piece to make boiled beef and vegetables, that's all. When I got married in 1927 I had never eaten beefsteak or fillet of veal. We didn't know what butcher's meat was.'

Not only did people spend as little as possible, but in times of plenty they made provision for the lean days ahead. The harvest of summer, gathered in the gardens, the fields and along the lanes, were in part left untouched and preserved in various forms – sugared, salted or dried. Duly prepared in this way, they were carefully stored from the cellar up to the attic. In the latter was put everything that had to be kept dry – pots of jam, dried fruit, sacks of dried beans, different kinds of flour: 'In the attic we used to put the flour for the pig which was ground at the mill here, and also the flour for ourselves which was ground at Beaunotte mill – it was finer and whiter. In addition the miller gave back to us the bran, which we put in the chickens' mash, and again the wheat chaff that was finer than the bran. We gave that also to the poultry.' From the beams hung, head downwards, the bunches of flowers and plants all wrapped up in newspaper to catch the seeds. In the cellar the vegetables for winter were stacked on the floor – beetroot, carrots, cabbages, kohlrabi, potatoes, with the earth still on them. The bottled fruit and vege-tables in dark green jars with wide necks were lined up against the wall at the back on rough wooden shelves. Next to them were two or three earthenware pots of melted butter and lard, and the jars of green vegetables pickled in brine and covered with a cabbage leaf: 'This meant that the dirt that came up with the salt was deposited on the leaf. So when you wanted to take the French beans out of the pot, well, you lifted out the leaf and the beans were clean. ...' In the middle of the cellar was the salting tub, and at the foot of the staircase the cheese container.

After the Second World War there was a change in ways of living. The gardens were planted with a number of new varieties, which came to vary the local cooking. Above all, the rise in family living standards combined with improved methods of distributing food produce enabled everyone, workers and farmers alike, to buy items of food to which they could not possibly aspire in the old days. Butcher's meat was no longer considered a luxury for special occasions. Meals were now varied and consisted of three or four dishes — hors-d'oeuvre (salad, raw vegetables or *charcuterie*), main dish (meat or poultry, eggs or fish) with a vegetable, cheese, and sweet (fruit or cakes). The little meals that break up a working day were now made up of bread and *charcuterie*, washed down with wine or beer. Coffee had long since replaced soup first thing in the morning. This culinary revolution has complicated the work of cooks charged with preparing formal meals: 'It's a problem what to give people. Fillet steak and leg of lamb, they have them every Sunday. What a problem! I tell you frankly, people don't appreciate things like they used to.' Feast days lose their sense of a food treat, an exceptional occasion to eat a lot and taste unusual dishes.

The day revolves round the same mealtimes. The company sit in the same places as before round the table covered with an oilcloth, and they each have a complete set of eating utensils. The mistress of the house brings the dishes and people help themselves in turn. The abundance of food and the new relationship between generations have caused good table manners largely to disappear.

However, these changes in feeding tastes and habits have not abolished kitchen gardens or gathering food in the countryside. As we know, this all goes on in the village much as before.[17] Just as in the old days, gardens and wild fruit provide, in fresh or preserved form, nearly all the food consumed at home throughout the year. Of course the arrival of the freezer within the last ten years has changed methods of preserving and the types of produce stocked. You can put anything in a freezer: a side of beef, newly plucked chickens, fruit, freshly picked vegetables, eggs, bread, cooked dishes, etc.

Like all novelties, the freezer provokes doubts and controversy. It is totally disapproved of by some who believe that a long conservation period is incompatible with freshness: 'I'm against it, it's disgusting. People who eat food out of freezers get liver trouble. I believe they cause indigestion.' Others, on the other hand, have adopted the freezer wholeheartedly and have made it part of their domestic economy: 'Madame Roget puts everything into hers – an omelette all ready made, wrapped in plastic, all her chickens killed at once at four months old. ...' Others are still wary and continue to go in for mixed preserving. The pig is distributed between the salting tub and the freezer, the same with vegetables and fruit: 'I've frozen mushrooms for the first time; I've also put some in jars. I shall do both for French beans too.' Above all, freezing enables the housewife to enjoy garden produce and wild fruit over the whole year and to manage the domestic budget economically. The mistress of the house kills, all at one go, the pullets that have reached the right weight. She thus saves on their feed. The farmer, who has to sacrifice an animal because he can see no profit in selling it to a dealer, cuts it up and keeps it in his freezer. The worker can buy his meat from a wholesaler at the most favourable price and at the right moment: 'The butcher's got lots of work. Everyone with a freezer buys off him. He makes pâtés, ham, black puddings, small sausages, and he has good meat. He doesn't sell retail. If he sells steak, it's ten pieces at once, and it's the same for slices of ham. You can't imagine how much he sells. Clémence, she buys off him and puts the meat in Marguerite's freezer. It comes cheaper. Anyone who's got a dinner coming on orders from the butcher. Everyone has a freezer and, thanks to it, gets better prices.' The freezer has taken its natural place in this subsistence economy. It is perfectly adapted to the new food habits. It saves time and money, and offers its households the possibility of living in a state of food autarchy, almost as in the old days.

Nevertheless the freezer remains an expensive object, and it frequently happens that several families group together to buy one. It is placed in the home that has enough space and is divided into as many lockers as there are owners, the volume of each locker being proportionate to the share paid. Each person uses her locker as she wishes and can, if she feels inclined, take in the supplies of a neighbour or relative who has no freezer. The draper is without one and stocks her few sacks of French beans or raspberries from one season to another with her cousin, who shares a freezer with her sister, or else with her neighbour. The group of owners can be either on a neighbourhood or on a family basis.

This co-operation of relations or neighbours in the matter of a freezer can be extended to other activities. Quite often several households combine to fatten two or three pigs and so reduce costs: 'At the Fleurots' three pigs have arrived: one is eventually for Georgette and Marguerite in return for feeding them, one for Mother Fleurot for providing the grain and one for the dealer for producing the animals. In that way no money changes hands; a piglet is worth fifteen or sixteen thousand old francs nowadays.' The neighbours who do not take part directly in this communal rearing bring their kitchen peelings and the remains of their meals for the animals; so they get a few good pieces at slaughtering time. 'I brought the milk left over from my cheese-making for the last pig. I don't throw away any remains but bring them along for the pig, so I had the right to a pork cutlet. At present I'm giving them to the dog, so people are saying, "You'll get a dog cutlet."'

These few examples of effective co-operation between neighbours and relations, these gifts of food between households, give a good idea of the subsistence economy. It places each household in a cycle of general exchange.

We should not forget that this garden produce, the bag from shooting and the pickings from the countryside are sufficient to feed a household. But that is not the main point; for the harvest of gardens and wild life enable people to take part in a circuit or reciprocal gifts. It is true that up to the fifties of this century the rural sector showed a precarious market economy, so that all food produce from the farm and the resources of the countryside were indispensable for feeding households. Furthermore, all sorts of saving and thrifty habits went along with this market economy. 'At that time one lived on one's farm. One didn't make any money, and one didn't need any – only enough to pay one's rent. One threw nothing away and one kept everything; everything was used and nothing was wasted. It would never have occurred to anyone to buy a floor cloth. In the village there was nothing much to throw away. Everyone worked to feed himself; nothing was bought, except perhaps shoes.'

Economy in material things, as in subsistence goods, was a real obsession at the time and the mainspring of all the domestic group's activity. Nothing was to be wasted. You saved peelings and swill to feed animals; you saved ashes from the cooker to soak the laundry and manure the garden. Every object that could be re-used was put aside and employed when required, both in the home and at the farm: 'When the sheaf-binder came we used string to bind the sheaves. Then with the steam threshing-machine, the straw had to be tied up, so we used the string from the sheaves again. Two lots of sheaf string were needed to bind up one bale of straw. You had to tie a reef-knot, because if you tied a granny knot, crack!, the straw burst open. We called it the idiot's knot! You had to work fast as the machine chugged on. And then this string, after the straw, we used it yet again to make tethers for calves. We plaited the pieces of string with a machine, three at a time; we used to do this in the evenings. Everything was used again. String was expensive. The same with grain sacks, which were provided by the merchant. But sometimes one needed them for keeping corn. Fertiliser came in cloth sacks, so we washed them and they came in useful. But what a job it was washing the sacks at the fountain! I'd like to see the young people doing that work nowadays. They'd rebel! We used to do it as a matter or course.'

This frugality in buying things, this economy in the use of possessions, all these habits acquired very young are reflected today in the gestures and behaviour of the old people in the village. The electric light is never put on before darkness has set in. So long as the daylight lasts one does without electricity. In winter the cooker is lit on rising in the morning and heats the parlour and bedroom: 'We are never cold. It's different with the young. . . . First of all I'm warmly dressed – woollen chemise, two pairs of stockings, socks. In our bedroom when it's cold we put the heating on an hour before going to bed, no more. We turn it off for the night. We heat a bit on Sunday morning to change our clothes and have the room slightly warm, that's all. The heat coming from the parlour is quite enough.' The old view with alarm the wastage and improvidence of the young, used as they always have been to husband their possessions and treat them carefully. 'I still mend clothes today. Dear me, women sometimes say, "You're not going to patch up that old thing once again!" But I can't throw things away; I've got so used to mending. The young don't like doing it. Lucille brings me her husband's socks. And then Judith – her husband has torn a brand-new suit. . . . "Oh", she said, "I'm going to chuck the shirt away." "Well", I said, "you don't really want to. Give it to me, I'll mend it for you." So now he's wearing it. Really, a new shirt, with only a tear in the sleeve, it really shocks me. One is so used to saving.' Present-day affluence makes these habits of thrift and this austere morality seem out of date.

Nowadays in the village the food resources are not so carefully hoarded, but they are still widely distributed within the community.

The art of exchange

The people with whom one most willingly shares one's food are obviously one's own near relations.

'Lucille gets all her vegetables at her mother's; she helps herself to everything. She goes and fetches them herself or for her sister when her sister can't come. In that way we sent Adeline some lettuce, potatoes, onions, garlic, parsley, everything in fact. ... The last time my brother came I gave him five kilos of butter, six day-old chicks, five older chicks. ... The other day I gave my sister a brace of ducks and some eggs.'

These gifts,which touch all types of produce without exception, are only exchanged between very near relatives – children married in town, brothers and sisters gone away, members of an ancient household now dispersed. This circulation of food goes well beyond the confines of the village community. These presents do not of course call for financial or material repayment; the obligation to return them is not pressing, and the reciprocal gifts, when they come, can be quite different in nature and long deferred in time. 'My brother, he comes to help me when I've got changes and repairs to do in the house. ... My sister buys goods for me wholesale. ... Lucille buys oil and pasta ... they're not so dear in the supermarkets. The girls never come empty-handed. Their mother feeds them every Sunday, and they know well what that costs. They bring sugar and coffee, or else it's a shirt for their father or an apron for their mother. Oh Marguerite doesn't lose out; her daughters are very kind.' This distribution of produce and exchange of services between relations preserve the cohesion of a group which has a destiny and interests in common in spite of its dispersion. It is noticeable that if too great a disparity of income comes between related households, the food exchanges come to an end and contact lapses. So long as they last, these economic ties between relatives weave a food distribution network between town and country whose existence is often forgotten.

Within the village community this nutritional circuit continues, but it diversifies according to the geographical and genealogical proximity of the residents. Everything circulates among the members of a neighbourhood who have long lived on the same street, or among close relatives – cooked dishes, remains of cooking, garden produce as well as poultry, earth from the *chènevière* as well as honey from the hives. 'When one doesn't finish a dish, one takes it along to the neighbour. Sometimes he is very pleased. Yesterday I made some floating islands, and Victor didn't want to finish them; so I took them to Gilles. Or when I make boiled beef and vegetables, I bring the broth to Clémence as we can't drink it. It'd be a pity to throw it away. It gives her a good soup. ...' The excuse given for these presents is that nothing should be wasted and everything should be eaten or saved. That's the way it's put. But in fact it looks as if nowadays the object of such exchanges is quite different.

To appreciate this you have only got to follow the language of the exchanges; for they really are exchanges under the guise of presents going from one house to another. 'We trade vegetables between neighbours. Look at Lise, she has peas at the moment, and she gives me some to make up a dish. I've got peas in my garden, but they're not ready yet. She has no lettuces or turnips, so I give her some. In the spring I had no lettuce, I suppose I sowed too late; well, Marguerite had some. Every two or three days I went up to her place to fetch a lettuce. Now she hasn't got any more, so I take her some. It's a friendly exchange of services between neighbours. It's the same with Julia who lives opposite.' It is not unusual for neighbours to share their crops. If one woman plants a mass of onions, the other will help herself to them as long as she herself sows some peas, of which the neighbour will partake in her turn. The garden forges links. Furthermore, this neighbourly relationship is so intensely lived that in daily parlance the word 'present' displaces the word 'exchange'. 'Here we almost live together. We don't exchange, we give, which is normal among neighbours.' In the narrow circle of the vicinity or of the family network, gifts are exchanged every day and cover all kinds of goods, material or spiritual: 'Look, our neighbour when she's sad and depressed still often comes and weeps on our shoulders.' Between houses such as these, as between near relations, it is not seemly to pay back at once or return the same thing. 'We lead our lives in common', says the draper about the first cousin who lives opposite her. 'For instance, I never buy eggs. They (the cousin and his wife) need to get out, so my husband takes them for drives. She will not pay the petrol. She gives me eggs or, when she kills a chicken, she gives me a wing or a foot for me to make some broth. If she kills a rabbit, I get a leg.' The present in return, which always comes, is never immediate or identical, for all sorts of things circulate in this narrow sector — food from the freezer, half a pig, or soil from the *chènevières*.

In former times every house was bound to possess a *chènevière*. The vicissitudes of inheritance, sales and lettings mean that now many homes are without them. Also those who do possess one offer the use of a few rows to others, either neighbours or relations. The draper has no *chènevière*, but her first cousin Nicolas owns a large one at a place called *le Verger* ('the orchard'). There he lets her use a few rows. Furthermore, the draper is not the only one who enjoys this privilege. Beside her one finds rows allocated to two nieces, to the sister of Nicolas's wife, to Pariset the garage proprietor whose workshops you see at the bottom of the *chènevière*, to Perron, the former woodcutter who regularly helped Nicolas when he was his tenant, and finally to the post office manager.

At the beginning of spring Nicolas gets the *chènevière* ploughed; in May he traces out the rows himself with his cultivator; then he allots each person his or her row. A split stick, into which is slipped a piece of cardboard showing the tenant's name, is placed at the edge of the plot and indicates everyone's ground. Thus the stick saying 'Postman' marks the post office manager's row. A few metres further down one finds a stick saying 'Chevenoz'; these are the rows allotted to the draper; and so on.

'In the country, rows are given', which makes it plain that no money passes for the use of a piece of ground. 'One pays nothing for the rows', but the owners and users enter or function in a circuit of exchanges made up of gifts and gifts in return, always more or less spread out in time. Nicolas runs a system of mutual aid with his near relations, who are neighbours in the *chènevière* just as they are in the village. The allocation of a few rows is just an entry in a long account that is never settled, a favour amongst many in a long cycle of reciprocity. Anyway, the bookkeeping, abstract though it may seem, is always meticulously up to date, and accounts can sometimes be swiftly presented. 'It is my nephew who ploughs because he has a tractor, but I don't pay for his petrol because they too have the right to plant there.' With tenants who are not relatives and with neighbours, the accounting is more formal and the favours in return come more quickly, although they are always announced in the language of giving: 'They're free, the rows, they give us nothing – well, father Perron, he gives us a basketful every year. . . . This year he even gave us two. . . . I go and do my repairs at Pariset's; he never asks me for any money.'

Services rendered, presents offered, ground lent; the balance is so finely kept that at any moment the cycle can be broken by a unilateral decision without animosity or bitterness. Everyone feels that he has received his or her due. The garage proprietor has warned Nicolas that he will not take any rows next year. He has bought a *chènevière* near his workshop. The terms of the transaction between them will change, but the relationship will remain intact. Nicolas will make up for repairs to come with a pot of honey from his hives. Between neighbours the exchange of goods and services can always continue, whatever the conditions.

Nicolas is a generous distributor of rows, yet he is not the owner of the whole of his *chènevière*. He rents part of it from a family in the village who do not make use of it. The total rent is 'three rabbits a year', rabbits that are fed by Nicolas's cousin who has the use of two rows in the *chènevière*. 'As I've got the leftovers, I raise the rabbits which are used in payment.' Exchanges can thus be transferred from one household to another, involving each in a cycle of trading, where food produce really comes to look like money.

In this way, within the narrow circle of the neighbourhood or close family relationship, all food is liable to be shared. Anything that helps to produce this food can also circulate. Concern for saving, which is the avowed motive for these exchanges, is less important than the solidarity that they establish between households. These gifts and the counterparts that circulate between old-established neighbours and close relations keep the links of blood and neigh- bourliness fresh and alive; they keep them, as it were, in working order by constant use and attention. Exchange *makes* cohesion among families and solidarity among neighbours.[18]

Beyond this narrow circle based on residence and kinship, ex- changes proceed actively with the community as a whole in a more formal manner; but they only concern certain categories of goods or very special plants.

It is *knowledge* that is the commodity most frequently exchanged in the community as a whole. Varieties of plants in a garden and ways of raising them are not turned into a mystery, unlike family

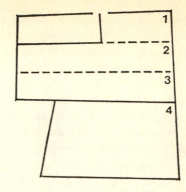

PROPERTY

The *chènevière* which Nicolas Demonet cultivates does not entirely belong to him. Part 1 was bought by his grandfather, then divided between his two sons (Nicolas's father and his uncle). Part 2 was bought by his father at the same time as the house (situated on the other side of the street), now inhabited by Nicolas. Finally Part 4 is let to some villagers in return for three rabbits a year.

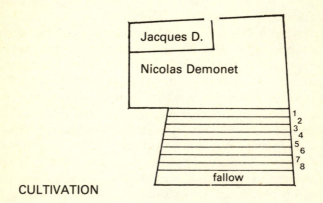

CULTIVATION

Fig. 4.   Nicolas Demonet's *chènevière* at Le Verger

1. N.D.'s first cousin. 2. Sister and niece of N.D.'s wife. 3. Other niece of N.D.'s wife. 4. N.D.'s first cousin twice removed. 5. The garage-owner. 6. The former woodcutter and N.D.'s ex-employee. 7. The postman. 8. N.D.

medicinal recipes that are jealously guarded and handed on under seal of secrecy. There are discussions between gardeners on the advantages of such and such a variety; there is exchange of information and tricks of the trade. The draper possesses a 'recipe book' in which, from earliest childhood, she has noted cooking recipes, knitting patterns, and detailed instructions on how to take cuttings of flowers. Between instructions on how to make dough rise and a recipe for Swiss roll, she has patiently copied out, from an old neighbour's dictation, the way to raise chrysanthemum cuttings. The information was recorded about 1930. Furthermore, admiration shown for a flower, a shrub or a fine-looking vegetable immediately leads to a present of shoots or seeds of the coveted plant: 'Passing by you say, "That's a nice clematis" or "Your geranium looks good", and you are given a cutting.' In this way cuttings of 'Greek moss' (*Campanula carpatica*), used as a perennial border for flower beds, made the rounds of the village. No one today knows who first owned the plant. In the same way there is 'slave-driver' (stag's horn sumach or *Rhus typhina*), a frail, slender shrub with downy, yellow, candle-shaped flowers that turn dark red in autumn, while its leaves become bright orange. Shoots of it are transplanted from one garden to another. It was brought to Minot about ten years ago by a woman who came from the Jura. Nobody knows its real name. Once introduced into the village and adopted, a plant is often given another name. It is as if the community finds it necessary to give its own name to anything that belongs to its universe. This tendency resembles the habit of giving to all members of the group a nickname which takes no account of their local status or geographical origin.[19] The individual's nickname marks his place within the community; the plant's name indicates its adoption locally. Besides 'Greek moss' and the 'slave-driver' one finds 'gherkins' for the small cacti used for borders, 'fleas' for busy Lizzie, 'milk-drops' for snowdrops brought from the forest nearby and planted in the garden. So there grows up a local, unofficial vocabulary, which ignores the dictionary and is common usage throughout the region. Thanks to this shared knowledge and to the plant shoots that are given away, novelties spread from garden to garden – until all the gardens end up by looking alike.

Herbs, those fragile plants that are indispensable in the kitchen and do not grow just anywhere, are passed around widely. 'Everyone comes to my garden for parsley, chives and sorrel – Marguerite's family, for instance, and the Fleurots when they've got guests. I don't mind, it grows again. Parsley doesn't thrive in all gardens; those who've got it have got it. Again, Madame Louchard comes to fetch tarragon for her gherkins; ... I've got no laurel; it's Murillo who gives me some. he's got a laurel bush in an old boiler. You have to bring in laurel in winter or it freezes. Rhubarb is only to be found in two or three gardens in Minot. One goes and gets it there – I've never been able to grow it.'

Garden flowers are also included in the exchanges that take place among members of the village group. They are given, in white bouquets, to the bride at weddings; and, arranged in country-style wreaths, they are placed on the coffins of the dead in church. They are the last offerings of the community to its daughters and its dead.

What is more important is that flowers establish a link between the living and the dead, between the sacred and the profane. Indeed, all through the year, flowers from the gardens are carried to the church. Lilac decorates the main altar in June; Madonna lilies adorn the statue of the Virgin; yellow flowers are laid in front of Saint Joseph. In the old days the girls of the choir were responsible for the church flowers. Nowadays Mass is no longer sung and the girls have no spare time; an old lady does the job. She looks in gardens for roses that have hardly bloomed, half-opened peonies, dahlias in full flower, and she asks for a 'bouquet for the church'. The request is never refused. Garden flowers are also cut to decorate the little shrine at home set up on the refrigerator or dresser, where photographs of the dead parents and the statuette of the Virgin stand next to each other. Then, on Palm Sunday and All Saints' Day, primroses, pansies and chrysanthemums grown in the garden are carried to the cemetery to be put on the family tombs.

Garden flowers offered to protective saints and placed in the church establish a link with the sacred. By decking the church with the harvest of the home one assures the protection of the whole household. Placed on the little shrine in the parlour or on the family tombs, flowers perpetuate the memory of the dear dead, are part of the care one should bestow on them and help to secure the bonds between living and departed relatives.

Society organises itself by family and by neighbourhood for the distribution and exchange of home-grown food. The first division comes in the difference between relatives and non-relatives. Among the former all goods are liable to be shared; among the latter only certain produce is circulated. In the village this family division is crossed by a spatial division. The local group is organised in a series of circles with the household in the middle, then the near neighbours, then the entire village; and, finally, beyond, the community of the dead and the world of the sacred. In each of these circles food produce circulates according to fixed rules. Hence the exchanges are intense between members of the same household or of the same district and consist of all sorts of goods. With the rest of the community the links are occasional, seasonal and limited to a few products. Finally the exchanges with the dead members of the group take a floral, ritual form. In these different circles the reciprocal gifts vary considerably. In the family sector they are often deferred in time and different in nature; in the village sector the return is less delayed and usually of the same nature; in the case of the departed the offerings are purely symbolic.

Nevertheless, certain foodstuffs, valued according to a group code, for example, eggs, poultry, parts of a pig or pots of honey, circulate just like money from one end of the village to the other. This movement tends to fix and confirm the different sectors of the community as we have just outlined them. So the services rendered, the tools lent, all the actions which in a village cannot be valued in money terms, are repayed with the help of these foodstuffs. For example, certain men have special gifts and certain women fulfil particular roles. Their indispensable services are always paid for in kind. The man in charge of bees,[20] who looks after the hives, captures the swarms and gathers the honey, receives as payment part of the honey supply or else a chicken. The man who kills the pig is rewarded for slaughtering and cutting up the animal by the gift of some choice pieces. He also takes part *ex officio* in the meal that follows the killing. The 'home-help', the one who used to be present at all the great occasions in individual lives, is now a general nurse, giving injections and visiting old people who are bedridden. She is never paid for her services in cash. Small presents — a pair of slippers, for instance, or a fowl — and odd services remain the usual way of rewarding her.

Accordingly a system of accounting, vaguely codified but variable, grows up, by which three eggs pay for a seat in a car to go to Dijon; a chicken thanks the postman for his good offices; a piece of black pudding recognises a favour done by the mayor's secretary. This currency role given to food produce means that it cannot be traded commercially within the community. Garden crops, poultry and the pickings of the countryside are never bought and never sold. The way these goods are in fact distributed has an effect on food production policy.

Because of these exchange networks and transactions one soon grasps the necessity for each household to produce more than what is strictly necessary for its own consumption. There must be excess production in the kitchen garden. You must dispose of a surplus in order to enter into a system of mutual exchange with other households. For instance, a couple without children produces far more vegetables than it can use. The surplus is either given to people one wishes to oblige, or made the counterpart of a present previously received, or used to start an exchange connection with another household. Another domestic group with a large family disposes of its fruit: 'We don't eat our fruit, so we give it away. I gave our redcurrants to Madame Colleret; she gave us a pot of jam, but in fact we don't eat it.' The nature of this surplus changes from year to year, from one house to another. What is important is to dispose of the surplus regularly.

Of course these transactions and exchanges are not absolutely necessary. Each household could supply its own needs, plant enough food to guarantee its survival or buy in the produce it lacked. But people recoil from using money for products that can be obtained in another way, and besides these exchanges express and confirm the links between households. These comings and goings between houses, these continual exchanges of goods and services between members of the community, put everyone in contact with everyone else. Each domestic unit is caught up in a network of mutual aid without the intrusion of social origins and professional status. The movement of garden produce reinforces the cohesion of the group and plays its part in forging the mechanism of village sociability.

This diversified distribution of food has doubtless always existed. But in former days it was turned upside down in times of distress, and also institutionalised on certain occasions.

We used to take food to people who were badly off ... my grandmother made me take supplies to people who had a lot of children, the woodcutters for instance. That was in winter, when the snow came, because at the farm, we always had plenty to eat, winter and summer. Nowadays there is no snow, but then there were months when you could not get to the woods, so they had nothing to eat because they lived on cutting wood. So sometimes my grandmother would say, "Take them a sack of potatoes" or some bacon when we killed a pig. ... We used to take food to Toussaint's, Kiki we called him, he burned charcoal. There was also Camille Malet, he had lots of children too. There were probably many others who supplied them because it was always the same situation. During the haymaking and the harvest such people used to come to the farmers as day-labourers, so they were known. One said, "Why, come winter we'll give you a bit of bacon if you need it." One wasn't going to let people die of starvation. They were in a bad way. . . . One said "Winter's hard, what are these poor devils going to eat? One must give them something or they'll starve." There were families who had ten or eleven children. It was sad to think of them having nothing, absolutely nothing. . . . We brought them potatoes, eggs, a chicken, a rabbit, especially in bad weather. You couldn't leave them to starve. When we saw that they couldn't work or that the mother was ill, we took pity on them. When things improved, one said "Ah, now he'll go back to work, and he'll get paid for it." He didn't get paid much, but at least he got paid.

From this long monologue we see the necessity of sharing food with those who need it, with the neighbour who is most in want and lives nearest, in the same village. By these actions the survival of the poorest is certainly assured. One eventually expects work from them, but above all the group shows solidarity and everyone is the better for it.

In the old days one didn't only bring food for the most needy:

One brought presents all the time. In the season of the Perpetual Adoration one brought food to Monsieur le Curé. I remember his maid Mademoiselle Gabrielle had drawers full of chocolate, butter and eggs. . . . It happened in May, when the Sacrament was exposed all day and people went on watch, each in turn. It made a ceremony. Monsieur le Curé invited other priests, so food was brought for him to make a meal . . . a chicken here, some eggs there, it depended . . . but there were always presents at each feast . . . one always brought dragées for a christening. For a wedding one gave anything that could be eaten. . . . Those who were invited generally brought poultry, others tapioca, a kilo of sugar, some chocolate – even the woodcutters brought presents, everyone did the same. . . . It was nothing much to give them, but they were nice to receive.

These gestures of bringing food on all religious and lay occasions seemed like real rituals of commensality. It was as if at these festivities which concerned only one household, all the village took part in the rejoicing by eating together. In this way social inequalities were obliterated, conflicts were smoothed out and mutual help was confirmed.

These customs have now ceased. Presents are no longer 'brought', apart from flowers for those getting married and for the dead. We know that flowers are not treated in the village like other garden produce and that they form part of a symbolic network of exchange.

For this reason they can be given without the gesture appearing archaic or charitable. The nature of the things exchanged has its effect on the relationship which they engender.

So household produce plays a key role in the village. It enables each group to live almost in a state of nutritional autarchy and even to have at home the flowers necessary for the proper functioning of rituals. This produce, generously shared among relatives and neighbours, and selectively distributed to the community in general as a method of reward, creates an active network among members of the group. It strengthens mutual help and is at the root of village sociability.

The habitat has very much developed, and so has the way of life; but the household's physical presence and its position in space has remained unchanged, as has a certain feeling of being part of the community. This rural society, which is said to have disintegrated, is made up of domestic groups apparently isolated from one another, but desirous of being in theory equal. One absolute imperative remains – to make exchanges. It is a fundamental, primary imperative since it is the one that builds up society.[21] To exist in a group you must exchange, for exchange establishes the connections between separate monads[22] and fights against the tendency to self-sufficiency, both as regards the individual and the family unit.

Exchange is a remarkable gesture in a society where each person is now capable of existing on his own. It represents an archaic solidarity in a fractured universe. As exchange links up with the immemorial and finds its justification in 'what's always been done', 'what's always been seen to be done' and in the 'custom' of the group, it endures so that the community may survive. Despite the isolation of individuals in their new homes, despite the autarchy of each household and the disappearance of a collective communal life, the village remains, thanks to the reciprocal barter of foodstuffs, a community where 'we get on' because 'we exchange things'.

2

Time of life

Life unfolds in a linear progression from birth to death, only punctuated by the transition from one age-group to another. It forms a series of stages of varying lengths that have altered with the passage of time. We know that every transition from one group to another is attended by rituals and celebrations destined to mark the withdrawal from one stage and ease the entry into the next one. Baptism enables the new-born child to enter the Christian world. It is only after 'burying' their juvenile life and then proceeding to the celebration of marriage that a boy or girl can pass into the adult world. In the course of our study so far we have left aside the content and significance of these 'rites of passage' in order to appreciate these stages in their daily content, which is placed by those we interviewed in two periods of time – 'in the old days' and 'nowadays'. An individual's life as it unfolds encounters this phenomenon of two sorts of time, and it is this encounter that we want to describe.

The world of childhood

The period that elapses between birth and the end of primary schooling comprises in Minot the two age-groups that in the old days were distinctly separate. The children from birth up to six or seven years old are the *papons* and *paponnes*. One talks about 'Jeanne's *papon*' and 'Rose's *paponne*', a term indicating that the little child belongs entirely to his or her mother. From entry into school up to the end of primary schooling the children are called *gachnins* or *gachnettes*. This word is then followed by the Christian name of the child, who in this period acquires part of his identity.[1]

During these years the child will get to know his domestic surroundings, both social and natural. But in what way and with
whom will this apprenticeship be carried out?

The ceremony of admittance   Up to the last ten years of the nineteenth century baptism took place immediately at birth. This haste
is explained by the very high death-rate at birth in days gone by. A
baby, if he survived birth, was taken to church the same day or the
day after and christened. This haste can be seen in the baptismal
records – 'Etiennette, born 24 September 1740, was baptised the
next day by us; Jeanne, born 28 May 1762, was baptised the same
day by us. ...' If the baby was surviving with difficulty, he was at
once christened at home by the midwife or the home-help,[2] or again
by the maternal grandmother, who was always present at her
daughter's confinements.

Angélique, who attended women in childbirth between the wars,
remembers: 'I did it once. I christened a baby who was about to die.
I poured out some holy water and said, "I baptise you in the name
of the Father, the Son, etc.", and then the child was buried in the
church. I was told one could do it, so I did it.' If the child survived,
his real christening followed in church; but by an emergency
christening[3] the new-born child escaped perpetual wandering in
limbo. But however strong the desire was to christen the child as
early as possible, one avoided doing it on a Friday, the worst day of
all, the day on which one did nothing that involved the future.[4]
Furthermore it was thought in the old days that as long as the baby
remained unchristened, he remained vulnerable and open to all
sorts of danger. Hence the reticence that surrounded birth. After
emerging from his mother's womb the new-born baby was placed
in a laundry basket and not in his cradle. One avoided looking at
him, one refrained from visiting him and one never uttered his
Christian name. The procession to church was sparsely attended –
the godfather, the godmother,[5] the woman 'who carried the baby'
(generally the one who attended the mother at the birth) and that
was about all. The mother was never present and the father was
often absent, judging from the parish records. It was only after the
christening that neighbours came to visit the mother and baby.

From the last decade of the nineteenth century one sees the time
lengthening between birth and baptism. This is probably due to the
inhabitants' growing distaste for religion and the weakening of

popular faith. Nowadays three, four, six months or more can elapse between the two dates.

In 1918, in *l'Almanach paroissial*, the *curé* already deplored this behaviour: 'Parents wait too long to christen their children. Christian parents, do not postpone your children's baptism. Death might overtake them, and then what responsibility and remorse for you! Children ought to be baptised as early as possible. To wait more than two weeks is mortal sin.' The last *curé* threatened not to have the bells rung for late christenings, a dire threat that could cause anxiety where the child might be illegitimate. For it is only when baptism has taken place that the bells ring out, announcing in their loud tones the birth of a new member. These bells, themselves christened, anointed with holy oil and having distinguished godparents, play a protective role for the benefit of the local community and the new-born baby. Besides, there is a connection between the language of the bells and the baby's learning to speak. When the bells ring out full strength, the godfather and godmother are required to kiss each other in the church porch: 'The godfather and godmother must kiss so that the baby should not be a dribbler and a stutterer with a snotty nose.' When this has been done, the godparents throw hazel-nuts, dragées and small coins to the crowd of village children. At Minot these showers of fruit and sweets are call *tricöts*:[6] 'The kids waited for the christening party to come out; then the godfather and godmother threw the sweets all over the place; the children were made to run about, and they picked the things up off the ground. In the old days there were more hazel-nuts than dragées, more small coins than large ones.' One calls down fertility and wealth on the village by throwing food around which the crowd of children jostle one another to pick up. By this sugary tribute the godfather and godmother discharge their debt to the young age-group, to which they have just added a new member.

On return from the church a meal takes place at the home of the baby's parents. In the old days there were few present – the baby's parents, the godparents and their spouses if they were married, and the woman who had carried the child to church. The copious but simple meal – there was only one meat dish – had been prepared at home without the help of an outside cook. After the meal the godfather and godmother walked through the village, visited houses and gave out dragées. By way of thanks the inhabitants said, 'If the baby falls in the mud we'll pick it up.'[7] Nowadays the godfather and godmother only visit the near neighbours. Also many other changes in the christening ceremony are evident.

The discretion surrounding birth and the precautions taken to protect the new-born baby have disappeared today. The christening ceremony, which takes place long after the child's birth, brings together a crowd of relations, who all go to the church with the baby's mother. Grandparents, uncles, aunts, godparents and cousins are invited to two meals – lunch and supper. These meals are prepared by an outside cook and consist of many dishes with fancy names.[8] There is now very little difference between the christening meal and the one served at first communions and weddings. These changes are recent. At Minot one can date them from the sixties, and indeed the two forms coexist – quiet ceremony with meal attended by few people, ostentatious ceremony with lavish lunch and supper attended by a crowd of guests. To understand these changes you must take into consideration all the rituals of an individual's life, for they form an indissoluble whole. The first communion, which used to be a simple ceremony with only close relatives present, has grown in size and brings much of the family together. Marriage, which used to be open to the community, is now restricted to the family and one age-group. Finally, death assembles relatives in church but does not give rise to huge family meals. So ceremonies connected with childhood and the beginning of life have taken on more importance than death and the close of life. Is this due to the all-important place taken by the child and adolescent in social life, or rather to the more reticent attitude adopted towards death in our societies?

As the festivals, which throughout the year used to bring the village and the various age-groups together, have disappeared or diminished, so the more specifically family ceremonies have expanded and become so ostentatious that many old people have objected strongly. Christenings and first communions nowadays involve lavish expenditure, usually provided by the fairly close relatives. People invite each other to the occasions, but they are also a means of showing off to the community in general. At once each household in the group situates itself in the local hierarchy; it has a position to keep up, and each family ceremony reflects the status which it holds or to which it aspires. In former days this lavish sort of festivity was confined to the local saint's day, when all households celebrated with meals at the same time and entertained neighbouring villages through the relatives they invited. Now the community takes second place to the family.

In the old days   At the beginning of this century breastfeeding was advised for the longest possible time. 'Everyone breast-fed. You persisted even when the milk did not come. It went on for at least a year and to make the milk pass you put parsley under your arms. When the milk ran really short, you fed the baby with bread soup. You boiled up crusts of bread for a long time in water, and you only gave the liquid. Then at about eight or nine months you gave some *panade*, i.e. crusts of bread boiled and then beaten up with fresh butter.'

If the mother could not breast-feed the baby, a wet nurse was sent for. If there was not one to be found, or if there was no money to pay for one, the baby was fed on boiled cow's milk, a system quite recently introduced in the village.

At the beginning of the century too, babies were wrapped from top to toe in swaddling clothes and cotton flannel. They wore bonnets and remained lying down most of the time until they could walk. In poor families where all the members went out to work, the baby was left alone tied to the cot with his bottle wedged against the edge of the bed. In farming families a grandmother, an elder sister, or indeed a young relation, was charged with minding and rocking the baby. Cradles were always surmounted by a large veil of tulle held up by a rod to protect the child from cold in winter and flies in summer; and they were placed on rockers so that they could swing. Small babies were rocked for hours, and yet they were often left to cry with the coarse words: 'Cry away, you'll piss less.' The recommended treatment was not clear cut. Moreover, this oscillation between two types of upbringing was evident throughout childhood. When he was older the child would find himself the receiver of both smacks and kisses, scolding and compliments, without always understanding why he was receiving such punishment or, on the contrary, escaping censure.

Once the child could walk he left his cot for the bed of a brother or sister, or of a widowed grandfather or grandmother. As we have already learnt, the same room in the house contained the whole household, regardless of age, until late in the individual's life and late in this century.

The child very early on took his full part in the life of the adults. His food was the same as theirs, except that one avoided giving him meat so long as he had not got a full set of teeth. His daily life went on in the common parlour, a space that was well filled, seeing that eating, sleeping, cooking, evening sociability and all conversation went on in it. So the child was placed at once in the heart of the family and never moved from it. The grandparents stayed more at home than the rest of the household, so they took charge of the child. In the company of 'Granddad' and 'Grandma' the child was gradually introduced to family and social life. There started a long dialogue between generations where the older generation imparted to the child their knowledge of how to do, say and recognise things. 'We spent all our time with the grandparents. It was by hearing them speak that I learnt the dialect, because my parents spoke French to each other. It was from my great-grandmother, the mother of my grandfather, that I learnt to count. She was ninety-two or ninety-three years old at the time, and she had come to die in her son's house. She couldn't read or write, but she taught me how to count. She used to say, "I'm going to teach you the Lochères vespers." So, as she sang, she repeated, "One stick and one stick make two sticks . . . two sticks and one stick make three sticks. . . ." It was like a chant, and thanks to it I learnt to count.'

The child explored his neighbourhood with his grandparents, visiting friends and relatives. In this way he got to know the topography and the family connections of the village, and he learnt the various links that bound one neighbour to another. 'In the afternoon my grandmother used to say, "Come along now, we'll go and see the François." She was on good terms with Mother François. At other times Hermance Jodelet, who lived next door, said to me, "Are you coming? I'm going up to see my Aunt Pélagie." As I was always ready to wander around, I went with her. We got on well with Hermance; indeed we're related, I'm not sure how, but she used to tell me, "You belong to our family, you're our cousin." I loved being at their house. I went to them often, staying for a meal.'

This apprenticeship in social geography and village behaviour was also pursued in other walks. The little child accompanied his grandmother to the cemetery very early on. There was always a departed member of the family to whom respects had to be paid. 'As soon as I could walk, my grandmother took me to Mother's grave in the cemetery. We went there nearly every day, especially as after Mother there was Albert my cousin, who died when he was eight.'

The grandparents had recourse to supernatural beings to frighten and discipline the grandchildren in their charge. The fear and panic inspired by these mythical creatures were thought to make them behave well. 'They frightened us with Mother Wind and an old man who roamed around. They told us about *la Mère Gaillon* who haunted ponds and reservoirs: "If you get too near, *la Mère Gaillon* will pull you in." There was *le Tire-Bigueu* who lived near wells and cisterns. We had better not go too near or he would pull us to the bottom. ... There was also Mother Wolf who would eat us up. There was *la Mère Lusine*, a bad woman who lived at the entrance to the village. When one went away, one had to remember one's handkerchief. My grandmother used to say, "Don't forget your hanky, because when you return you'll have to wipe her backside." She took your handkerchief off you to wipe herself. "Don't forget your hanky. Mother Lusine won't let you in if you haven't got it."'

This imaginary mythology told to the child was confined to the locality. These harmful beings guarded the boundaries and water-points of the village territory. Quite apart from being a psychological phenomenon (which we do not deny),[9] we feel it is essential to underline the educative aspect of this mythology. It was a question of warning the children against the real dangers they ran by going too near wells and cisterns or walking across the fields. At the beginning of this century wolves still roamed the undergrowth; the lakes and wells were hardly protected and remained a serious danger. Memories of these dangers are still current: 'When I was a little girl I saw a wolf. One felt scared in fog and was told that wolves still prowled in the woods. I still have a bedside rug made out of a wolf killed around 1900.'

There were very few toys made outside the village to amuse the child in these alarming surroundings; only a ball, a hoop or sometimes a doll for the little girls: 'I had a doll that had been bought, not made by my mother, with a china head, and she could go to sleep.'

However, the universe of children's games was much richer than might be supposed from this poor supply of toys. To start with, the world around the child gave scope for play. A whole world of familiar animals filled their lonely hours and their leisure: 'In the old days, on the way out to the fields, you caught crickets and put them in the hearth. And then there were owls ... we tried to raise one when I was small. Quenesse who rang the bells for the time of day, the angelus in fact, he often found owls that had fallen from the belfry. So he gave them to us. But of course they died. Yet we'd given them mice, but it was no use.' Often the child brought up a cat who was always known by the generic name of 'Minette'.[10]

Besides, young children were rarely left to themselves. For brothers, sisters or a cousin come to spend the winter at the farm, surrounded them, amused them and introduced them to all sorts of parlour games. 'A young niece of my grandmother's came to stay for a whole winter to learn dressmaking. What a good winter we had! What games of cards we played! We used to play at *Cinq sous*. I wouldn't know how to play it now.' And the ever-present grandparents kept the children supplied with tales and wonderful stories. 'When I was small, I slept with my grandmother, so in the evening, when we went to bed, she told me tales of *Tom Thumb*, *Little Red Riding Hood*, *Beauty and the Beast* and so on. . . .'

Just as they 'recounted the family' and passed on the details of their descent, the grandparents provided the cultural memory and thereby had an educational role to play. Through these popular tales, the rules and practices of society and its powers were handed on from the oldest generations to the youngest. Through these stories and the fairy-tale mothers who filled the world around them, children were taught their destiny – which was to obey and submit.

So it was an early childhood that was spent in the closed world of the village, a world that was rich in knowledge and legend. It was surrounded by old people who were attentive and ready to teach. It was lived in certain defined localities – the parlour, the house and the near neighbourhood. So the universe of the home and the village gradually unfolded itself to the child.

Up to this point we have seen the grandparents involving themselves in the child's socialisation; the parents have hardly appeared. The father and mother certainly did supervise and care for their children from birth onwards, but they were very much occupied by work at the farm and only took part in the educative process when the children were old enough to take part in the general chores. This stage was reached early, for many tasks were entrusted to the child from the time he was six or seven years old. This age marks, with entry to school and sharing in domestic work, the child's entrance into the group of the *gachnins* and *gachnettes*. At this point appear the parents, whose role is essentially to deal out work, supervise and punish. 'As children we were always kept busy: "You'll go and fetch some wood, then you'll clean up the potatoes, prepare the straw for the stable, feed the rabbits, and so on. . . ." Oh we never had a moment's rest. Sometimes I used to say I'd like to have some fun, but there was always something to do, for the boys as well as the girls.'

There was certainly no lack of work on the farm to keep children and grown-ups constantly busy; but it did seem as if parents were as much concerned to counter idleness as to employ their children usefully. The great principle was to 'keep them occupied', to allot them tasks which would keep them in one place, far away from the fairly crude aspects of village life and from bad influences. This explains the parents' horror of idle moments and their exact distribution of tasks to be undertaken. So the child's time was divided up and organised by the parents. These young boys and girls were always on duty and required at any moment of the day or night to carry out jobs. 'During the war we were only women at the farm, and when a cow was about to calve Mother used to say, "Go and get Uncle Victor." He lived up in the village. How scared I was going there! The streets were not lit, so I had to run in the dark. I always thought I heard someone running behind me. I was afraid of my shadow. My grandmother used to say, "Well, so you're afraid of your shadow at night!" This was another of my grandmother's educational ploys – irony. Fear and fright were used with small children, mockery and derision ("You're afraid of the dark!") with the older ones.'

Grandparents disciplined children with words, but the father and mother mostly used corporal punishment to make themselves obeyed – smacks for the smallest, slaps in the face and blows with a stick for the older ones. Some preferred to seize a handful of nettles and give their offspring a good hiding on the calves, or beat them with wet rags. 'One day, instead of looking after the cows, I was playing at boats on the river over there. It was at the time of high water. My mother came at me with a stick and belaboured me from the river to the house. I couldn't sit down for a week. Then she called the gendarme who said to me, "Pick up your belongings, young fellow", and he took me away, adding, "You'll eat flies' legs and grasshoppers." We went like this to the edge of the village and there he sent me back home having given me a talking-to. I'll remember it all my life. When the gendarme came, it wasn't funny. It was an old gendarme who knew us all. But I made myself scarce when I saw him arriving. Each time he came in to ask if I was behaving myself.'

So, in addition to these frequent hidings (they beat each other too!), the parents had recourse to very real individuals. The make-believe beings who filled the disciplinary world of very small children were forgotten. Every age had its terrors. Between seven and eight years old the child took on numerous responsibilities. He drove the animals out to the fields and helped with the work of the farm. There was no longer any question of frightening him with those imaginary but alarming characters that peopled his early childhood. The child was sent with the herd to the other end of the pastures and told not to return until sundown. He was then faced with real dangers. 'The cows got stung by flies and bolted, and you had to look for them in the dark. There were also vipers. ... One was afraid of wolves ... Mother had seen some in her time. She had a job on a farm and wolves came every night to the sheep-fold. Once she held a sheep by its head and the wolf had it by the hind legs. ...'

The severe punishments meted out by fathers and mothers did not exclude real tenderness felt by them for their children, and affection that showed itself in warm-hearted gestures: 'We were always getting up on Father's knee. Mother also cuddled us and kissed us, taking us in her arms. But my uncle, he was really nice. We were always hanging on to him.' These fathers and mothers, whether fierce or tender, did not communicate very much with their off-spring. They were always busy in and out of the farm; they were often away; and they had little time for chatting. It would be wrong to think that parents did not hand on their knowledge and skills, but in their presence apprenticeship was pursued in silence, almost entirely by watching. 'We learnt to do things because we saw them done. We sat on a bale of straw watching the cows being milked, then at six or seven years old we were told to do it ourselves.'

This importance given to learning by watching involved a certain degree of discipline. Not everything was suitable to be seen. So one advised children not to stare at people who were unusually ugly or were weak in the head. Certain skills could be acquired by watching, but corruption could come in the same way. Similarly, suggestive sights were hidden from the gaze of the youngest: 'The stallions were fine horses. ... The stud farmer rode through the villages. He arrived mounted on his horse all decked with bells and fine blankets. But we children were sent packing. When the stallion arrived, we were told, "Go away, children, go shopping up in the village."'

In this training through watching there was no dialogue, and no explanations were given or asked for. This suppression of talk between generations was to be found not only within the household (there was no talking at meals), but also in public or semi-public places where children lingered amid the grown-ups. There the children watched and listened, looked and learnt, standing at the edge of the adult groups.

The girls spent long hours in the workshop of Mélie Morelot the dressmaker. 'The mother and her two daughters had the same workshop and, in addition, they took apprentices. I often went there. I was very young, perhaps seven or eight. Sometimes I said to my grandmother, "Well, I'm off to see the dressmakers." They were pleased to have me because I picked up pins off the floor. Later they had magnets for this, but they had none at the time. And then they got me to do little jobs, and we laughed a lot. I was in amongst them, and I watched and listened. Oh she was nice, was Mélie.'

The boys went to see 'Nouël', a sabot-maker during the week and hairdresser on Sunday, or the wheelwright. 'Wheels were beaten out near the Creux fountain. It occurred in the spring before the busy season. The wheelwright asked all the farmers who had wheels to forge to help him. The boys came down in a gang, especially on a Thursday. Girls were not allowed there. A tall pile of faggots was set up and you saw the hoops turning red in the fire. Then they put the wheel on a block, picked up the hoop in large pincers, adjusted it to the wheel and tapped it on with a sledge-hammer to make it fit. Then they fetched pails of water, and there was noise and steam. It was an event.'

In the workshop, while she picked up pins, the little girl listened to the love stories told by the apprentice dressmakers. It was said in the village that they were flighty and ran after the boys, like their needles through their material. The young boy would hang about the craftmen's place, where men gathered, and would listen to stories of game shooting, the fixing of elections and all the local news. Each sex had its own places of initiation from childhood onwards, and there was a big difference between what was told to boys and what to girls. Tales of the chase and the hurly-burly of politics were recounted to the boys, while the girls listened to the secrets of love and intrigue. From the very start the destinies of boys and girls were marked out separately.

So the activities of the craftsmen and the talk of adults were observed by the children. The wheelwright who ringed his wheels at the Creux fountain, the blacksmith who shod the oxen in front of his workshop, the weaver in his cellar by the window at ground level, all were watched by groups of silent children. By watching adults in this

way, boys and girls got to know how things got done locally and how
jobs were shared out. Above all they learnt to moderate and restrain
their speech.[12] Only those who wielded power, i.e. the adults, were
allowed to talk, and they used speech in their children's presence
solely to inculcate elementary rules of conduct. From his father or
mother the child heard the same lessons constantly repeated: 'Say
thank you, say good morning, say goodbye, don't speak at table,
finish your bread, don't ask questions.' Apart from these rules,
children were given very few explanations, and there was little verbal
communication between parents and children. The transfer of
knowledge was effected indirectly, by practice and observation.

This law of silence was only disregarded between the old and the
young generations, and this is where the grandparents came in again.
With them the children enjoyed great freedom: no need for 'thanks'
or 'good morning' or 'goodbye'; no excessive politeness, for with a
grandparent anything was allowed. The dialogue that had started in
early childhood continued its course. With the grandparents apprenticeship proceeded slowly but surely as the child grew; the tasks
became distinct and the skills more complicated. The little boy
dawdled with his grandfather out shooting or in the woods; he tried
the art of twisting string to make tethers for the calves, or he learnt to
make stacks in the fields. The little girl stayed with her grandmother,
and became adept at cooking, knitting, picking herbs and gardening.
'It was my grandmother who taught me to garden. We children
worked the garden as she couldn't manage it. She showed us how to
handle a spade, how to turn the soil over and break it up. That's how
I learnt. We were about ten and six years old. We were made to weed
the paths and at the same time we were taught "That's good grass",
"That's no good; not to be given to the rabbits", "That's tarragon,
and that's parsley." We were told what had to be removed and what
left untouched. Grandma always said, "Go and get me some parsley,
but don't bring me back hemlock." We learnt in this way how to
make beds not too large, and how to trace out rows – two or three,
not more. When I was a bit older, about fourteen or fifteen, my
grandmother taught me how to sow, how to collect seeds and
recognise them one from another.'

These educating grandparents were also a refuge and shelter
against severe relatives. 'It was with Nicolas's grandmother that I
learnt to knit. In the winter, when she had finished with the animals,
she came and sat there near the window and she "heeled" socks, that

is, she knitted just the worn-out heels. One day I took off my boots and there were no heels left at all on my stockings. My aunt saw this and slapped my face hard, saying, "You could have taken your stockings off earlier. Now you're going to mend them as a punishment." I was about ten years old; I cried and hid behind the clock, because Justine said, "I don't want to see you crying, or I'll give you two more smacks." Grandma was near me and said when Justine went out; "Look, you can't mend that, the hole's too big. I'll pick up the stitches for you and you can knit a heel." And so I learnt and I was very pleased. I made a heel and then I sewed it on the stocking. It was like that I learnt to knit.' As protectors and teachers, grandparents also played their part as special mediators in conflicts between parents and children. They always acted with kindness and affection, and seldom were their services refused.[13]

Just the opposite of the occasionally strained relations between parents and children, or between kinsfolk, the ties between grandparents and grandchildren, were usually imbued with gentleness and tenderness. The old people as tireless teachers and educators gave protection and understanding to their grandchildren. Throughout childhood and even beyond, grandparents held an all-important place in the socialising process, a place that has long been unsuspected because it was marginal and unobtrusive.[14]

In the same way the joint life of age-groups and local community action have not been taken into consideration. Yet these two groups influenced behaviour and attitudes and were important factors in socialisation.

The community exerted its influence either indirectly, in the guise of known characters outside the family or directly, by the intervention of its members. You will remember the gendarme, the versatile figure in the countryside who crops up in the memories of old people today. Parents called him in to back up punishments that had been inflicted. Apart from the gendarmes, many other figures appeared regularly to reprimand boys and girls. 'The schoolmaster came to the parents to say that the children had answered back. The *curé* or Mother Huguenin who took catechism came to say that we had misbehaved at Mass or had not known our lesson. So we were given a spanking. The *garde-champêtre* inspected the fields every day to see if we had trespassed with our cows. If we had, we were sent to apologise. You had to go to the owner of the field and say you were sorry. According to the people's characters or tempers you were greeted with a couple of smacks or treated to some goodies.'

The child encountered at the hands of these strangers the same sort of treatment, which oscillated, as we have seen, between brutality and kindness. When he went to 'apologise', the child never knew what to expect, just like at home. Blows and endearments were dealt him in the same generous and mysterious manner.

The same educational procedure flourished at school. The same method of teaching by signs was applied – when to sit down, when to get up, when to keep silent – and there was the same compulsory silence: 'We were not allowed to talk in class.' As at home, corporal punishment rained down thick and fast on the heads and fingers of the young schoolchildren. 'Mademoiselle Briset was very severe. She used to beat us with hazel branches. Mademoiselle Laurent, who taught me in my last years, beat us with a ruler. She made us close our fingers together and she hit the ends; and she also hit us on the head. As for the boys, their teacher Monsieur Arety was very strict, but he beat less. He only beat his own children. But when the boys saw him in the street on a Thursday they avoided him, because if they didn't know their lesson next day or had not done their homework, things went badly. Sometimes he even boxed their ears.'

At school the master showed the same determination to keep them occupied. 'We had a lot of homework. Every evening there were two mathematical problems to do, an essay, a grammar lesson, verbs to conjugate, history, geography, recitation, civics. At school we worked all the time.' School was an extension of home and gave the child certain domestic tasks. 'In the evening, after four o'clock, we had to sweep the school out and get rid of the dust. In the morning, before eight o'clock, there were two of us for this job, a big girl and a younger one. We also had to light the stove, bring in wood and keep the fire going. Each girl was on duty for a week.'

The schoolmaster was universally respected and lived in the village all year. He held the job for years and did not cease his supervision when lessons were over. He continued to watch over his pupils' behaviour in the street and during the holidays. He sought our parents to tell them about their offspring's conduct. The tactics of the school and the family were the same in education and there was close agreement to keep the child under strict social control.

However, we must not get mistaken ideas and imagine that this identity of views on discipline was extended to an intellectual influence of the schoolmaster over the families. His advice on children's careers, for example, was rarely followed, especially among the farmers who needed labour on their properties. Many, now advanced in years, or even just grown up, complained of having been prevented from continuing their studies: 'I could have been in the post office! My teacher wanted me to carry on studying. My father said, "I need my daughter to work." So I had to stop.' In educational institutions parents looked for an apprenticeship in discipline as an extension of home discipline rather than the inculcation of knowledge and skills. In this period and social group, hopes for promotion or social improvement were not centred in the school. Let us simply emphasise this harmony between family and school discipline. Knowledge was imparted at school in much the same way as habits of work and the duty of obedience were inculcated at home.

Furthermore the church, through the *curé* or the lady in charge of catechism, used the same methods to make the children work and to punish them. Finally the neighbours also acted as surveillance. Wherever he was or whatever he did, the child was caught in a watertight, coherent system of discipline.

A close relationship was woven between home and other places of socialisation – the church, the school and the village – and all these played their part in the normalisation process. The child was in a way caught in a trap by this network of informers; but in addition local society imposed its control on the education of its members. The child passed from a social control in infancy exercised almost exclusively by the home group, or even simply the grandparents, to a control exercised by the whole community. The second stage of childhood was marked by an ever closer integration into the local society, which in its turn imposed its own code of behaviour more and more strongly.

Politeness, self-effacement, self-control – these were the essential virtues preached by village society and aimed at as a priority in young children's education. They acquired these modes of living through a carefully organised programme, through imposed behaviour and certain compulsory activities. This discipline probably explained the prudent silence of the young villagers.

There remained only one way of escape from the world of adults – the age-group in which boys and girls shared work and celebrations. Also there was the farming countryside as a place of freedom, which sometimes led to truancy.

The lay and religious festivals throughout the year brought the children together in a jolly band that went asking for things all over the village. At Carnival time they were dressed in gladrags and went from house to house begging for *gargesses* (doughnuts). At Easter they carried *bruands* (rattles) and posted themselves at the cross-roads to announce the church services, then they claimed the *roulée*. 'This consisted of fresh eggs which were given as a reward for our services. We took them along to Monsieur le Curé who divided them up between us; then we went and sold them to the hotel.'

The distribution of holy water on Easter Saturday gave rise to a general request for money, which in each case resulted in a few *sous* and took the young crowd to the far-flung farms. Boys and girls, still in a mixed group, joined together on Christmas Day to wish the inhabitants 'Good health, a happy New Year, and Paradise at the end of your days.' A few goodies – a couple of prunes, a piece of sugar or chocolate – were given to them in return for their greetings. The less generous inhabitants found themselves being wished 'Paradise at the end of this year'.

Young boys and girls roamed far and wide behind their flocks. All the children of the village drove cows to the fields. The children of the farmers and craftsmen were put to work in the evenings after school, while the woodcutters' children were sent out as early as six or seven years of age. This went on from May to November. The smallness of the plots and the free run allowed for the herds once the harvest was over gave the little drovers the chance to get together and have some amusing escapades: 'At the end of the season we went to the fields all day. They were all open; we could mix our animals up and we would get together to play. I remember there was young Boudart, he was always ready for pranks. He lit a fire, we milked a cow and made hot chocolate. He had a little bitch and he sheared her with some clippers intended for cows. How we laughed! At Fresnes farm, which belonged to my uncle, I minded the cows, sometimes accompanied by my cousin and then by one of my brothers. We had a good time; we jumped about and ran. We were sometimes four or five of us together. The girls always had something to make or mend, but we boys we did nothing except tease the girls. . . .' In the fields, far from the paralysing talk and the inquisitorial looks of the grown-ups, the first moves in sexual play were rehearsed.

Far from adult supervision, the idle children played truant in the shelter of hedges and copses. As they followed their herds or strayed off unseen, the boys and girls foraged in search of food, such as pungent berries to eat and herbs to suck, or livestock that could be traded in, such as magpies' eggs, various birds and vipers' heads. For the mayor paid them a few *sous* for vermin. The other children guided the younger ones in this natural apprenticeship and everyone put into practice the lessons taught by his grandparents not long before.

The farming lands were a place for amusement and a refuge for gangs of enterprising children, but in spite of this they are chiefly remembered as the scene of tiresome work grudgingly carried out: 'As children we went haymaking, raking up the hay that fell from the carts. At beetroot harvest we had to go and dig up the roots and then split them. We children were put on this job as soon as we were twelve years old. We had to pick up stones in the fields and stack them at all times, even when we were minding the cows. Our parents put us behind the plough to pick up potatoes or glean when the wheat had been cut. We went off at about six, or half-past, in our clogs. There was dew on the ground, we had no boots, so we got our feet wet. We certainly had a tough life as children in the old days.' Then festivals and games always seemed like interludes stolen from work, which remained the essential system for training children and inculcating rules of conduct.

As he passed from one age-group to another, the child found his play activity reduced in favour of a heavy daily programme of work; but his space and horizons started to widen. The young boys and girls left their neighbourhood and roamed round the village, even making their way to distant farms. Gradually they began to find out about the subtle divisions of the built space. As they followed the herds and joined the gleaners, and as they took short cuts in their search for wild food, the children got to know the part of the countryside that was cultivated or carried cattle. They left their marks on this new territory. The trailblazers wrote on the winter snow: 'We passed here' to warn those that followed. They found each other by using their voices: 'We called from one valley to another with a long modulated cry, and the other replied. So one said to oneself, "So-and-so must be there" because we recognised one another. It was the same when we came home. We called out, then the other said, "Hallo, they're coming along." We waited for one another; soon we heard the bells of the herd and we then came home together.'

The forest on the horizon marked the frontier of the territory. The children never penetrated it. Their first expedition there was led by the *curé* who took the group 'exploring' in the forest during the retreat before the first communion. This initiation into wild country marked the end of childhood. After the communion the boys and girls were separated and became two groups of adolescents.

At present   This time of childhood as remembered by the villagers came to an end about 1950. It was then that the *veillées*, the festivals and the community activities ceased, and so did the traditional ways of bringing up children.

The dramatic technical changes that took place on the farms, as we know, changed the life of women there. The farmer's wives were rid of all work in the fields, and so they could look after their babies themselves without much trouble. To ensure a peaceful life, they now see to it that the sleeping times of the baby coincide with milking times. The young women of the village who have taken up a job that keeps them out of the house leave their child with a relation or some other woman confined to her house and without occupation, in return for payment. This solution helps to make up for the lack of a crèche or nursery school. The mayor's wife looks after the baby of her husband's secretary; the schoolmistress entrusts hers to the postmaster's wife. But for preference one asks one's maternal grandmother or some other grandparent, a sister or a sister-in-law to mind the baby. As in everything else one prefers to turn to relatives first, then afterwards to neighbours. Nowadays the father and mother seem to be the main educators of their children, even in cases where children are handed over to a minder in the morning and taken back in the evening. Parents have recovered a role which in former days they had to delegate to others for economic reasons.

In early childhood it is the mother who takes care of the baby. Her housekeeping tasks are reduced by convenient household appliances, and she uses baby products such as cellulose napkins, plastic pants and prepared foods, so that she can devote herself almost entirely to her child. She brings him up in accordance with modern principles of child-rearing, which are widely publicised through magazines and radio. She breast-feeds if possible. The baby very soon has freedom of movement, and after fifteen days is no longer wrapped up. He is soon taken out of his bed and parked in a playpen. Toilet training is systematic and starts early. The baby is always with his mother. At night he sleeps in his parents' bedroom; in the daytime the mother keeps him by her and takes him wherever she goes. If he cries, she picks him up, makes a fuss of him, talks to him tenderly and gives him a biscuit or a teat to suck. This intimacy between mother and infant during the whole of early childhood certainly makes for a harmonious development of the affections, but it is neither educational nor particularly stimulating.

Parents talk to their child in 'baby language' for a long time. They do not try to give him educational toys or involve him in creative games. They are content with kindness and try to inculcate pleasant manners and politeness: 'Say thank you, say good morning, say goodbye ...', a complete code of behaviour which they themselves learnt in the old days and which remains the model to follow today. The young child has not acquired a real status. He is always treated as a primitive being who must be coddled and brought up gently. Indeed the grandmothers are amazed at this leniency: 'Rémy's daughter, she's always whining. It's the parents' fault for being too kind. You must know how to give smacks occasionally. They're always picking her up.' Grandparents are now, paradoxically, the advocates of a stricter education. Antoine and Gertrude Morelet often look after their grandchildren and brandish a small whip to make them obey — without much effect. For today, as before, the grandparents spend time with their grandchildren. They mind them in the mother's absence and, if they live next door, the child steals round to see them when he has started walking. Then the grandparents resume their role of special teachers and tellers of tales of days gone by. 'I've taught Gilles ...

> The fog is coming down,
>> Sweet glow-worm
>> Quickly, quickly
>> Light your silver torch.
> When it snows, it's God who is plucking his geese.
> When it thunders, it's the Devil who's beating his wife.

I tell all this to Gilles.'

They wander off at dawn with the children looking for mushrooms or snails; for they still introduce them to the natural world. 'Yesterday I found a glow-worm. I picked it up and brought it to Gilles. He likes insects and plays with them for hours. I'm looking for a green grasshopper to give him; one no longer sees any. He would like a cricket, but I can never manage to catch one.'

Expeditions along nearby paths are also resumed on fine summer evenings. Several grandmothers, all hearty walkers, take their grand-children walking 'on the plain'. Approaching by sunken paths, they stroll along the river as far as the Mill, to Saint-Roch's chapel and the Buge track. As they walk they tell the children the place-names and show them their fathers' and their neighbours' fields. Gradually the children learn the names and recognise the properties. And as they go along they pick up good grass and find out where mushrooms grow. Just today I took part with a few grandmothers and their grand-children in one of these evening educational walks. I went to see 'Grandpa's animals' in the fenced pastures and learnt with the children how to call the cows at milking time. 'Come now ... come now.... ' Two words uttered quickly and shrilly, in two different tones. Is all this knowledge going to be lost? Very few of these young children will stay in the village and follow their fathers' or their grandfathers' profession.

The cemetery remains, as of old, the favourite place for grand-mothers' walks. There the children run about among the graves without embarrassment, jumping from one stone to another. The villagers are familiar with the dead, for there are close links between the living and the departed, centred on this cemetery, where people walk and forge the group memory. The grandmothers pass from grave to grave, reading the inscriptions to the children and recount-ing the lives of the dead. In this way the communal memory is handed down from the oldest generation to the youngest. And this intimacy with the dead enjoyed by children from their earliest years is in no way traumatic. On the contrary, these walks are a form of apprentice-ship for life and conduct. It is hardly surprising that a language of death still exists in the village; for people talk about it without reticence or embarrassment.[15] So early childhood has hardly changed in its time span, for the absence of all nursery schooling has preserved the limits. Also the people who educate the children remain the same, but the parents have recovered a central and all-important role.

Is this role now played by the nuclear family the reason for the discovery of the child in village society, or its consequence? Bear in mind the sumptuous christenings nowadays, the lavish first com-munions, all those celebrations connected with childhood which have become more important than those connected with life's end. Yet this rediscovery of their children by parents forms part of the general withdrawal into the nuclear family that has been noticed in many other contexts.

Entry into primary school marks, as in earlier days, promotion into the higher age-group, but participation in domestic tasks now ceases. Within his family the child is freed from all duties. The daughter no longer helps her mother in the kitchen or the garden or the cowshed. As for the boy, the mechanisation of agriculture prevents him from taking an active part in farming work. In fact parents ask very little of their children – to bring back bread on their return from school, make their beds on holidays, and that's about all. Furthermore they arrange their own programme so as to allow the child to take part in activities far from home or in the town. There is the father who takes his children every week into Dijon for them to attend accordion lessons, and he waits for them for two hours. Nowadays parents are anxious for their children to leave the village world and take part in life outside. 'My Aline is spoilt. Everything has changed in a few years. It's now skiing at Les Rousses and dancing at Recey. Other grown-ups say, "You're spoiling Aline", but I reply, "Look at life nowadays."'

Although affection and kindness are unsparingly given, just as in early childhood, and although corporal punishment has ceased, there is still little dialogue between generations. In answering my question about what sexual education they planned to give their daughters, mothers showed themselves at a loss and distressed at the prospect of facing these difficulties: 'I really don't know how I shall set about it. My mother never spoke to me about such things.' Enlightenment about sex comes from the age-group, as before. The older ones initiate the younger ones, and the most extraordinary tales are current. 'My mother never told me anything. I only learnt by watching animals, and then we talked about it among other boys and girls. The older ones in the class told me how babies were born. One girl told me than when one had periods, one had to spend two days sitting on the lavatory – and I believed her.'

The school has developed too. The new teachers have introduced modern teaching methods which call for dialogue, verbal skill, initiative and imagination on the part of the pupils. The teacher's desk is placed at the back of the class behind the children, who hear but cannot see him. This is a visible sign of the new pedagogy based on verbal communication. Discipline has followed suit. The children themselves lay down the scale of punishments and apply them to each other. The teacher himself does not escape this general law. Having forgotten to put on his slippers before entering the classroom, as is the rule, he had to write out fifty times: 'I will put on my slippers.' Hierarchy has disappeared and the superiority of the adults has faded away in favour of free discussion between generations. The child's imagination and free judgment are developed by building up a personal file at school, in which he makes a note of everything which interests him – history, poetry, literature, nature. Furthermore all the pupils contribute to the making of the class's central file where they keep the documents used in class, for example, leaflets, newspapers, photographs and collections of insects. Special attention is paid to the locality and to village life. History, geography and science based on observation are learnt on class walks, which take the children from one end of the area to the other. The weather chart is compiled by the pupils themselves and has various headings – temperature, atmospheric pressure, state of the sky, life of men, life of animals, life of plants, the events of the day – which are filled in every morning by the children. This sums up and illustrates the special attention paid to the world around the youngsters. The modern school leans towards the intellectual and personal education of the child rather than the acquisition of skills, so it becomes liberal and discovers the environment – the village and its history, the work that goes on, and the inhabitants.

This new-style teaching is not entirely to the liking of the parents, especially when it is pushed to extremes, as it is by the present mistress who has done away with class books and does not set homework. 'Things are going badly at school and the parents complain.[16] The children have no book, no homework, nothing – it's all wrong. With the modern methods children don't learn anything. They can't read or write any more, and don't even know their multiplication tables.'

Nowadays parents expect school to provide a social promotion and a means for their children to acquire a trade and a job. 'Parents are ambitious. They want their children to go on to higher education and leave this place.' They expect the school to help their children find a place in society. In a farmer's family only one child will follow his father's occupation: the others, both boys and girls, must find themselves a job elsewhere. Hence the importance attached by parents to the practical side of schoolwork, which according to them ought to be carried on at home if it is to be regarded as serious. Such work nowadays seems like the only sort that one can or ought to inflict on a child. Hence also the importance attached to a regular ascension of the educational ladder. In 1976 certain parents were in conflict with the schoolmistress about children being refused entry into secondary classes – a disagreement that had to be brought before the primary school inspector.

From the primary school onwards parents desire an intensive preparation for the professional and urban world in which their children will be required to live. In short, parents cannot see how these new teaching methods, by making use of play, verbal communication and personal reflection, can pursue the same goals as the old methods and provide the same training; and the new methods can do this while, at the same time, paying special attention to the child's personal development. One remembers the important place that the book held in rural families – the evenings of old when the young schoolgirl read aloud on winter evenings to the whole household listening attentively, and the oft-remembered blue paper in which the textbook was covered on the day of return to school, an act that amounted to a ritual of initiation. It is understandable that parents are shocked by the abolition of all textbooks. There is at present a sort of gulf between family and school, to such an extent that the former sometimes contradicts the latter. The criticisms and the recourse of parents to the mayor or inspector are proof of this disagreement. For parents mean to remain masters of their children's destinies, just as before, and never submit meekly to the decisions taken by the school authorities.

So there is a cleavage between the world of school and the world of home, just as there is cleavage within the local community. The village continues to watch and judge the behaviour of the children, but refrains from making any comment to the families concerned. 'In the old days we were perhaps too strict with children, now we're not strict enough. When one sees kids that rude. . . . There must be a limit somewhere!' The villagers criticise but hold their tongues and withdraw into the family fold. The world of coercion, in which the child used to live, gives way to tolerance and even laxity. It is no doubt this easygoing morality to which adults refer confusedly when they talk of young children today. 'They don't learn the same things as we did. First of all, take catechism, it's not the same thing now . . . it's not at all what we learnt as children, it's quite different. Dash it, one sees good and bad, but one finds a lot of things which are very bad. ... I can't help saying that there is something missing in these children.'

For one is bound to wonder how harmonious development can result from this new family freedom, which does not bring real dialogue between parents and children, and from this schooling which is deplored by parents, putting the children in an ambiguous position. To whom can they turn? How can they decide on their training and their future? For some children, things are simple. Their innate taste for nature, their feeling for agriculture, marks them out naturally as their fathers' successors. In a family there is always an elected member. But what about the others?

This is where the age-group comes in as an essential centre for socialisation. Boys and girls, now liberated from all domestic and agricultural work, find themselves free to do what they like, how they like. The village and the farmlands now become the scene of their casual wanderings. In neighbourhood groups they dress up in masks and old-fashioned clothes at Carnival time and go from house to house proffering their boxes for money and their baskets for *gargesses* (doughnuts). Most of the other annual festivals have disappeared. No matter, a variety of informal games bring them together in the countryside, where they have their rallying points. One is secret and hidden – a cabin built in an old oak tree at Curtil: the other is visible and open – the edge of the football ground on the outskirts of the village. That is where the days of childhood are spent, there the first signs of sexual play occur, as of old. The girls hang by their legs from the balustrade and the boys, as they pass by, nimbly remove their knickers. The country remains the children's playground, the place of initiation and of their first emotions.

The entry and departure to secondary school, which happens at about twelve or thirteen years of age, marks the first break with childhood, which only really comes to an end after the first communion between the ages of thirteen and fourteen years, i.e. at the same age as before. The period of childhood has not changed between yesterday and today. The village still lives according to the same cycle and the same rhythm; only the contents of people's lives have changed.

The days of youth

On leaving primary school at fourteen, boys and girls joined the ranks of *la jeunesse*, filling a period between two breaks from the family circle, and indeed sometimes from the village area. This period opened with a departure, which was temporary, and closed with marriage, which was final.

Before the years of upheaval following the hostilities of 1940, the girls went away in the winter after leaving primary school to complete their domestic education in a private or public institution, or in a dressmaker's workshop. The more well-to-do went as boarders to the Institut des Soeurs at Châtillon-sur-Seine; the rest chose to go either to the free domestic science school which ran in winter at the *sous-préfecture*, or to a bespoke dressmaker's. There were many of these dressmakers in those days in all villages, and during the winter they welcomed the daughters of farmers and craftsmen in return for a small fee.

Sewing was the main skill taught both at the dressmaker's and at the school. The girls learnt to make clothes and look after household and personal linen. Mending, embroidery and knitting made up the main part of their apprenticeship. In fact they became skilled in what was to be their main task over the next few years – the preparation of their trousseau. At the school they also learnt the rudiments of housekeeping and 'good form': 'You had to know how to lay a table attractively, how to wait, the right side to serve, and so on. ...'

In fact, whatever the curriculum, the real object of this spell of training was quite different. This period of separation from the family and village group was meant to make a break with the world of childhood, where boys and girls worked and played freely side by side. From now onwards young men and women were each to develop within their own sphere, one entirely masculine and the other entirely feminine. From this age onwards meetings between the two sexes could only be on an individual basis and as part of an accepted friendship. On their return to the village the young people would form two groups, 'the lads and the girls', each with its own activities, all opportunities for meeting being strictly formalised.

During this training time, the girls broke with their past habits and for the first time tasted that feminine life made up of mutual help in the face of common problems. They would meet among themselves at the school or the dressmaker's in a strictly female setting where were forged the first networks, those first friendships that linger long in the memory, and the first tentative collusions: 'At the school we learnt to make our first layette, our first bootees. More than half the girls didn't know how to knit. It was I who made the bootees at our evening gatherings and brought them in next day ("Oh, Tine, *you* know how to knit!"). And then there was a week of ironing, and I'd rather have been almost anywhere. There were some girls who were good at it — Marguerite, for instance, she knew how to iron, so I used to say to her, "You'll iron my linen and I'll do something else for you." And I kept some good friends. I saw one of them only the other day. We formed gangs. We got on well with each other in ours, and we've remained friends. We were girls who knew each other a bit at home.'

Finally, this journey at the end of childhood occurred at a time when adolescents first became aware of the mysteries of their bodies, and the sexual education of those days tended to emerge from their private conversations. 'My mother never told me a thing about my periods. We slept in a dormitory of 150 girls at our school, so things happened. Word got around about periods. Mine began at college and I was proud of the fact. I told the other girls, and they told me about theirs. . . . I only informed my mother much later.' Friends of the same age made up for mothers' silence. Indeed it was sometimes only once this stage was over, and the information acquired, that there was any dialogue between mother and daughter. So a mother only found out after the interlude at school that her daughter was developing late, and then started to worry: 'It's not normal, she's not yet a real girl', thought one of them about her daughter, who was to start menstruating late at the age of sixteen and was sent the following winter to see a doctor in Dijon.

During this absence from home the girls got to know their biological destiny and were initiated into the code of sexual behaviour: 'At the beginning we went and fetched milk from a long way off. We had to cross the whole of Châtillon, so some of us made eyes at the boys. The trip was therefore stopped and we were no longer allowed to fetch the milk.' This admission that the tender glances were soon suppressed, and budding flirtations stopped dead, shows that there was disapproval, but one gathers also that these doings were commented on at length among friends. Girls just emerging from childhood were discovering the relationship between man and woman.

It was a moment of transition that led to a new world, and a break with the past. The journey to the brink of adolescence was a real initiation, and at the end of it the girls were aware of the mystery of their bodies. They learnt how to behave with the opposite sex and were ready for the tasks and roles of tomorrow.

The programme was the same for most of the boys. They went in for apprenticeships related to their future activities, leaving for the Institut Saint-Joseph in Dijon or the the school of agriculture which operated one week a month in the main town of the canton. There they learnt the rudiments of accountancy, manual crafts, and farming, and like the girls they started to integrate themselves into the masculine world.

Spring saw the end of this winter escape and the return to the family fold. This was inevitable because, up to the nineteen-fifties boys and girls had no other choice after primary school but to take up their father's or their uncle's trade, or help their mother in her household activities.

In farm or shop the young people took an active part in the work, often replacing the assistant, the labourer or the servant. They worked hard under the direction of the head of the family, just like the other members of the household. They got up at five in the morning and only stopped at nightfall. The girls milked the cows and helped in the house: the boys cleaned out the stables and spread the manure, while others went to the fields to weed out the couch grass and take stones out of the soil. The work was trying and endless, and it kept the young people busy most of the time. Furthermore this work was assigned hierarchically according to age. The tasks that were most esteemed, either because they demanded skill and experience, or because they conferred dignity or power, were reserved for the adults. The young were restricted for a long time to subordinate tasks.

In the first decades of the century, work on the farm or in the shop was still entirely regulated by custom and tradition. Although the jobs complemented one another, they were systematically organised by rank, with adults occupying the important positions. Of course the most vital jobs – ploughing and sowing on the farm, and making things in the workshop – required a long and laborious apprenticeship, especially as the training was entirely based on observation, attention to technique and imitation of older people's movements. 'A good sower cast seed over twenty feet – ten on one side and ten on the other. You walked forward matching your leg and arm movements, you had to get the knack. . . . It was the old folk who taught us to use a seed-bag, which was just a satchel with a shoulder-strap. You tied up the two corners and then put in three or four bushels of seed – it depended on what you were sowing. Seed was always sown by hand. You had to avoid taking too much if it was small seed such as lucerne or clover. You took it between three fingers, and then you opened up your fingers so that it spread well. You opened your fingers and the seed passed between them. It was a knack.'

The old grandfathers, if they were around, came to the rescue of the young, for there was very little communication between parents and children during the transfer of knowledge. In fact silence reigned between them during adolescence. Apprenticeship in techniques remained entirely based on watching and imitating movements. And, as at a younger stage, obedience to parents was still imposed on boys and girls by physical violence. 'I had a hiding on my eighteenth birthday. . . . I remember it well. . . . It was the last one, but I got it all right. I didn't even know what I had done.'

The slow pace of traditional apprenticeship meant that the young were kept away from jobs that carried prestige, just as they were forbidden all tasks that involved knowledge of a 'secret', that is to say a trick or recipe that had made the reputation of a craftsman, a farmer or a cook. For everyone in those days had his or her private dodge. 'There was a secret way of killing a pig; there were secrets in the kitchen, such as putting fourteen different herbs in your black pudding; there were private recipes for sausages and pâtés.' The blacksmith had his secret for tempering steel which he would only reveal to his successor. The saddler had his, too, which he would only hand on to his son. 'Each saddler had his speciality. My father's was horse-collars – that was his secret. Right up to his death he never really taught me how to make them, and when I finally learnt the knack, horse-collars were no longer made.' It was only at the last minute, when the possessor was on the point of dying or retiring, that the secret was unveiled. The chosen recipient was already mature in years and settled in life. You never gave away secrets to the young.

Women's activities also had their hierarchies and their secrets. Girls at home found themselves given unpleasant and unpopular jobs like sweeping, peeling vegetables and washing underclothes. They never got near to the stoves or the cooking, which remained their mother's exclusive department. 'With Mother I was not allowed to touch the saucepans. I helped with the washing-up, but I was never allowed to cook. She never let me.' Cooking and food conservation (a daughter never went to the salting tub) remained closely guarded secrets. For the whole of their youth girls were kept in semi-ignorance of the main household tasks. The following scene of tragi-comedy shows up the consequence of this state of affairs: 'I married at twenty-two, and I cried the first evening because I didn't know how to cook.'

So all the important jobs, whether secret or complicated, remained for a long time beyond the reach of the young. Fathers and mothers reserved for themselves the right to continue doing them for as long as they thought fit.

So young people were confined to secondary activities throughout their youth. A saddler's son recalls, 'I mostly did repair work as long as my father was there', and a farmer's son could say the same. This inferior position accorded to the young, this subordination to the head of the family in the allotment of work, was accentuated by their financial dependence. The young man or woman received no wages for their work and had no right to any reward. A little pocket money to go out on Sunday was all the thanks they got, but the head of the family could even decide against this. 'My father never gave me a sou, not a centime. Once I went to a wedding and I had the misfortune to say I was going to be twenty the next day. "So you must buy us a drink", they said. I hadn't a centime to pay for it. We were drinking lemonade, and I had to borrow two francs.' Between parents and children the settlement came later, at the time of marriage or when the inheritance was apportioned. Then the son or daughter who had spent his or her youth with the parents was rewarded by the gift of two or three animals or by some material compensation. The draper's son said, 'There was never any question of a wage before my marriage. I worked for my father and was fed, lodged and clothed. I got pocket money. As I had worked for a long time without being paid, my father, when he distributed his property, as an extra gave me a van well stocked with goods and a horse with it.'

To buy themselves a drink or some bauble, boys and girls only had their 'pin money': 'It was the tip that a dealer gave to those who looked after his animals.' This practice, current in the old days, enabled young people to build up a small nest egg that was carefully mentioned in the marriage contract: 'The future bride brings to this marriage a gold chain coming from her gains and savings and valued at fifty francs' (1848 contract).

So throughout their youth boys and girls remained financially and morally dependent on their parents, who were masters of their offspring's destiny for as long as they pleased. In this way the young person's entry into adulthood was postponed as long as possible.

Indeed the consequences of this situation are to be found in the age-of-marriage statistics and, more subtly, in matrimonial choices and the rate of bachelorhood.

What we must emphasise at once is this ambiguous status in which young people were kept. Boys and girls entered very early into the adult cycle of work, whether domestic or agricultural. As soon as they left primary school, they took part in the economic production of the household or they carried out essential tasks in the running of the home. So the young seemed indispensable for the functioning of that traditional economic system where each member of the household carried out complementary tasks. In spite of the important work they did, the young did not enjoy any corresponding autonomy. They were kept for a long time in inferior jobs and economically subjected to their parents' control. However important they were to their family's production, they had no recognised economic status and remained inferior and dependent beings.

They had to wait for the middle of this century, a time of economic and social unheaval, for the status of youth to develop. About this date boys and girls began to have access to further study and apprenticeships, which brought them independent professional jobs far earlier than in former times. They neither of them now remain at home after primary school; they mostly prolong their studies and go to seek their fortunes in some place other than the family workshop or farm. Only the son and heir, who will take over the business, remains with his parents, but he now receives a wage and is described on administrative documents as 'family help'.

Nowadays the young win their financial independence very early. At the same time the progress of mechanisation and the disappearance of crafts has upset the traditional hierarchy of tasks. The tractor and combine harvester are the department of the son rather than the father, or at least they require the co-operation of both. Today the young have not only acquired an economic status but they are considered professionally as equals. These changes in status, admittedly facilitated by other social adjustments such as the shortening of military service, affect the man's age of marriage and his choice of mate. The young now marry earlier and are less restricted in their matrimonial choice.

These changes have brought in a different attitude that is paradoxical. Formerly the young were at an early age regarded as men and women where work was concerned. As soon as primary school was over, even in the last years of childhood, they carried out heavy work and were used for exhausting daily tasks: 'Once one was seven years old one was somebody. At ten one was a man.' This early committal to work was not accompanied by any assumption of professional or financial responsibility. Access to adulthood – 'we were not allowed to wander abroad before we were sixteen to eighteen' – was postponed as long as possible. Nowadays the young start to work later, but they win financial and professional independence sooner and so arrive earlier at adulthood. The time of youth has been shortened. The prolongation of school or apprenticeship spreads over several years. Once this marginal period is over, the young are at once involved in an active professional life and quickly attain financial independence. They can then, if they like, get married.

Marriage, that other escape from the world of the family – this time final – always brings the time of youth to a close.

From dances to marriage

Today as yesterday, once their work is done, young people retain one privilege – to enjoy themselves. There were, and still are, many opportunities for doing this; for the lay and religious festivals spread throughout the year, and family ceremonies give youth an excuse to get together. For what we must now consider are the social arrangements which officially enable young people to find and meet one another. We will leave aside all ritual events which separate girls and boys into two 'gangs'.

Courting The dance which goes with most types of rejoicing, whether public or private, is the main occasion for young people to get together. So it is hardly surprising that it is the main place for future couples to meet. 'My mother met my father at a dance at Recey ... I met my husband at a dance at Aignay. . . .' In one dance or another, from generations back, father and son, mother and daughter, met with adventure. But was it at the same sort of dance?

Before the fifties, which was when the community started to break up and the departure of the young increased, boys and girls did not enjoy the same liberty of movement, and the chances of 'going dancing' differed for each group.

The girls as a rule attended only the village dances. Indeed there was a choice of every sort of local dance, both formal and informal –

the May dance, Saint Catherine's, Saint Nicholas's, the dance on the patron saint's day, weddings, and finally the dances decided impromptu on Sunday evenings. 'Oh, it really was the good life. There was a dance every week or fortnight. Sometimes we said to the accordionist, "Give us a dance on Sunday" and we decided among us boys to hold one. We asked Bertrand for the hall and permission from the mayor to go on after midnight. To get the girls we approached the mothers, we spread the news around, and we had to ask the *capitaines*.'[17]

So all these dances, whether organised in advance or impromptu, brought together the youth of Minot. Some of them, however, were open officially or unofficially to the neighbouring youth. At the weekend dances, for instance, boys from nearby villages took the chance of gatecrashing. These incursions were bound to happen and were expected in that the neighbours made a point of honour of having a go, and the organisers obviously failed to make the holding of their dance known. 'We decided among ourselves to hold a dance in the evening and we found a violinist. The boys of the village nearby heard about it and came in a gang. As it was our party and we wanted to dance among ourselves, we were inclined to chase them off. We chucked pieces of charcoal at them, but it didn't go any further than puncturing bicycle tyres.'

The invasion of boys from the neighbourhood upset the balance of the sexes and was an affront to the male sense of owning their girls – hence the fighting. But in fact the girls of Minot seized an additional opportunity to find a mate at these dances. Furthermore these invading boys, who were craftily retained by puncturing their tyres, came from the region, from that group of places with which there were close marriage links.[18] At this period there were marriages between inhabitants of villages which fought with one another. In the same way the boys of Minot on the following Sunday made a point of invading the dance being held in the neighbouring village. The girls did not go with them under threat of losing their reputation for ever: 'We boys went to the dances on our bicycles, but the girls did not come with us. The ones who did were not worth much.' The girls remained in the village without moving. Leaning over their embroidery and sewing their trousseau, they were held back and stayed put. Meanwhile the boys roved round the surrounding countryside.

The festival of the patron saint had a quite different character. It was an important celebration that lasted three days. It was above all a family party since each household invited their *parentèle*[19] from the country around: 'We invited aunts, uncles, cousins, who came from afar and stayed the night.' All the youth of Minot and the villages around gathered together as relations, and not as members of this or that village. For this reason fighting was unthinkable at the saint's day festival. On the contrary, cousins and neighbours got to know one another and forged links. The festival brought together all the young people who made up the marriage world – the neighbours (in the sense of the inhabitants of the villages around), relations and more or less remote cousins.[20] So the girls from neighbouring villages came along, just as the girls of Minot went when the festival was held in a village where they had relations. 'In the old days we generally only went to three festivals – our village's and those of our grandfathers.' Family relationship was the only pretext for a girl to leave the village. Of course she never went alone, for her mother or a brother went with her.

The wedding dance was like the festival dance in the sense that it brought together members of one age-group and relations. However the cousins invited were more numerous and came from further away, beyond the 'matrimonial area'.

So, for the inter-war period, we can classify the various village dances by types, starting with the one that assembled the narrowest circle of young people and finishing with the one that brought the largest number together; in other words we go from the most endogamous to the most exogamous. There were the age-group dances and the improvised dances reserved in theory for Minot boys and girls, but in fact open unofficially to invasion by boys from other villages. There was the dance held on the occasion of the saint's day festival, to which all the neighbouring youngsters were officially invited, but in a family context. Finally, in the same spirit, there were the wedding dances more wide-open to the outside world.

Nowadays most of these dances have fallen into abeyance. If some of them continue the same in appearance, the spirit behind them has changed. According to the people of Minot, the reason why they have disappeared or changed is because the groups of young people no longer 'hang out together'. It is indeed noticeable that in this age-group a new *fact* has come into play – the departure of the young to 'schools' – and new *habits* play their part – from being static in their village, even in their home, girls now go out and about. Both changes are linked to the general opening-up of the village to the outside world. More and more use is made of educational institutions in the regions, and there has been the vast increase in transport facilities.

In the last two decades the departures to *lycées* (high schools) and technical colleges have increased. Children not suitable for secondary education are the only ones left at the village school. All the others try for entry into secondary school at twelve or thirteen. If they are successful they become boarders and only return to the village at weekends or for the holidays. So the young people reach the town very early, and then get jobs that are essentially urban. For once their studies are over, the local firms have few jobs to offer, and in any case most of the young stay in town. The only ones in the thirteen-to-twenty age-group to go on living in Minot are some boys — future farmers who attend the canton's agricultural school during the winter months, farm hands placed by the *Assistance publique*, and young operatives at the dairy depot or the garage. And there are a few girls employed at the atomic centre at Valduc. 'Formerly all the young people were in the village, so it was possible to organise a dance. What parties can be set up now, and who would be present? At Minot there are only small dances of no size at all.'

So there is a real thinning-out of this age-group over long periods. There is imbalance of the sexes because proportionally more girls go away to pursue their studies and work in town. Social diversification is more noticeable than before, and the spread of professions is wider: 'The farmers, the dairy workers, the builders and the garage hands go together, there's no difference. Those who have pursued further education are a separate group.' Clearly the young fraternity is split apart and does not 'hang out together'.

But above all, in this reduced and dispersed group, boys and girls enjoy the same freedom and privileges. Nowadays the girls who work in towns and who have 'gone out' of the village, only come back there at the end of the week and then 'go out' again at once. There is no longer any question of keeping them anchored. Accompanied by a brother or a cousin, they go, like the boys, from one dance to another. Boys and girls today are mobile in two senses of the word. As *nomads* they attend dances and they are also *motorised*, with a car that takes them further and further away. So the area of leisure activities has widened, and boys and girls explore it together.

This radical change in the situation of girls, who are no longer held in their work or in their play, has had many consequences. As they are free to go to dances wherever they like, they have ceased to be partners reserved for the boys of Minot. As this is so, the latter have no reason to defend them. We shall never again see the 'lads of Minot' fighting for their girls against the 'wolves' of Saint-Broing.[21] Why should they when the girls are no longer theirs and not destined for them? All possibility of marriage between boys and girls of Minot now seems excluded. This situation is so intensely lived and so clearly perceived that, when the young people arrive together at a dance in the region, they do not recognise or address one another. 'At a dance we don't dance with Minot girls because they don't accept us. Rather dead than invite a Minot girl! At dances where one is very well known one cannot dance any more. Ten or fifteen girls refuse you. When they haven't got an escort from outside, they dance among themselves.'

Just as in the village, boys and girls no longer speak the conventional language of their age-group,[22] so they do not talk to each other at the dances where they meet. That is why the young have to push out ever further in search of a dance 'where one is not known'. It gets to a point where movement becomes sheer movement for movement's sake: 'When one is at a dance at Recey, one gladly goes on to Baigneux or Saint-Seine or Lery.' And everyone starts complaining: 'Dances are tailing off. The young are exhausted, they're always motoring. They spend all their money on transport.'

So the quest for a mate drives on the young ever further. Or is it a need to drug themselves with this newly acquired freedom?

The village has therefore ceased to appear as the only possible place for these boys and girls to meet a future spouse: 'A Minot girl doesn't go out with a Minot boy. . . . They know each other too well!' The village seems too narrow an area compared with the broad spaces now freely travelled. Because of this no one feels the need to organise impromptu dances or those that marked age-group celebrations. These dances belonged to a time when girls collected in a group in the village, when the boys hung out together, when the youth organised games and livened up the life of the village with its parties and its rounds. The young now feel themselves living in a social void: 'Minot is dead and boring. What can you do in Minot?' The void is a sign of their lack of understanding and cohesion as an age-group and is shown up by the colourless aspect of the village on to which today's houses look out.

However one evening we saw the young getting together and re-establishing contact. It was Carnival day. As soon as night fell, the young boys and girls passed silently through the streets all dressed up, and made a house-to-house collection. In the evening they improvised a dance in the parish hall. One brought a record-player, others records, while others had bought cakes and drinks with the money they had collected. Did this impromptu dance indicate that the break was not complete? Was the group going to find its cohesion again? Would the parties and dances be resumed? Absolutely not. This improvised dance had in fact the look of a family party. It was as if some facetious cousins were meeting after a long absence and remembering their childhood together. Each one showed off his talents as a dancer and acrobat. Instruction was given and new steps demonstrated. Frenzied dances bringing all the young people together in a joyous farandole or two swaying lines were more in evidence than couples dancing together in a haze of tenderness. These boys and girls were not there as possible life partners, but as childhood friends and members of the same family. On the next Saturday these same girls would refuse with disdain to partner these same boys at the dance in a neighbouring village.

Now the group of young people has disbanded and dispersed beyond the village territory. There has to be a redefinition of the group of potential marriage partners on a different geographical scale. The network of dances during the course of a year certainly offers a first approach.

As for the saint's day festival, which in theory remains the same, it now appears in a different light because of the changes in behaviour. In the old days it saw the presentation of the village girls to the assembled boys, whether neighbours or relations, but now it is only a dance like any other. For the young it is not characterised by any special solemnity or rejoicing. It is open to everyone – relations, neighbours, strangers – and there is fear of noisy and violent invasions by groups of young boys who rush on their motor cycles from dance to dance spreading disorder. The prudent café proprietor closes his iron shutters after eleven at night.

There remains the wedding dance. Now that the official and unofficial festivals have come to an end and the dances are open without restriction to the whole region, the wedding dance confines itself to the family group. It has become an exclusive preserve, closed to invasion from outside, a gathering of two family worlds, and the meeting-place for future marriage partners.

Contacts and alliances must be forged betwen the two sets of relations on these occasions. Every marriage must lead perforce to others. 'Marriages occur in series.'[23] Hence these complex stratagems, these secret confabulations to form couples, because at a wedding every young unmarried person must have his or her escort. 'We wondered at the time of Robert's wedding who we were going to invite as escort for Robert's brother Paul. Colette, the future bride, said, "Invite Marie-Hélène Pautet." We hadn't thought of her. Then there was a question of Paul not being able to attend the wedding, so one of Marie-Hélène's brothers came to tell us, "If Paul doesn't come, my sister won't come either."' This remark implied that one did not pair up with any old person. For each pairing has an important matrimonial potential, starting, for example, with the pairing of the best man and the chief bridesmaid, which brings together the groom's younger brother and the bride's younger sister.

'At weddings you see each other and get acquainted', and one finds these pairings leading eventually to further marriages. Also the genealogical peculiarities of farming folk begin to manifest themselves – double marriages which join two brothers to two sisters, and series of marriages between cousins following on one another.[24]

So it is at dances that young people meet each other and couples are formed. There they make each other's acquaintance to the tunes of the dance and under the watchful eye of mothers and brothers: 'He invited me to share the last waltz and then afterwards we saw each other again at other dances. ...' There then begins a long odyssey for the young people before they arrive at the final marriage ceremony. After having 'met', they are then 'on speaking terms' – a very short preliminary period in which they encounter each other again, apparently by chance, and get more acquainted. 'He sought to know my name and he hung around the house in his car without my knowing. He agreed to go to the same dances as I did.' As every relationship between a boy and a girl gives rise to jokes and comments among their friends, the partners lie low and separate themselves from their age-group. The 'speaking terms' stage is a secret time in which they decide between themselves to pursue the adventure.

'Walking out' The 'speaking terms' period is succeeded by the 'walking out' period. This begins with the idea of marriage being revealed to the parents. 'We decided to get married and we both told our parents. I talked about it first with my mother, who had a word

with my father. He agreed to it, so I mentioned it to him jokingly. The boy was then invited to dinner. It was the evening of Saint Catherine's day and we went on to the dance together afterwards. . . . He asked my father's permission to "walk out" with me.'

'Walking out' amounts to a precise status, but above all the term signifies that there is a commitment and that marriage is definitely intended between the boy and the girl. So the discussions between the parents and the young people assume a great importance, hence the precautions taken. A well-disposed and impartial intermediary is chosen, for the proposed partner is at once scrutinised in his family and social setting, and the parents accordingly give their refusal or their consent. 'When Monique announced the name of the boy she was walking out with, her father immediately found out that they were related (they were third cousins once removed). So it was known to what family he belonged.'

If the verdict of the parents is favourable, the young man literally 'makes his entry' into the girl's home. From now onwards he has the right, and even the duty, to enter her home and then take her to the dance. He is sometimes even invited to dinner or supper. During this period, all goes on between the boy, the girl and her parents. The boy's family is kept informed, but does not take part in the proceedings.

This right to enter the girl's home is the sign of official recognition by both the families and the community. From now onwards the girl is called *la bonne amie* and the young man *le petit ami*. Our grand-mothers had the charming expression: *un(e) futur(e) qui vient*.

'They are walking out', they say, which means that they obey a code of conduct which has not changed for decades, except in small details. It is a code made up of obligations and taboos. '"Walking out" means that you are in duty bound to go out with one another. You dance together, and it is at dances that you show off you relationship. You kiss each other, but you do not go to bed together.' This last assertion lays down a rule. In fact, as we shall see, it is not unusual for young people to have sexual relations from that moment onwards.

One vital prohibition marks this 'walking out' stage – no pairing with any third person. At dances the girl can only partner her 'friend'; indeed no other young man would risk inviting her. If a mar-riage is planned in one of the two families, young people who are 'walking out' do not lightly let themselves be partnered by others, even though custom might expect it. 'At Suzette's wedding her sister was bridesmaid while the bridegroom's brother was best man, but she was already walking out with Jojo, so she ended the wedding with him. So it was Suzette's brother-in-law who managed the wedding and was in charge.' Sometimes the situation is even more clear cut. 'Matthieu refused to be best man at his sister's wedding because Marie-Hélène, with whom he was walking out, was not bridesmaid.' The relationship between bridesmaid and best man is so fraught with matrimonial possibilities that members of such a sensitive relationship as 'walking out' cannot allow themselves to get involved in such a dangerous situation.

This duty to remain together is however attended by one taboo. The boy and girl who are 'walking out' cannot be godparents at the same christening. If they infringe this rule, their relationship is in danger of breaking up: 'My daughter's godfather and godmother were walking out before the christening, but it ended simply because they were godparents together.' This incompatibility between 'walking out' and being spiritual parents is hard to understand. Godfathers and godmothers belong to one or other side of the new-born child's family, so they hold the same position favourable 'with a view to marriage' as the ideal couple. But, on the contrary, society excludes marriage between the godparents of the same child.[25] Also, the suspicion of incest in a couple who are 'walking out' but are not officially engaged is intolerable. The couple are placed too early in the position of parents and are bound to separate.

The importance of these duties, these taboos and this code of behaviour becomes obvious if you remember that the walking-out period can last between six months and five years according to circumstances. It is a trial period during which the two families who are to be allied in the future never meet each other officially; so a break between the young people remains possible and will lead to no irremediable consequences. The 'walking-out' period is the period of reflection.

Hitches and disasters Usually these matrimonial encounters developed, and still do develop, without a hitch. The young people get to know each other at a dance, they choose freely, and the parents agree to their choice.

One might suppose indeed that the game was settled in advance, that the boys and girls only choose partners who have a good chance of appealing to their respective families. Doesn't the mother say to her daughter before she sets off for the dance, 'My girl, you'll dance with someone of your own class'? Furthermore each family builds up in its collective memory a store of marriage tales, accounts of matches, real family sagas handed down from generation to generation. Each clan builds up a fund of knowledge about its genealogy on which children draw very young. They hear talk of family and inheritance, and so acquire a sense of their part in the issues at stake. When they come to make a choice, they conform to the family ideals. So the son of a landowner knows that he can only marry a girl of substance and, before getting involved, he makes enquiries and calculates her expectations. A girl's recent disagreeable experiences show that such practices survive: 'I had partnered a boy at two or three dances. He came to the farm and looked around everywhere, the stables, the house.... Then he asked me, "How many hectares do you own?" I said that we had none and were only tenants. The boy never came back. Another one asked me to come out with him through a girl I knew. I said to her, "This boy wants a rich girl." "Yes, but you are rich", she replied. "No, we're only tenants", I said. The boy never again asked to see me.'

In fact some rich families of the canton have the well-established and openly admitted reputation of organising lucrative marriages in advance without their children's agreement: 'Even now there are families in which the children from the age of twelve or thirteen know whom they are due to marry. They are families in which the inheritance must not be divided.' In these cases the strategy is clearly proclaimed; in others it is more muted, but is no less effective. The weight of upbringing, the strength of parental authority, and social constraints[26] implicitly dictate the choice of a partner. The parents remain, frankly or covertly, the masters of the marriage game.

It would not be surprising if there arose conflict between parents and children, and trials of force with dramatic results, for the parents may categorically refuse to accept such commitments.

The refusal is indicated at the preliminary discussions when the first revelations are made by the young people. The stories of separation imposed by the parents are more frequent than those which show resistance on the young people's part to the parental will. The situation is now changing, but it required, and still does require,[27] exceptional circumstances, the support of family or powerful friends, and unusual courage and character to go contrary to the plans of the parents. In the course of three and a half centuries only two marriages are recorded in the church and civil registers in which parental consent was not obtained. One was celebrated in 1912 uniting a woodcutter and a linen maid: a child had been born a year before. No doubt the poor reputation of linen maids was at the root of the conflict. The second, concluded in 1927, brought together in marriage the daughter of a farmer and the son of a travelling draper. The bride's father refused his consent because the proposed marriage did not suit him. So it happens that children ignore their parents' will. Sometimes the latter find themselves forced, by the arrival of a child, to accept the marriage. They then show their disapproval by symbolic signs that are not recorded in the documents. 'My father would rather have seen me dead than married to Pierre, so he refused to lead me to the wedding.' In cases of disagreement 'there was no wedding', and the marriage ceremony is reduced to the minimum without any party or rejoicing. A quiet, secret wedding (we shall return to this later) starts the married life of the young couple off under poor auspices.

Furthermore these forced marriages are always followed by a break between the parents and the disobedient offspring. The young woman who married in 1927 without her father's consent never saw him again until she visited him on his death-bed. Another woman saw her brother for the last time when he married a flighty foreigner and left the village. Departure often remains the only possible answer to the rift. In this way descendants separate and families disperse.

Resistance to parents sometimes turns to tragedy. The young man hangs himself: 'Look at Robert Saunier, who hanged himself in the barn down there. The Sauniers were richer than the Pierrets – that was the trouble too. The girl he was in love with was a maid and was paid by the day. The Sauniers were tenant farmers and were fairly well off, so it was certainly that. She went away into service at Grancey. Then he went and hanged himself in the barn down below there, and it was his sister who found him. The girl never married.' In despair the young woman throws herself down a well or into a tank or, like that unmarried mother who could not marry the father of her child, ends by committing suicide. 'Look at the Dubost daughter, it was just the same. She didn't marry Monsieur Malet. His mother made him sign on for Africa so that he shouldn't marry her. She had a child who didn't live long, perhaps two months. She was a maid at the Bouvet's. He used to go and sleep with her every night, and one fine day she found herself pregnant. Oh she was terribly unhappy: her father threw her out, poor girl. She got married later, but had a tragic end. She burnt her head in the cooker and had a horrible end. Poor girl, she didn't deserve it, for she was a good worker. The same story – Mother Malet was very proud and didn't want the match. . . . He, the young man, signed on in the army at 22 to go to the colonies.'

Another of these tragedies was the infanticide perpetrated in 1947 in a neighbouring village by a father on a baby born to his daughter. He did not want her to marry the child's father.[28]

These sad stories tell of the struggle of love against reason, of the heart against money and family respectability. It is not always for reasons of inheritance that parents insist on relations being broken off. Self-interest is not always the motive force. Every family, however humble, has a name to defend and a place in society to preserve. In other words, each has a 'symbolic capital'[29] which is put at risk with every marriage. Matrimonial strategies and total refusal of certain matches are not only the practice of the rich or simply the result of calculations aimed at increasing the family's economic capital. 'Vincent Bacherot was in love with a girl in Recey, niece of a notary who made off with the till. His father refused to let him marry the girl, yet it was not a close relative but only a collateral who had besmirched the family name.' The disgrace of a relative reflects on the whole kindred, and a reputable family would lose caste if a daughter married into the guilty family, even if she would profit materially from the match. When it comes to the point, an honourable marriage has more value than sure financial gain.

These criteria of honour and prestige are hard to grasp, and they rarely passed through the minds of the people we interviewed. They are so mixed up with criteria that aim at an increase in economic capital. 'Take for instance your godfather's attitude to his daughter. She wasn't keen to marry her husband, but her father said, "He has fields and a farm; he has money. You won't find anyone better." She wasn't thrilled, but she married him just the same.'

In a society which is often dedicated to possessions and increase of landed property, it is hard to distinguish in a marriage between what is symbolic and what is economic, particularly as the latter is explicitly indicated. 'At that time it was the parents who said you'll take that one because she has land that adjoins ours . . . so it will increase our holding.' Economic capital is more real and tangible than symbolic capital. The latter is only really evident among the poorest, whose only asset it is. In their case public opinion often finds that they give themselves too much importance and that they need not show themselves so haughty. People cannot understand why they should take a stand on such arguments. Thus no explanation could be given to us for certain refusals of marriage among humble families. There was no estate, no inheritance, only honour to be saved.

In fact in every family there is a prudent outlook in marriage matters which excludes foreigners, frivolous girls and unreliable young men, and imposes equivalence, both professional and social. Hence this concern for marrying one's equal. You should neither marry too much beneath youself nor too much above: 'I never wanted my sons to marry girls richer than they were. One can blame oneself if things go wrong. You can be told, "You brought nothing and you've got nothing to show. I've restored your house's fortunes."'[30] This requirement of equality and parity among marriage partners is thus forcefully expressed. Between families you must 'marry the same'.

We must not deduce from these examples that all unions are the result of elaborate strategy on the part of parents and that sentiment never brings the partners together. But, until recently, love did not triumph in every case. In the old days, challenging the parents' refusal meant separation, banishment and sometimes even death. Also children, being financially and morally dependent, usually submitted to parental pressure and broke off their relationship. 'I got on very well with the young man I was walking out with, but we broke up because he had a grandfather who was an old horror, a really dreadful fellow, who said, "If you marry Olga I shall hang myself. One doesn't marry a girl with 'that' on her face."' (The girl had part of her face covered with a birthmark.)

When a courtship ends unhappily, the boy and the girl reluctantly accept another partner, often chosen by their parents. But sometimes the years go by and they remain unmarried, because of the strict requirements imposed by the parents. Pierre Auffray, only son of small farmers, is fifty-five and unmarried. His plans were twice thwarted by his parents, who refused him permission to marry a girl from the town. It was his duty to carry on the farm. There is this imperative obligation to 'work the land': 'one has land, one is bound to stay and work it' – a requirement that hinders many vocations. 'I would like to have become a butcher, but my parents were against it.

The farm had to be run, so I stayed.' This dictates matrimonial choice and echoes another obligation that is just as restrictive: 'One must stay with one's parents and look after them.' 'Pauline had parents who did not want her to continue her studies. Her first boyfriend was killed in the war. A second one would have liked to have married her, but her mother had died and she stayed to look after her father.' 'Mademoiselle Valentine had a mother who was left a widow at a very early age and had no other children; so she couldn't abandon her. She had even found a fine match, a gentleman who worked in Paris at the post office; but because marriage would have meant leaving her mother, she remained single.' This type of bachelorhood was not uncommon in the depopulated countryside at the beginning of the century, when families became reduced in numbers.

So an unmarried man or woman is bound to stay with his or her parents in a society where a child can only reasonably leave home by starting a family. While the parents remain active, they are in charge of the household and run the farm or shop. So, whatever his or her age, an unmarried child remains subject to the parents, who always treat him or her like an adolescent. Two unmarried sisters of over fifty live with their parents, and their mother always refers to them in public as 'the little girls'. Indeed both of them are sinking into neurasthenia.

The place of the unmarried person in society is not an easy one. The man becomes the target for all sorts of jokes at the café. He is given the role, or he assumes it, of public clown. His real or imaginary sexual adventures, and his escapades when drunk, hit the village headlines. Gradually, as the years go by, he becomes an eccentric. Unmarried women come to be regarded as victims and to be pitied. If they have no relations in the village or are not disposed to render all sorts of services, they are gradually left to their solitude. The bachelor in these societies that are rigidly divided into age-groups with precise roles, has no social status of any sort.

Usually parents want their child to avoid this sad fate. Also, when the child shows himself incapable of finding a suitable partner, or to avoid a disastrous choice, the parents themselves take the matter in hand. The search for a spouse becomes the mother's job within the family. Failing her, a close female relative such as a grandmother or a sister takes on the task.

The mother proceeds in various ways, according to the circumstances and the type of match required. She generally starts by

Leaving church (H. Amiot, 1900, L. A. S. collection)

A traditional craftsman's house (F. Zonabend, 1973, L. A. S. collection)

At the foot of the parlour stairs (F. Zonabend, 1975, L. A. S. collection)

The *agöt* (F. Zonabend, 1974, L. A. S. collection)

Grandparents and grandchild (H. Amiot, 1900, L. A. S. collection)

Parlour in the old days (H. Amiot, 1900, L. A. S. collection)

Children collecting on Carnival day (F. Zonabend, 1973, L. A. S. collection)

The traditional wedding photograph in front of the church and the cemetery (F. Zonabend, 1974, L. A. S. collection)

The draper on his rounds (anonymous, 1912, L. A. S. collection)

Twenty-five years later, the draper's son on his rounds (anonymous, 1938, L. A. S. collection)

The saddler at work in a lane (anonymous, 1902, L. A. S. collection)

The grocer-baker (H. Amiot, 1900, L. A. S. collection)

Mors omnia resolvet, 1582
(F. Zonabend, 1975, L. A. S. collection)

The mourning shawl (F. Zonabend, 1973, L. A. S. collection)

searching among her own relations, looking for a near or distant cousin who might fit the bill. 'My marriage (it was a woman who married her first cousin living in Paris) was fixed up by my husband's mother, my aunt in fact. She knew that he would find it difficult to live alone. He was shy. She said to him, "But why don't you marry Olga? That girl will always earn her living."'

The mother has the family history at her fingertips and tirelessly looks through the list of relations, knowing well how to make use of them when necessary. She quickly ferrets out the suitable partner from among the scattered relatives. 'My brother and his wife were distant cousins, and the marriage had been arranged by their mothers.' Within the extended family there is no need for an intermediary to 'arrange' marriages. The mothers agree among themselves and enter into direct negotiation.

If the mother fails to find a suitable match within the close family circle, she has recourse to an elderly relative who enjoys a comfortable social position. This relation then looks through the kindred to try and find a match. She usually ends up by finding the required partner within one set of relations or in one family circle.

In a few difficult cases, such as an heir who is physically or intellectually handicapped, the mother approaches someone outside the family. She turns to a person whose profession enables her to know the situation of the families in the region. Nowadays at Minot one is glad to approach the cattle dealer – Dominique, a woman – or the retired post office employee who lives in the next village. 'Oh, at Saint-Broing there's a mad keen matchmaker. She fixes up a lot of marriages, and they work. If you knew how she loves marrying people off! For instance, not long ago there was a young man who got married at Châtelnot. ... He came to see her and said, "I'm worried. I want to get married, but I'm shy." So she said, "I know a girl who will do you nicely. From the point of view of position and tastes I can see that she'll fit the bill. They're friends of mine. Tell you what; they have hens and sell eggs. We'll go along and ask if we can buy some." They went and bought a dozen eggs, the young man saw the girl and liked her. So he went back next day while taking a walk, and the marriage was arranged.' This role of intermediary is very precisely limited. She comes between the two families and acts as a go-between or excuse to bring the young people together. But she never takes part in the marriage discussions or in the official contacts between families. Once the introductions are over, the intermediary withdraws and the mothers take the negotiations in hand. By way of thanks the matchmaker, nicknamed *croque-avoine*,[31] is invited to the wedding.

This choice of a spouse clearly shows the preponderant role of women in the arranging of a marriage. Matchmaking mothers, female intermediaries, quarrelsome future mothers-in-law ... . We shall see how they make and break marriages. Within the immediate family, in the narrow circle of relations among whom matches are decided, mothers, grandmothers and sisters lay down the law. They 'arrange' unions or break them up: 'It was the mother who didn't want him to marry this girl.' These women in their official positions can enter on marriage negotiations without a failure – always possible at this stage – being felt as an affront to the family. In the same way they can break up courtships without the families concerned taking offence. Discreet and hidden, they manage meetings and hatch plots. In fact they hold the real power within the family, even if appearances are misleading, and give husbands the pride of place in public. When agreement has been officially reached between families, and when the time of courtship is over, then the future bridegroom's father goes to the girl's father and asks for her hand in marriage.

The marriage proposal   At this stage of the discussions, and if the future couple and parents are in agreement, the first step towards uniting the families takes place – the marriage proposal. On this occasion the young man no longer enters the young girl's home alone, but accompanied by his father or mother; or if they are both dead, by a male representative of the family, his uncle or godfather. Although this step is in accordance with a strict pattern, it tries to give the impression of being impromptu. Informed by letter, or through the young man, of the date of the interview, the parents of the young girl keep the visitors to supper without actually inviting them. During the meal the father presents his 'demand' which is generally accepted. It is unusual for custom to be flouted and for the candidate to be refused the girl's hand. It is an embarrassing situation which can occur if certain official contacts and preliminary discussions have been omitted.[32] After the marriage proposal comes the period of engagement.

Engagement   A time of many exchanges and favours on both sides, the engagement lasts a short period of four to eight months at most, except when the young couple decides to become engaged before the boy has completed his military service. This practice, now more and more frequent, is frowned on by parents. 'When Paul announced to me that he wanted to become engaged, I was shocked. I didn't want a boy who was going off to the army to be involved with a young girl. I said to him, "Think, you've only got two months together. You don't know the harm that can be done when a young girl abandons a boy on military service."' The separation aggravates the delicate nature of the engagement, and, for the adults a break that is unimportant at the time of courting becomes socially dangerous during the period of engagement; for the official situation implicates the whole family. At this stage any break can become the cause of a rift between families.

In addition, the time of the engagement opens up a period of relative freedom for the future couple. 'When you're engaged, you're free; you can go out alone together and go off for the day. But people would be shocked if you went off for two days. You kiss, but you don't sleep together.' As at the time of 'walking out', this last statement describes things as they should be. The truth is completely otherwise: 'Nearly all girls go to bed before marriage.'

One is bound to recognise the fact that many girls – boys of course are free to exert their virility – have sexual relations before being officially engaged. Besides, they risk no reproaches provided the affair ends in marriage. 'Nearly all girls are no longer virgins on marriage, but they have only had one fellow. They marry the boy with whom they have been carrying on. There are girls who get pregnant on purpose in order to get themselves married. As the boy always marries her, there is no serious problem. It starts tongues wagging, but the girls are not looked down on.' The virginity of a girl does not call into question the honour of a father or a brother or even of the whole family, as it does in Mediterranean countries. It is an individual and not a social capital, and it is up to the girl herself to dispose of it as she thinks fit. Some are proud to have been married virgins. 'My first was my husband. I had never slept with him before our marriage. My husband was proud that I was a virgin. He never told me so, but I'm sure of it. It was only then that he trusted me. Before he had been jealous as I had had affairs with boys, not going beyond kisses. He had said to himself, "The first one who hasn't let herself be had, she'll be my wife."' Others cheerfully admit that they had to advance their wedding day: 'We wanted to wait to get married

until 23 June, the date of taking over the farm. But I was pregnant, so
we married earlier.' And the tale is told with much laughter of the
baby who was born, to the surprise of the guests who had noticed
nothing, on the night of his mother's wedding. 'It was a Venot girl
who gave birth the evening of her wedding. Nobody knew there was
a child on the way. That evening there was the wedding party, and I
went with the others. We dined and started playing cards, then all of
a sudden the doctor had to be called bang on five o'clock in the
morning, and there was a boy!'

The old priest, who does not like to condone breaches of the rules,
now refuses to bless engagements. 'The Church used to recommend
engagements to be officialised with rings exchanged and a document
signed. I've stopped all that, as they think that they are then allowed
to do anything, and the baby appears two months after the wedding.'

Public disapproval is only shown when girls misbehave – those
who run after boys, flighty girls, easy girls, those who used to follow
boys from one dance to another, and today go conspicuously from
one boy to another. The group has, or used to have, ways of
censuring such misbehaviour. 'It was an insult to a girl to have no
shots fired at the wedding. It showed that she was not worthy of it.'
'Instead of a may bush, a pile of manure was tipped in front of the
door of a girl who had misbehaved.'

But scandal only really broke out when an illegitimate baby was
born. In a society where the basic cell consists of the father, the
mother and the children, where each member of the family group has
a role to play, any unbalancing factor – the bachelor, the woman
without a man, 'the child of a girl' – results in reproach or pity,
sentiments that one can easily expend on marginal people. As we
have seen, the bachelor, the unmarried mother and the love-child
have no recognised standing in the village. Their paths are strewn
with traps and difficulties. Some families, for reasons of honour or
money, refuse to allow their sons any possibility of regularising the
situation and ending the affair by marriage. 'There were those who
said, well, things must be put right, but when the difference is too
great ... mothers aren't easy. It is above all the mothers.' So the
abandoned girl is shunned by society. 'My father said, "I'll show you
the door, if it should ever happen to you!", so I knew what to expect.
There are girls who would not even tell their parents.'

Then on the birth of an illegitimate child the mother does not
know where to turn to find godparents. She cannot turn to the two

families, paternal and maternal,[33] from whom godparents would normally come. One does not exist and the other has backed out, so she has to call upon the children of neighbours. This role of god-parent can be assumed without too much difficulty by children as they are scarcely touched by the social system. 'Nobody wanted to be godfather or godmother to these children, so you had to sacrifice yourself. My grandmother said, "You come to us, the children will take care of you." So it was that, when Nanette's child was born, I was godmother. The baby died. It did not live long, perhaps two months, that's all.' When the godparents were finally chosen, it sometimes happened that the priest refused to ring the bells for the ceremony; for a bastard is not entitled to be consecrated with bells. Such a child can only enter the Christian world surreptitiously. When the child survives and the mother does not leave the village, he is given a nickname by the group recalling his origin. 'Brunet, his mother, had been servant to one of the Bruns. So he is pointed out.' 'The Englishman, his mother had him by an Englishman in 1944. The kids amongst themselves called him *l'Anglais*, so he got angry and went home crying, "Why do they call me *l'Anglais*?".' Although such 'accidents' only occur occasionally,[34] one understands the eagerness of parents to shorten the period of engagement.

The engagement, a period of relative independence, is the time for many exchanges, material and symbolic, which will gradually unite the engaged couple, link the families, set interdependence in motion and firmly bind the union.

Shortly after the marriage proposal, a more formal, more cere-monious meal takes place at the home of the young girl's parents. This meal, called the *repas d'entrée*, assembles together the future couple, their fathers and mothers and some close relations such as grandparents, godparents, uncles and aunts. On the girl's side it marks the 'official entry' of the young man into his future wife's family circle. At the end of the meal the young couple exchange engagement presents – a ring for the young girl, a signet ring or a chain bracelet for the young man. Fifty years ago the latter would have received a tie-pin, twenty-five years ago cuff links. As opposed to the ring, the traditional symbol of alliance, the girl's gift in exchange seems to have followed changes in fashion since the First World War.

A week or fortnight after this first official meeting at the girl's home, a *repas de retour* takes place at the young man's home. It is the girl's turn to make her entry into her future husband's home and to get to know his relations. The same relations, but on the male side, are invited, and the young girl on this occasion receives her *cadeau d'entrée*. 'It is table silver or a small piece of furniture; in fact a gift for the couple.'

These compulsory stages and formal occasions to herald the coming marriage and make contact between the two families continue unchanged today. However, more and more often, an 'engagement meal' bringing the two families together at a local restaurant is added to the earlier repasts. Presents are exchanged on this occasion. This new series of *fêtes d'entrée* has in no way altered the protocol of the past. It has simply added one more family gathering to the existing ones. The present tendency to multiply private ceremonies is due to the disappearance of village festivals and class reunions. You no longer see in villages joyous gatherings of boys and girls having their 'stag parties'. 'The Sunday before the wedding the priest at vespers used to say a rosary for the future couple. At the end of it the engaged girl invited all girls present to a *goûter* which she had prepared beforehand. The boy used to invite the local lads for a drink at his home, at the café, at someone else's house, or more or less anywhere in the village.' Now festivities of this kind take place in the family or at work, outside the village. So now you see a tightening of the family group and an opening-up on the world outside. The village has ceased to be the only place where its members spend their lives.

During the *repas d'entrée* the young people amuse themselves while the parents of the future couple discuss their contributions. For the establishment of the new couple is based on these contributions, consisting of gifts of furniture and real estate and coming from both sides. These gifts vary in quality and quantity according to the wealth and circumstances of the parties concerned. Real estate, i.e. land, houses, farm equipment, shops, and furniture, in a word the family estate belonging to the parents of the future couple, is seldom divided up at the time of the marriage, even in the case of an only child. Two things may happen. Firstly the married child leaves the family farm – which most often happens in the case of a bride as in this region married life is usually spent on the man's domain – and consequently receives as a dowry an advance on the eventual inheritance. This consists of money, furniture, linen, or shares in the estate, which will later be deducted. Secondly, the young people come to live and work on the farm of the parents of one or the other.

The child receives the same benefits but, in addition, the conditions under which the young couple install themselves are laid down, for example, salary, housing, hours of work; in other words their rights and obligations.

Formerly these conditions were duly put on paper: 'In consideration of the aforesaid marriage, the future couple promise to remain in the home of Mother and Father Sentier and to work for their profit in any matter which is lawfully and honestly ordered them; in return for which the above-mentioned Mother and Father Sentier shall nourish, maintain, house and heat the future couple, in health and in sickness, as well as any children that they may have, and furthermore they will receive all the profits that the husband may have earned at the end of the year's work from the aforesaid father and mother, in particular for the months of *vendémiaire, brumaire, frimaire* and *nivose* of each year. However, the husband will be obliged to help his father-in-law during the above-mentioned months should he so require. In case of disagreement the future couple shall withdraw themselves to wheresoever they may wish, taking with them their dowry and any profits that they may have withdrawn.' (Contract signed in the month of *pluviose*, year VIII, 1799.) It goes so far as to foresee the results arising from mutual lack of agreement. Today these conditions are often agreed to by word of mouth: 'My parents discussed and decided where in the farm we were to live and how much we were to be paid.' It now no longer seems necessary to have a contract drawn up before a lawyer.[35] Modifications in the relationship between generations are perhaps the reason for this change.

The trousseau consists to a large extent of household linen, collected by the mother piece by piece over the years. Hemmed and embroidered by the girl since early adolescence, this linen forms part of the family's contribution. Its financial standing is shown in the number of sheets, towels and tablecloths, and in the quality and quantity of embroidery embellishing them. Its social rank is indicated by the monogram.

In well-to-do middle-class families the girl only embroiders her personal linen. The fine pieces — tablecloths for a dozen or two dozen guests and towels — are made and embroidered by professionals outside. On the linen the initials of the couple are entwined in matching colours. This is certainly a sign that the two families are going to found a line. Daughters of farmers and craftsmen embroider the whole of their trousseau themselves. On each item they mark out their initials in red cross-stitch. It is here that each family shows its autonomy and demonstrates its assets.

Nowadays girls still prepare their trousseaux, but they embroider them less. They buy linen with their earnings, either salary or family remuneration, taking advantage of bargains offered by big shops during white sales, or bargains and lots offered in catalogues by mail-order firms. The mother makes up the numbers at the time of the marriage. Then as now girls collect their trousseau piece by piece.[36] Same actions, same behaviour: they all tend towards the same destiny, 'to marry'. 'To be married is a girl's pride.'[37]

Sometimes the boy brings some fine pieces of linen, more to mark his rank, it would appear, and the position of his family, than to provide for the needs of the couple. 'The boys also have a trousseau, but less complete than the girls' and often not new. It's extra family linen that the mother has. My husband, for instance, had several pairs of pretty sheets, with pillowcases, embroidered by his grandmother.'

Finally, furniture traditionally completes these possessions and effects. The girl's parents supply the couple's bedroom furniture: 'When I was married in 1965, my parents bought me a complete bedroom suite – bed, wardrobe with mirror, dressing table and bedside table.' The bed is always complete with mattress and blankets. As fashion and tastes change, the wardrobe and bed made by the village carpenter have been replaced by mass-produced furniture bought it town. The straw mattress has given way to the woollen mattress, the feather eiderdown to the quilt, then to the woollen blanket.

The boy's parents are responsible for the kitchen. They give the cooker, the refrigerator and the kitchen furniture. The man is responsible for providing the household food and looks after the heating. To the woman is given the role of providing for the intimacy and well-being of the couple. To the one the food, to the other fertility – the roles are assigned from the start.

The engagement period draws to an end in an atmosphere of happy and feverish preparation. During the month before, the wedding invitations are sent out, the last arrangements are made and the last services rendered. The wedding clothes are bought or made. They are never decided on long in advance, in fact the future bridegroom is never allowed to see the bride's dress before the day of the wedding. The wedding dress, long and white, the head-dress and the veil that goes with it, are bought by the girl's mother. The 'day after dress', the dress worn by the young bride on the day after her wedding to attend the mass said for the dead of both families, is given to her by her mother-in-law, 'My parents-in-law gave me the "day after dress" of brown satin, and my father-in-law bought me a plush coat as well. I still wear it: I turned it into a jacket.' Dressed and adorned by her new family, the young woman now belongs to them. She will wear this 'day after dress' for a long time on all ceremonial occasions. It clearly shows from now on where her new attachments lie. Right up to the last decades of the last century the bride at the 'day after' mass was dressed in black and wore a large cashmere shawl in warm, dark colours. 'The shawl was the garb of the day after the wedding and it was given to the young woman by the bridegroom's parents. The shawl was carefully kept and used as a table cover.' So the same symbolism dictated yesterday's gifts.

The engagement period ends on the eve of the wedding. Up to that moment all arrangements may be questioned and promises broken. 'My sister was engaged. There were rumours about her fiancé, so she broke it off. She has never married.' The rupture always brings dissension between the families. Bachelorhood, a late marriage or a stupid one, will generally be the lot of young people who have to break off an engagement. The sad story of a rich landowner's daughter illustrates this danger. Anne was engaged to a solicitor's clerk. A few days before her wedding, her father received a letter from the fiancé's 'mistress' informing him of her relationship with the boy and threatening to make a scene on the day of the wedding. The marriage was cancelled. The years went by and Anne fell in love with a Polish immigrant, a farm labourer on her father's farm. The father began by opposing the misalliance and then gave way, faced with a public scandal; for his daughter was living openly with the farm labourer. The marriage took place, but fate was in the offing. Anne was shortly afterwards killed in a motor smash with her husband driving, and a few years later he was found hanged from the beam of the barn. It was a wedding party who discovered him. 'Nevertheless it was a fine wedding and we laughed a lot.'[38]

Silence and noise The wedding ceremony marks the end of a long odyssey, which with its unofficial stages and its official procedures leads the young couple up to the altar. The boy and the girl get to know each other and are approved within the family. They then walk out and are admitted into the circle of close family relations. Finally they are officially engaged and are introduced to other relations. On the day of the wedding they will be presented to the whole community. So, step by step, all the social circles concerned by the projected alliance are involved and informed.

Why this long and slow advance, why all these procedures fixed as so many indispensable stages for the correct unfolding and conclusion of the union? As we have seen, the achievement of a marriage is no trivial affair. It requires reflection, information and strategy. These manoeuvres cannot be carried out hastily for fear of losing their effectiveness.

The whole business could of course be conducted, if not faster, at any rate without all these formalities, these halts, these formal stages. But is it not through all these that families keep control of time? Time to think things over, to collect information, to refuse, to break off or to go on. Time also, thanks to these ritualised procedures, for the disturbance caused by the creation of this new family to be smoothed out. As Lévi-Strauss has shown: 'Every marriage threatens the equilibrium of the social group.'[39] Bearing this in mind one can see that no stage can be omitted; for time would not be able to do its work and integrate into the stream of social practice what looks like disorder and disturbance.

This engagement period, used for social and symbolic ends, is also turned to account to publicise the projected marriage to the various family circles, one after the other. This publicity is necessary so that everyone informed of the plan can express his agreement or disagreement, tacitly or explicitly. This publicity comes to a head on the day of the wedding when the celebration bursts forth noisily before the whole community.

All along its route the procession is accompanied by noise and shouts, by screams of children, the applause of the spectators, gunshots and clanging bells. In an atmosphere of noise the procession goes through the streets and enters the church. After the Mass the meal takes place. It lasts for several hours and is interrupted by songs, cries and laughter – the shouts of men telling ribald stories, the laughter of slightly tipsy young girls, the scream of the bride when the best man pinches her calf under the table and rises brandishing the 'garter'.[40] In a stream of words and songs and a whirl of noise the banquet goes on until the late afternoon. Then the dance starts and music escapes from the wide-open windows of the village hall. Towards midnight the young couple fade away, followed shortly afterwards by the young people of the wedding party who attempt to 'run them to earth' in order to 'turn them out'. During the night the village echoes to the cries of the pursuers; they bang at every door and beat against the shutters demanding the couple. 'Oh, they always find them. There is always someone who follows the couple, or the bridesmaid knows, but she has lost them. Then they knock everywhere. We fled on foot. We went behind them and hid in our own house. We were discovered around five in the morning!' The pursuers had carried off the 'brew' prepared by the cook – a chamber-pot decorated with an eye, smeared with chocolate and sticky with toilet paper, into which champagne was poured. 'The couple are pulled out of bed and the mattress is upset. The bottle is emptied into the chamber-pot. The bride has to drink first, then the bridegroom, then the bridesmaid, then the best man, and finally everyone drinks. The wedding has come to an end.' The party finishes in a last outburst of laughter.

The rowdy nature of these weddings is very evident. We must, however, add that noise is considered a highly desirable feature. The shouts, the laughter, the tears[41] are all part of the rejoicing, and some now complain, saying: 'People no longer know how to enjoy themselves. There are weddings nowadays where one hears nothing.' Every wedding, past or present, becomes a highly coloured, noisy epic, which one remembers for the rest of one's days. Silent, speechless weddings are tainted with suspicion. Are the couples' parents having a row? Has the bride behaved in an unseemly fashion? We must not forget that those are the two main reasons for a wedding not to be celebrated to the sound of shots, songs and din. We see why everyone wants to give a wedding the maximum éclat and in this way guarantee it the widest publicity. Noise obviously has the prime task of informing everyone that a new couple has been constituted and that the ritual has been duly observed.[42]

In our view the noise and the din have other functions. In a number of European rural societies noise is synonymous with fertility and fecundity. The shots, screams and shouts which accompany the procession call down prosperity and abundance on the couple.[43]

The greater the uproar, and the more noise there is, the more fertile the bride will be and the more the couple will be blessed with descendants. But the marriage, as we have seen, marks a moment of unbalance in the social group. It is a break in the sociological chain. Noisy behaviour in these critical circumstances is supposed to chase away the evil spirits.[44] Noise then becomes protective. The uproar during weddings shields the couple from all harmful influences.

Both beneficial and protective, noise is also a mediator. To convince oneself of this one has merely to listen to the gunshots. Two or three boys hidden in the gardens which surround the *mairie* are responsible for 'firing the wedding'. A first volley resounds at the moment when the procession leaves the bride's father's house; a second, more intense, greets the couple's consent at the *mairie*. So a succession of shots covers the moment when the young girl leaves her home for ever and is completely detached from her family. The firing doubles in intensity when, having said 'yes', she starts to belong to her new relations. So gunfire bursts forth at a crucial moment in the ceremony, the short but very dangerous interlude where the vulnerable girl is between two sets of relations, detached from one lot but not yet taken over by the other. The noise plays a double role, that of protector and intercessor. It protects the young girl during those moments of change and separation. It also ensures a smooth transition and favours the passage from one group of relations to another.

All weddings are, moreover, places of encounter. They join the young couple together and unite two groups of relations from amongst whom other marriages will result: 'One gets to know one another at the various weddings.' A wedding is above all a meeting-place, a gathering; and amongst those present there must never be a moment's silence. Noise means communication.

This uninterrupted flow of words only ceases a while for the traditional 'wedding photograph' which fixes for eternity the assembled members of the wedding party. On leaving the church, after the congratulations which are offered beneath the porch in an atmosphere of joyous exuberance, everyone gets ready for the photograph. The photographer has set up some steps in front of the cemetery gate, and there he places the guests. So the wedding party, which the moment before was scattered in small, noisy, chattering groups, suddenly coalesces, becoming a close-knit, solemn group. The united family at that solemn moment assumes all its importance. Moreover, this ceremonious photograph[45] is the only one which is given to the relations, present or absent, the only one that is shown to strangers and exposed framed on the sitting-room sideboard. For this photograph expresses the *alliance*. On it is clearly inscribed the field for social relationships and matrimonial

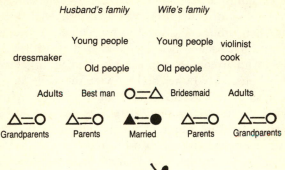

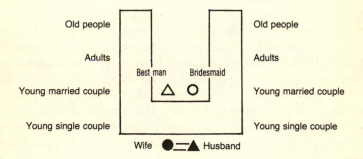

Fig. 5. Seating plan of relatives
on the wedding photograph and round
the table at the wedding meal

The positioning of the relations on the photograph is doubly reversed round the table – the young people take their places around the married couple and the old people occupy the ends of the table – the relations are thus intermingled, and the union is complete.

strategies, the circle of family affiliations and the invitations policy.

'At the end of the first row, that's Isaie Courtot; he was my parents-in-law's first neighbour, so he was invited. Higher up is Clémence Janin, a neighbour too; she lived next door to my mother-in-law, so of course she was invited as well. We too had invited our neighbours. We lived in rue Paluet, so we asked the Brisots, who lived next door. We invited a Moret, also the Guillaumes who lived just opposite us. On our right was Félix Toussaint's house. My father and he were the same age and they got on well, so he was asked. After them was Louis Grivot and his wife, invited by us. After that there was no question of more neighbours, they were too far. ... Behind us is the best man, Georges Camuset, the groom's brother and next to him the brides-maid, Albertine Lamarche. The bridesmaid and I made our first communion together as we were the same age. As I had no sister, and all my cousins were married, I took my friend. I would have invited her in any case. My husband was the same; his fellow conscript, he invited him too. ...'

The couple are in the centre of the photograph and directly behind them the best man and the bridesmaid; so they too are in the position of the couple. Their future is all marked out! On the bride's side her close relations are grouped in the first and second rows. The same arrangement prevails on the bridegroom's side. The third and fourth row are occupied by more distant relations and young unmarried people of the same age-group as the couple. So a double division governs the composition of the photograph – one horizontal separates the young and the old, the other verti-cal the relations. On one side an age-group, on the other the family – the two circles between which the young couple's life will take place.

Finally, at the ends of the rows, close to the relations and the young, we find the organisers of the ceremonial – the cook, the dressmaker, the violinist, not forgetting the person whom everyone looks at and who is not shown – the photographer, whose role, however, is very important. Intermediary between the families (he places the relations) and between the living and the dead (the picture is taken just in front of the cemetery gate), it is he who has the power and the duty to impose silence on the noisy assembly at this juncture, when the welding of the families is taking place. So noise is replaced by silence.

Men and Women

Once they are married, the young man and young woman belong to the adult world. However they only acquire their full adult status after the birth of their first child. Up to then they are under the guardianship of either the husband's or the wife's parents.

Mothers-in-law/daughters-in-law Nowadays, as in the past, the parents do not give up the running of the farm on the marriage of their heir or heiress,[46] and for a period, which may vary, the parents and the young couple live together. In remote farms, two buildings, one large and one small, giving out onto the same court-yard, house the two establishments. At the beginning of their marriage the young couple live in the small house, the old couple remaining in the big one. With the passage of time, children are born in the one and young people get married and leave the other. Then the old parents move to the small house and the young couple take over the large house. At this juncture the farm passes from one generation to the next. In the village farms, or amongst the crafts-men, parents and married children live together, 'same hearth, same kitchen'. After the birth of the first child, the old parents leave the house for a smaller one, either rented or bought, close to the farm or the shop and, if possible, on the other side of the street. At the same time the business is transferred.

This more or less prolonged period of cohabitation between two married generations is obviously a source of friction and latent conflict. As long as the old parents continue to be in charge, it is they who are in command of all and sundry. So the old father continues as in the past to manage the business and divide the work among his assistants and his son, who does not dare to impose himself. 'My father-in-law was hard and strict. He was the boss. We were going to be married on a Saturday and Blaise had said to me, "I shan't do the rounds during the week; I'll stay with you." On Monday his father told him to go off and do the rounds. He sulked, but he went off.' In the same way the mother-in-law keeps her domestic prerogatives: 'It was the mother who cut the bread and served the soup. When a small piece of bread was handed out, one said, "It's a slice cut by a mother-in-law", which meant that a mother-in-law was not very generous when it came to feeding her daughter-in-law.' The pun which underlines the mother-in-law's pettiness towards her daughter-in-law runs: 'The moon is an aster, the mother-in-law a disaster'. This describes at once the type of relationship which grows up between the two women. If one remembers that the phases of the moon rule the farm as well as the domestic year, and regulate the biological cycle of a woman's body, dominating the intimate and economic life of the couple, the association of a star and a mother-in-law indicates the important role the mother-in-law plays in her daughter-in-law's life. She programmes her work and dictates her leisure activities as well. 'The day of the Minot holiday my mother-in-law decided that I was not to go and that I would remain at the farm with her. My brother-in-law was at home and my husband went to the fête with him, but I stayed at home. Oh I cried my eyes out!' But above all the mother-in-law keeps an eye on the young woman's morals: 'My husband shortly after we were married had given me some pretty, short, embroidered shifts. I wore them during the day and slept in them at night. One day my mother-in-law, as she was doing the laundry, saw my shifts and said, "Do you go to bed in those shifts?" I replied, "Of course, what else could I go to bed in?" "You should be ashamed of yourself, showing yourself to your husband like that." I replied, "Oh sometimes I wear nothing at all!" That really tore it! My mother-in-law went to my mother and said that I was cheeky and immodest. To tell you the truth, I never slept naked, but the words just came out like that. In fact it was none of her business!' In those days, to show one's arms or an ankle, or the hem of one's shift, was a sign of depravity or coquetry, unworthy of a well-born young woman. Even between husband and wife morality imposed strictly modest and dignified behaviour. So the mother takes over from her son, acting as the guardian of her daughter-in-law's morals. Sometimes she goes even further and assumes the right to interfere in the sexual life of the couple. 'She reproached me for not having a baby. It wasn't my fault. I never did anything not to have one. .... I was never able to. ....' By interfering and scandalmongering, some mothers-in-law even succeeded in separating young couples. 'Old Mother Bénodet, for example, she made Georges and Jeanne's sister, the one who's dead, divorce. She forced her son to divorce, and how much else! The mother-in-law was always there between them, and so one fine day they separated.' These evil mothers-in-law can be compared to those selfish mothers who break up their son's or their daughter's marriage plans in order to keep their children by them.

Considered as an outsider and an intruder in the household, the young daughter-in-law rarely confronts her mother-in-law directly. It is through a third party that they clash. The husband sometimes acts as a go-between, but more often it is a close relative (a daughter or a real niece) who intercedes for her. 'I dared say it to Estelle (the brother of her father). "She works hard; you ought to be glad to have a daughter-in-law who helps you. When you know how to work, you have gold in your fingertips." I dared speak to Estelle and take up Clarisse's defence. When I found her crying, I went and tackled her aunt, but I never dared do the same with my mother-in-law.'

The names which they gave each other reveal the coldness of their relationship. The young daughter-in-law had no term of address for her parents-in-law until the birth of her first child, when they became *le pépère* and *la mémère*. When she referred to them, she spoke of them irreverently as *la mère Demonet* and *le père Demonet*, or more curtly as 'the mother-in-law and the father-in-law'. The parents-in-law called their daughter-in-law by her Christian name and used the familiar *tu*, whereas she always used the formal *vous*.

This latent opposition between generations was not helped by the economic dependence of the young couple, whose work was not remunerated and who drew no salary. 'We didn't have a penny, she never paid us anything. . . . She didn't even pay our social security, and that is why we now only have a very small pension. . . . She paid for our clothes and our food. We were treated like children. We worked, went into the fields, milked the cows and were scolded because we didn't do our work properly, just as if we were kids. . . .' The old mother managed the household expenses and did not hesitate to make decisions for her daughter-in-law. 'When I needed something such as clothes or slippers, she (the mother-in-law) said to Jacquette (a niece who is a seamstress), "You'll bring an overall for Gabrielle." I wasn't even allowed to choose it; she did it for me. She even chose the wallpaper for our bedroom!' The mother-in-law made her position felt even more strongly when it was she who had arranged the marriage, or if her daughter-in-law came from a more humble background. 'Béatrice was reproached for the fact that she had contributed nothing, and her mother-in-law continually told her, "You should be happy to have found us. Especially when one thinks where you came from!"'

The training received throughout childhood and adolescence bred passivity. The decisions of the grown-ups were accepted without argument: 'I can tell you we were patient in the old days. We behaved like meek little lambs and never thought of rebelling. If someone had said to me, "You've got to go and sleep with your mother-in-law, not with your husband", I would have said, "That's all right."' Sometimes a courageous young woman with a mind of her own might dare to answer back, but practically inadvertently. 'I was cheeky, I couldn't help it ... it just came out.' So daughters-in-law did not dare to stand up to their parents-in-law, and the sons, their husbands, did not have much more courage. 'Pierre never said anything to his parents. He didn't side with them but remained silent. But your husband, Sylvaine, he was always on his mother's side!' What is criticised here is not so much failing to reply or answer back to orders and insults, but failing to put up a silent and united front to parents. In this society where men and women were considered equal, the married couple was expected to put up a show of solidarity.

Today such troubles are rare. As soon as he is married, or even before, the young farmer is paid a salary and quickly acquires financial independence. Things are arranged so that the young couple immediately set up house separately from the parents, and they make sure that, when both houses are on the farm, they are built on the same alignment but far enough apart for spying on comings and goings from a window to be impossible, or opposite each other, one blind gable facing the other. This is a strict application of another proverb the people of Minot like to repeat: 'Each pig to his own sty.'

In fact this pre-eminence of the older generation over the younger ends very quickly, and then one sees a complete reversal of the situation. As soon as the old parents have left the big house and handed the farm over to the young couple, they are deprived of all authority, and the relationship of subordination between generations is reversed. Any idea of continuity of authority in the family, of the pre-eminence of aged parents, is foreign to the spirit of the village. The inheritance is divided up during this transfer of power from one generation to the other, and the parents give up the ownership of the farm or the shop when it is theirs. If they maintained this ownership, they would possess a hidden but nonetheless real power over their heirs. This is not done.

The parents estimated the property – the cattle, dead and alive, if it was a farm, the goods in stock if it was a shop. They then shared it between the children and left the main house for the small house nearby. In fact they continued to come to work on the farm every day, but now under their children's orders. 'The grandmother spent the whole day at her daughter's. She cooked the meals, did the housework, and dealt with the poultry. It was her daughter who told her what to cook and what to buy from the travelling dealer. The grandmother asked her every morning. As for Father and Mother Demonet (the husband's parents), one took the cows out to the fields and the other the sheep. Every morning it was Antoine who decided what each was to do.' The old parents enjoyed no privileges. Even if they shared the meals, they no longer sat in the place of honour. When they were ill or widowed and no longer able to look after themselves, they were forced to live with their children and were relegated to a disused part of the farm. 'Grandmother Emmeline died there, over the barn. A room had been fixed up for her; we children went up to see her and took up her meals.' In the same way as the parents maltreated their children, the latter did not hesitate to bully their old parents. 'Often my grandmother was scolded so severely that she left her daughter's house in tears.' One understands why old people, treated like this, has no wish to return and live with their own children. 'So long as I can manage on my own, I don't want to be dependent on them. ... ' Those who had the economic responsibility exercised authority over all the members of the household.

The situation nowadays has changed very little. The parents, once they have retired, lose all economic control over the farm and all power of decision. They are barely informed of plans and their advice is rarely asked. 'My father did not farm the way we do now, so we cannot discuss things.' When the son takes over the farm today, he goes in for technical changes and decides on how things will be managed in a way which often displeases his father. The latter is not consulted, still less listened to, and yet he still provides the necessary financial guarantees. 'Father Roget's son took out some loans, and they made the old man ill.'

Such situations and such family behaviour underline the position and strength of the married cell, which makes up the standard way of life in this rural society. A family cell is closed in upon itself, away from outside influence and protected from interference. Here life as a wider family group can only be short-lived and temporary.

Husband and wife   Shortly after marriage the young couple became their own masters. On the farm or in the shop, husband and wife played different roles and carried out different activities. We will not repeat all this. What we want to analyse here is not so much the details of the tasks accomplished than the spirit in which they were carried out, and the kind of relationship existing between the couple and the other members of the community. Bearing this in mind we must begin by emphasising that the tasks of men and women complement each other to a large degree and the separation of these tasks is more apparent than real.

We know that for things to be well run both husband and wife are needed. The dramas resulting from bachelorhood or widowhood in rural societies are there to remind us of the indispensable complementarity of the roles played by each. The tasks of a couple are allotted according to sex and are territorially divided. The wife is occupied in the house and the farmyard or in the shop, while the husband is busy in the fields, in the market or on his rounds. So the wife is by tradition attracted indoors to the intimacy and private life of the home, whereas the husband's activities tend more to the outside world and the open spaces. This traditional opposition between indoors and outdoors, between the confined space of the home and the freedom of the fields and the village is in fact less true than one might think. It belongs more to theory than to practice.

Of course to outward appearances each sex has its own field of activity, exclusive in theory, but at times these fields impinge on one another. When the work requires it, the wife goes into the fields with her husband and it sometimes happens, as we shall see, that the latter helps in the house. From all accounts the feminine world appears to be less highly regarded than the masculine world. Public opinion in the past forbade men to do women's work for fear of their being teased or scorned by their contemporaries: 'They said of a man who made the soup or did the washing, "You're a Jean-Fanoche" because in principle it was only women who ought to do that sort of work.... In those days it was lowering oneself. It was the same with milking cows. My father would never have milked the cows, or even learnt to, because it was *fanoche*!'[47] The women we spoke to interpreted these masculine attitudes as a refusal to carry out menial tasks: 'It was lowering oneself.' In other words the tasks were degrading and dishonourable. On the other hand they retorted that women did men's work perfectly well without there being any public criticism.

'No one made fun of a woman who went to work in the fields with her husband and then went ploughing and the rest of it. Oh no, on the contrary this was thought to be perfectly natural. "She's his wife after all, and there is no reason why she shouldn't do it." A woman must do everything.'

It would be wrong, in our opinion, to follow this interpretation too closely and to think that women only carried out menial tasks, leaving the rewarding work, which carried prestige, to men. Of course, the comments of the women we spoke to tended to make us think this: 'We were, however, looked down on. Women were really servants, and even lower. In the home the woman was the slave, the underdog. The man would not even have carried a pail of water to help her and relieve her, oh no. In the old days the old women had a hard life, a very hard life.' In a society which is dominated by male values, but is also influenced by the feminism spread by the media, the women we interviewed unconsciously recalled the past in a biased fashion. They forgot that, if a woman's task was never-ending and tiring, the work a man had to do was heavy and arduous, and many of them, as we shall see later, had to put up with the surly temper of wives who treated them like servants. The reality was not so clear cut.

In their respective spheres the husband and wife were in turn master and servant, when they found themselves side by side. In the home the husband could only carry out certain well-defined tasks. He could deal with the salting tub when his wife had her periods,[48] or he could do some quick cooking. 'In the evenings we had omelettes and it was Father Dumonet who cooked them. Of course he bickered with his mother-in-law: "It's always he who has to make omelettes", she used to say. But he had the knack. If you had seen him flip the omelette, he was skilful; he never let it fall. He tossed it in the air and caught it in the frying pan.' When in the old days a wife helped her husband in the fields, 'she picked up the sheaves behind the scythe, loaded the bundles of hay and sorted out the beet'. But beyond this distribution of tasks, the couple both at home and outside enjoyed the same power. Marriage for these rural farming families was and still remains a symmetrical association within which husband and wife assume different but complementary tasks, without one being subordinated to the other, or regarded as carrying out menial tasks. Moreover, the couple share the responsibility of managing the enterprise, the accounts and planning of the family budget being entrusted to the wife, and the husband taking over the outside work, for example, sales, orders and deliveries. But all decisions involving the economic future of the household are discussed between them. Neither has precedence over the other. They are of course called *le patron* and *la patronne* by the farm hands and those outside the family. Husband and wife call each other by their Christian names, and each in a possessive and reciprocal way refers to the other as 'my man' and 'my woman'.

'You must understand that here there is only one master, your mother and I' said a father one day to his son, thus unconsciously revealing the true position of the couple. In this society subordination exists at the generation level, the young and the old coming under the adults, rather than between the sexes. This distortion comes from the fact that, contrary to what happens outside the farm, the events and things said within the privacy of the home must not be revealed publicly for fear of ridicule. Nowadays this co-operation is openly appreciated. 'Now things are much more balanced. Today a man can do the washing-up just as well as a woman. He cooks too and is not looked down upon for doing so.' Whatever may have been said, this 'balance' has not really been achieved; for although the husbands help their wives in the house, the wives no longer go into the fields. The fact that agriculture is now mechanised and in the hands of men prevents them from going there. Men and women no longer work side by side in the fields, so now a whole area is closed to the wife. A whole world and a special type of relationship now no longer bring husband and wife together.

There remains the intimacy of the home, to which the wife is much more confined than in the past. But this intimacy is not referred to openly, just as one does not air one's family quarrels in public. Everything that touches the home is secret and concealed. The code of the group forbids one to reveal anything that concerns this feminine enclave. Given this attitude, one can understand that the worst fault that one can ascribe to a woman is to be a 'gossip', because one immediately thinks of her as relating outside what goes on in one's own home. The wife, as the guardian of this privacy, must act with discretion. She never takes any official initiative, and never exerts pressure openly. The steps she takes always remain private and unofficial, and she allows people to think that the decisions and public demonstrations of family power are the work of her husband. When the wife announces a decision affecting her household, she never reveals it under her own name; she shelters behind that of her husband. The wife's message is transmitted through the mouth of her husband.

On his side, the husband must also protect this intimacy and not talk about his private life outside the home, nor must he make affectionate gestures to his wife in front of a third party. This position that the wife occupies in the centre of the home, these discreet practices observed so as to maintain her position, certainly restrict her freedom of movement, but for all that do not put her in an inferior position. She shares real power with her husband, even if, seen from the outside, she spreads the illusion that only the head of the family holds this power. If power is considered as a weapon in life's struggle, husband and wife exercise it in common.

Although family politics dictated such niceties of behaviour, there was often a certain roughness of manners between husband and wife: 'My grandfather used to hit her and beat her. I had to come between them. I didn't want her to be beaten. Now old Mother Jauffray, who died the other day, I said to her son, "Such a hard time of it your mother had. What she had to put up with, good Lord. Her first husband drank, and then she married again, another drunkard, who beat her as well. ... "'

Yet it was not always the men who were brutal. Some households were terrorised by real termagants. 'Now take Mother Barey, she was a woman. Her poor husband had to leave, taking his cow with him,[49] to go and live with his children. ... And then Mother Bouchet and Mother Fleurot of Courlon, and Mother Perron ... what women they were. They made everybody work; their men had no say in anything and the poor old things never dared open their mouths. ... Now take Lucille, she had everybody shaking in their shoes, the grandmothers, her husband, the children and myself. ... What a time she gave us. Everyone had to work, and at the end of it none of it was any good.' So in the old days there were forceful characters among both men and women. The women of today relate this upsurge of feminine authority to the experience of the 1914 war: 'First of all it was because of the war. With the men away they took charge, so they thought they could do anything. They had done all the work, driven the plough, pulled the harrow .... Mother Demonet never stopped saying, "Whose fault was it if I had to do everything? Without me you would have had nothing to eat." So these women got used to running things. They wore the trousers, you might say.' This view of things, though interesting, can only be partial. Violent, aggressive behaviour was not typical of just one particular generation of women, but of a whole period in which life for adult men and women was a hard struggle, and both personal and family relationships were different from what they have become since. It is enough to remember what the rules of behaviour and the teaching methods were in those days. They reflected conditions of life in which aggression and tenderness, brutality and gentleness, hard work and fun were constantly mixed. Violent relationships between husband and wife were therefore not exceptional, neither was the opposite. The uncertain economic conditions of the period, the rough conditions of life, the ceaseless toil of the farmer and the craftsman, were important elements in this behaviour. In this context one can understand why family life was accompanied by a certain brutality. There was work to be done and it had to be productive; such was the imperative that weighed down on the different generations within the family, and upon the husband and wife. Then 'the economic factor became a mode of intimacy".[50] On the whole one can assume that in those days physical violence between generations and between the sexes was one of the ways in which they communicated.

These habits of violence no longer continue. Violence against children or within the couple is now socially frowned upon. It has vanished from the private household, yet still erupts elsewhere, at local dances, or on the roads ... .

As can be imagined, roughness of behaviour between husband and wife did not preclude sexual intercourse. Yet this was carefully controlled among farming families. Inheritance strategies and a desire not to share an estate among too many heirs demanded, and still do demand, a limited number of children: 'Once you've got the driver, you stop', as they say in the Châtillon district, i.e. when there is a male heir who will be able to drive the horses, and therefore take on the farm, there is no need for further children.[51]

In the past, birth-control was practised in many different ways: 'Oh it's quite simple, they sleep apart. Now take that family at Louesme where the young man has got married recently. His grandfather had only one son and then his wife died. Well, he never married again. The father had only one son; his wife is still alive, still young, barely fifty and their son who has been married two years has no child yet. They now own two-hundred hectares.' Sleeping apart, putting off the birth of the first child, not remarrying after becoming a widower – all these practices were widespread as means of birth-control among the better-off families. For the rest, with less room at home but the same desire to limit their offspring, they resorted to late marriages,[52] or possibly to forms of abortion.[53] This must have greatly hindered intimacy within the couple, and the chief anxiety for women seems to have been another pregnancy: 'Now take Claire Grasset. Every time she was pregnant there was a drama. She always said it was something else. When she expected Blanche, it was an abscess of the liver; next time it was a cyst. She didn't want to be pregnant, yet she was pregnant all the time. So she would invent any old story.'

Nowadays young couples plan the size of their family carefully: 'I want two children, perhaps three, but with a five years' difference in between' and they have access to up-to-date contraceptive methods. It is hard to say how far the emotional link between husband and wife was, and still is, affected by such attitudes: the distance between researcher and interviewee is still too great. One thing however must be stated – in these farming families marital conflict seldom comes out into the open. One does not get divorced, but in extreme cases there is a separation later on, when the children are married and the settlements have been made. Then one may leave – with the cow that by custom accompanies one throughout one's destiny. The preservation of the patrimony is paramount. And yet long acquaintance with some of these couples shows that between man and wife there does exist a mutual esteem, a benevolence expressed in little teasing jokes and a quiet understanding. With responsibilities shared and roles to some extent interchangeable, man and wife probably find it easier to get on together. The only marital conflicts to become public, and recognised as such, are to be found among couples in the worse-off social categories.[54]

The drinking party   Changes in the living arrangements of the family have resulted, as we have seen, in a concentration of family life within the home, a home henceforth protected from the outside community and its possible intrusions.

And yet this closing-in of couples on themselves does not mean that they live in isolation. They have complex and lively relations with other couples of their choice. The choice is one of affinity, either professional or family. There are, for instance, the four or five couples, more or less closely related by blood, who constantly help one another and meet together on all family or ceremonial occasions. Or again there are the three couples of young farmers who share their work every day and often meet together: 'We take it in turns to invite each other, not perhaps every week, but pretty often. We discuss things a lot . . . about our work and our daily life. The men and the wives together, we talk about our lives.' Also, all the young couples are intensely involved with their near relations in Minot and the neighbouring villages. Now that the parents are no longer 'in the way' – separate living arrangements at an early stage have prevented habits of authority asserting themselves – they are often paid friendly visits. In any case the parents are very much in demand for looking after children, or for other forms of help that may be needed.

The social life of village couples seems to be rich and lively; yet it is entirely centred on the home. They entertain at home, and they go to a few chosen friends to be entertained. The village community has lost its attraction as the natural place for gatherings and rejoicings. The old *veillées*, which brought neighbours together for jolly evenings, 'making waffles, the men playing cards, the women knitting', the civil or religious festivals, the impromptu dances, the loose informal groupings, the varied events which brought the village or part of it together, have all vanished. 'When I was young, there was much more fun than now. There were wonderful dances and life was really good. There was the theatre[55] and there were village parties for which we made cakes and sold them at auction, and with the money in the kitty we went on trips. We amused ourselves more in the old days, and the young admit it. They say to us, "Only you know how to have a good time".' The village activities, which used to bind all the families together in one brotherhood, have now dwindled to nothing. In their place, as we have seen, there is a close network of social exchanges and mutual help, which keeps the village together as a solid, lively entity. Now the families are dispersed into a series of small groups bound to one another by links of good neighbourliness.

The women have followed the same path. In the old days, under the vigilant eye of the priest, they belonged to various pious associations[56] who prayed together, or celebrated the feast of St Barbe, or went round the countryside in procession. Every week at the washhouse near their homes the women did their washing, exchanged news, and worked off their grievances. Today there is no resident parish priest at Minot and the washhouses are deserted. In fact the women do not meet together. They run into each other at the grocer's or the post office, they nod to each other at the church on Sunday, or have a quick chat over the garden gate. There is no public place where they can meet, no association, religious or otherwise, to bring them together.

Of course there are networks of women in the village who meet together regularly, but again within the groups of friends or relations already formed. The wives join up without the men to share in some domestic chore or in leisure activities: 'I go down in the afternon with the baby and we help each other. We like to be together, and we do a bit of sewing or embroidery. And then I like to go to Dijon and so I take Madame Ferlet in the car as she doesn't drive.' These meetings take place in the home, the outings in the distant town. Exceptionally the women will saunter along the streets of Minot or take a stroll together on the outskirts. The village is now under scrutiny; there are no comings and goings; its streets are empty and quiet. The women who have no friends or relations seem to lead solitary lives.

This description of women's lives and their families as centred on the home and partially cut off from the community, sheds a rather different light on the statements we heard at the beginning of this study: 'Everyone stays at home; there is no need of neighbours any more.' In fact this is how the women themselves see life as lived in the village today. It is a vision tinged with nostalgia for the old festivals and social evenings, and with regret for the past when women, as a group, took part in work and leisure together, and thus exerted their influence. For the relations between the men of the village present a very different picture.

For the men, anything is an excuse for going out, meeting together for a drink and setting up drinking parties. Of course they still have a meeting-place – the café. There farmers, workers, and craftsmen meet and drink every day. Nobody drinks alone in the café except the stranger and the drop-out. As for women, if they enter the place at all to buy a paper or a box of matches, they never linger. Even if they see their husband in a group of men, they will leave the place without speaking to him. They rarely appear there in any case, but prefer to send their children, who never stay with their father, for what is needed.

The café, then, is a place where men can meet out of their wives' hearing, and have a drink, talk and discuss things. Up to six men get round two or three tables, call out to another and, amid noise and rowdy fun, exchange spicy or serious comment, or discuss local news. Most of the men of the village will spend half an hour or an hour there each day in company. On special occasions – it may be 14 July, or election day, or somebody's wedding – a dozen men may find themselves together in the café, and each in turn will pay for a round of aperitifs: 'The other evening Mercier was there and Luret too and some more, and then the *maire* who'd come to buy *Télé 7 jours* for his wife . . . he got home at six in the morning!' It is on these occasions that the drinking party, or '*embuscade*' takes shape. For the fifth or the tenth time the café owner fills the glasses and healths are drunk. . . . The noise increases, the atmosphere warms up and the hours go by. Then one of the gang decides to invite the rest to supper at his place. He rings up his wife to ask her to prepare a meal for all of them. They all scramble into one or two cars and off they go, but on the way decide to make an uninvited call: 'We stopped at Loulou Mery's and had an aperitif. His wife Hélène was there; she locked the door and said she'd make us a meal. After the meal, off we go again to Poncey, but on the way we stop at Desliens'. He opens the door, and while he's fetching drinks, we rush to the bedroom and turn Eliane out of bed. She was screaming mad, but afterwards was ever so happy. We drank bubbly there. We went on to Poncey, where Marie-Jeanne had prepared a snack for us. From there we wanted to go to La Grange . . . but we made for home instead.' So from house to house, from aperitif to slap-up supper, from bubbly to omelettes, the *embuscade* catches a good many of the village couples in its whirl.

The *embuscade* is an impromptu, informal, egalitarian affair: 'You never know at the start who's going to be there. Anybody can join in and no house is out of bounds. It may involve all the married men of the village[57] with a few exceptions, as well as confirmed bachelors. Starting from the café and calling at one house after another, the *embuscade* bursts open the privacy of home and family life as described above. This is the only time when the home is opened to the village community, which now assumes the right to view people's private lives, judging and sanctioning any unsociable behaviour on their part. The ransacking of the house will be all the more ruthless if the master of the house is known to be stingy; the manhandling of the wife will be rougher if she is thought to be a shrew. In fact through this *embuscade* the community enforces its social control.

This kind of masculine foray started recently when the established associations for men lost something of their former importance, were opened to people from outside, and to younger men. The fire brigade for instance, which all men back from military service used to join as a matter of course, has lost some of its appeal, and its annual dinner, although festive in the old manner, is rather poorly attended. Shooting, which used to be the occasion for a great gathering, has now ceased since the 1940 war due to internecine quarrels; also the shooting rights for the village woods have been sold to outsiders. As for the football club, the pride of Minot, founded around 1932, many of its members are recruited elsewhere and of course are young unmarrieds. Furthermore none of these groups have premises in the village where they could meet, and they have no institutional status which might be an attraction. For all these reasons, and no doubt some others, the *embuscade* came into being. The term means three things all at the same time – an ambush into which fall men who have drunk too much, an expedition into the countryside and a trap for women of doubtful virtue. The *embuscade* is in fact a game played essentially between married men and women, a game for grown-ups.

Woman, although she may not appear to be part of it, is nevertheless the object of the game. First of all because all the talk of the men on these boisterous forays centres on woman and sex. 'Among ourselves we decide which woman we fancy among all those of the village, even including Mademoiselle Desgrange (an old spinster). But it's mere talk, we never pursue the point!' The mystery is how the men manage to combine these verbal flights of ribaldry with the reserve they feel bound to observe around the privacy of their own lives. Either the wives of the men present at the *embuscade* are kept out of the salacious review, or the husbands' sense of humour, verve or quick repartee are enough to defuse any embarrassing attack. However this may be, it is probable that many quarrels are both bred and settled by the *embuscade*. The following tale would seem to prove this: 'The other evening, Loulou Mery was terrified he might be taken to the Rigaults' and made to drink too much, so he bailed out of the car and walked home. Now Cochois was dead drunk when we took him home. ... Madame Cochois was not pleased, but Madame Mery was delighted. So Cochois swore publicly that he would take his revenge on Loulou. And he did – at the Crédit Agricole dinner. The whole party, including the women, flung themselves on Loulou Mery. We each spent 25,000 old francs on whisky. Mery was very ill. He was sick all over the place, then collapsed into a car and we all escorted him back to his wife. We then all trooped off to the Galskis' for an omelette.'

From one *embuscade* to the next, accounts can be settled in this way. The man who thought he could cheat and avoid getting drunk in public will be caught out on the next occasion. The woman who boasted too openly about her husband coming home still sober will quickly be put back in her place. Actually the wives are put to the test through their husbands' behaviour. They are reminded that they must not display too openly either their feelings of satisfaction or for that matter their marital grievances. 'After the elections there was quite a gang of them. They went round all the farms. Follin was with them. He came home late, but they say that his wife was upset and told him off. So he went out again and returned at six in the morning. But the gate is under electric control and he couldn't open it. He rang and she wouldn't press the button. All this in pouring rain. He jumped over the gate, fell and broke his leg in two places. She never came out to pick him up. The woman doctor arrived and treated him out there. No, really, that was beastly. I would have opened the gate and said we should settle this tomorrow.'

Women must avoid disapproving of their husbands' behaviour in public. They must do it in other, more discreet ways, if only by using the weapons at their disposal in their private relationship. The husband is denied access to the double bed: 'Cochois, when this happens, goes to sleep in the back room.' Or they can refuse all intercourse: 'Oh I gave him a piece of my mind all right. It was six when he came home. He made a lot of noise and pissed loudly ... he was cold all over.' 'She rejects me' was the husband's comment.

It is hard to say how far these male escapades affect the lives of couples. As we have seen, the close links between men do not weaken the strength of family life between parents and children. Nor do the wives' complaints or anger about the husband's absence seem to result in real conflict. The women in any case keep the upper hand, for they can refuse themselves as sexual partners. It is also true that the women are not entirely excluded from the *embuscade*. The game is played partly at home, under the wife's vigilant eye. For all these reasons, the freedom enjoyed by the men does not seem to bear too heavily on the couples' lives. If quarrel there is, it remains a private matter. The women have their own motives for this tolerance: they keep watch over one another's reactions and, unconsciously or not, try to turn these *embuscades* to their own advantage in competition with the other wives. Hélène, who locks the door on her group of visitors and asks them all to supper, knows that another wife in a neighbouring farm is expecting their arrival. But she will not have it said that she could not cope, or that her house was unwelcoming. We must remember that, with a few exceptions, the wives of the village do not see a lot of one another. While the men still remain gregarious, their wives are isolated and, when the occasion arises, they have to face these gangs of men alone. Hence this secret warfare in which women challenge one another. Lastly, their reputation is won or lost in the course of these *embuscades*, when they are turned out of bed, pushed around and verbally assaulted. 'Hélène is a good sort and likes a bit of fun.' So a list is established of wives who are not prudes and can take a joke but still keep themselves respected; of hypocrites who never get tumbled out of bed 'because they're only waiting for it'; of strong personalities, usually older women, who know how to keep gangs of men at arm's length. 'After Matthieu Cochois's wedding they came at two or three in the morning to take all our eggs for the omelette. Then Jeannot said, "If you don't get up, I'll turn you out of bed." And I replied, "Try that on and you'll see what's coming to you." Well, he laid off!'

The men too in these *embuscades* are tested in various ways and are thus assessed by the group. A man must show generosity; he must be able to give in order to receive and contribute as a member of the group: 'If you get out of paying for your round of drinks, you're said to be stingy and your purse is made of hedgehog hide.' The man must also 'hold his liquor' well and be able to drive in hazardous conditions.

The *embuscade*, however, is more than an eccentric romp. It goes back to a vision of the world that was held by this society, and it still bears the imprint of the past. Drinking to excess in company, careless generosity, careering through the countryside, hustling wives and snaring men, such are the rules of the game in the *embuscade*, a mixture of alcohol, money, women and danger.

It also goes back to a tradition of manly fun. In the old days, the conscripts, young men accepted for military service, roamed the countryside after their examination. With a trumpeter leading the way, and wearing a badge that said 'fit for the girls', the group went from house to house collecting eggs, a hen, a piece of meat here and there, to end up at the café for a night-long celebration. At every house where they stopped, the conscripts were offered food and a drink of wine or spirits. 'Bridal nights' were other events, when a group of people advanced noisily through the village looking for the newly-weds and turning them out of their beds to drink their healths.

However, the *embuscade* is above all an echo of the shooting parties in the woods, which the men of the village attended with passion until after the last war. Like a troop of soldiers they ran the boar to earth and chased the stag into the depths of the forest. Death blows that were followed by public rejoicing.[58] Not infrequently (for the village obituaries mention several accidents) the hunter himself was mortally wounded: 'Barrault died out shooting. He'd propped his gun against a tree. He slipped and fell and the gun went off. His femoral artery was severed, and he died of it.' Danger at the hunt or in the *embuscade* is not to be taken lightly.

Each *embuscade* has its dead man – a metaphor or sometimes a reality. A man who falls dead drunk into the omelette, 'it's the end, no image, no sound' they say, using the language of television, a daily presence in their lives. He is then carried home, humped on somebody's back, helpless like the carcass of an animal. Sometimes the party ends in tragedy: 'Loulou Mery was driving home from the Crédit Agricole dinner; he was found in a ditch at five in the morning. He must have passed out. We hope he'll recover, but he's been at Garches for two months for special therapy.'

Today as before, men in their amusements will face death. For death, it must be said, is a familiar presence in this society: it is neither forgotten nor suppressed.

Epilogue

This familiarity with death is at the origin of a whole system of gestures and social practices, as we shall now see.

Life Even today, before consulting a doctor, people in Minot still use a whole array of recipes, mostly made from herbs and plants. 'Against a cold you take an infusion of wild pansies. Our grandmother drank some every morning. Then the lesser centaury, "that's good against headaches", she used to say. I gather all that sort of thing and use it.' This preventive or curative pharmacopoeia is still very much alive. In June in all the houses there is the same pungent, heady smell of elderflowers put out to dry on top of the stove.

'Elderflowers in a compress are good against a swelling. I use them on the cows' udders, or, if one of us has toothache, on the cheek.'

Walks in the fields or around the village are made the occasion for picking up plants: 'Now take cornflowers, they have become quite rare. I gather them, and camomile too. I boil some water and throw the flowers in; they're good for the eyes, very soothing.' Celandine is picked from the banks at the roadside – 'the milk from the stem is rubbed over warts'; artemisia is found in stony places: 'you soak a bad boil in it, and it's very effective'; you pick mullein flowers – 'they're recommended for a sore throat.' Honey, another natural product, is used in various preparations: as a poultice it helps in the healing of cuts and wounds. Beeswax melted in oil is a sovereign remedy for cracked hands or udders. The bee itself is looked upon as a healer; its sting helps with rheumatism. However, bee stings can be too much of a good thing. 'One day the bees got into my pants, and I got stung all over. They are brave beasts and won't give up. Their poison thickens the blood. One thing you must never do is lie down, for you'll never get up again. You must walk to keep your blood active. Back at home I made myself a poultice of breadcrumbs and vinegar.' A lump of sugar dipped in the slime of a slug is a cure for tuberculosis. Open cuts heal more quickly if treated with a poultice of cobwebs.

At Minot, anything that partakes of raw nature is highly regarded. Wild animals are said to be superior in intelligence and incomparable in flavour: 'Animals that live in the natural state have a bigger brain, are more alive. A fricassée of hare's head, cheeks and eyes is a very tasty dish.' From being delicious to the senses, wild creatures and plants gradually become endowed with sovereign virtues. Also, in order to alleviate suffering, people turn to plants that grow without man's help and to animals that live in freedom. But although the curative properties of wild flora and fauna may be universally accepted, there is no uniform body of knowledge concerning them. Each family has its own recipes, its own plants, and its own methods for their use. In one family an infusion of mullein is used for a sore throat, in another for stomach pains. Artemisia is used for soaking a bad boil, and again as a drink 'to bring out the blood and bring on women's periods'.

This varied pharmacopoeia reflects its multiple origins. This medicinal knowledge has been assembled by each family either from 'their grandmother's recipes', or read in books and newspapers. The travelling salesmen brought with them all sorts of books and almanacs, for example, *Matthieu de la Drôme*, *Le Bon cultivateur*, etc. In them everything was laid down – the day for taking a laxative and how to set about it, as well as the day for killing the pig. Other secrets were revealed by certain village characters.

Long ago the wife of the *notaire* was the one to consult: 'Women from all around would come for advice when their children were unwell. She had a recipe for a poultice, and for a wild violet tea against the cough. ... ' After her it was the parish priest: 'Our good *curé* knew all about plants. He maintained that a tisane of dried hawthorn flowers was good for the heart.' His successor is now a woman of an old Minot family, who spent part of her life in Paris and has now come back to the village for her retirement. Because she has been away from the village for so long and has consulted a great number of homoeopaths, her advice is eagerly sought after and her erudition acknowledged. 'Madame Garnier will have nothing but plants prescribed to her. She goes to Nice every year to consult her doctor. He gives her nothing but tisanes.'

This knowledge, like all popular knowledge, results from a combination of oral tradition and book learning, of erudition and family experience. Whatever their origins, these methods of treatment are absorbed into the corpus of family lore and became part of the family's collective memory. They are then passed on, within the family, as customary or even immemorial, in the same way as the grandmother's recipes for cooking or the grandfather's special skills, and they are revealed to strangers under the seal of secrecy: 'I had a bad boil on my hand and came across old man Wiltz one day who said, "I'll tell you a secret. Boil up some artemisia and soak your hand in it."' A recipe, mysterious in its origins and given in confidence, becomes all the more potent.

To cure their daily ills, the villagers turn first to wild Nature rather than to the doctor. Nowadays they rarely seem to seek help from the saints of the church, as they did at the turn of the century, at least in individual prayer. The saints were, and are still appealed to for the benefit of the community in processions and pilgrimages. In the old days, the whole village went round the countryside in a procession at fixed times in the calendar year, so that the people, their land and their crops might be protected against natural disasters. A party will now travel to Lourdes in a chartered bus for no other reason than the luck of the draw. Every year the parishes in the canton set up a tombola, and the winners get a free trip to Lourdes. The Lourdes pilgrimage, or some other one, may incidentally be linked to the hope of a personal cure, through the vague notion of a miracle. The draper who has no children said one day, remembering her visit to Lourdes: 'A miracle might have happened there.' But illness is never the reason for going to the place of pilgrimage.

No faith is placed in God or saint or sorcerer[59] to ease one's pains. At Minot one turns to Mother Nature — or one trusts to one's destiny. For illness is above all a family matter. Every family has its own share of suffering and its own private illness, handed on from one generation to another by subtle hereditary influence. There is 'the asthma of the Barraults', 'the alcoholism of the Cortots and the Camusets', 'the madness of the Toussaints', 'the tuberculosis of the Barbrets' . . . . Now cancer, which was only mentioned for the first time a few decades ago, had now come to join the rest. There are the Cochois who have died of cancer, from maternal aunt to niece, for the last three generations. Every illness has its origins, and these are mainly family, rarely the result of chance or an accident. So illness appears as part of one's destiny. These afflictions single out each family like distinctive signs, which they do not admit. Most of them are considered shameful and are hidden away from outsiders. You will never hear it said by the Barbrets that two members of the family suffer from endemic tuberculosis, or by the Toussaints that the young son who committed suicide by burning himself was mad, or by the Camusets that the old father is in hospital for his alcoholism to be dried out. It is through gossip that one hears of the real reasons for deaths and periods in hospital. Yet one complaint, asthma, is openly claimed. It is the 'village sickness' and suffering from it is like a sign of belonging to the community. 'My husband has asthma and wakes up in the night choking. It's very common in Minot. There's Paul Cochois; he's so asthmatic he can't play football any more. There's a lot of it in the village . . . it's the climate.'

Death Whether illness is hidden or admitted, each family accepts its destiny. That destiny is death, and it is the women who are charged with attending to it. In the old days women assumed the symbols of this charge on their marriage. From their mothers came the ample black shawl that they wore at the funeral of a relative, and the 'family candle' that they lit at the death of a member of the household. From their mothers-in-law they received the 'day after dress', the dark dress that they wore on all ceremonial ocasions. As soon as she marries, a woman is ranked with the dead. Death and life are familiar topics. Not many years ago the same woman attended child-births and laid out the dead.[60] Life and death are constantly confused in female ministrations. For being a woman involves giving life, but also knowing death, accepting it, mourning it where necessary,[61] and attending to the needs of the departed. Every mistress of a house-hold keeps the family graves in the cemetery in order. She sees to the great gatherings of relatives which twice a year, on Palm Sunday and All Saints' Day, bring together the relatives and children who have gone to live elsewhere. It is always the women who arrange to have Masses said in memory of dead relations. In the old days the women used to be active in the fellowships of Notre-Dame du Rosaire and La Bonne-Mort, pious guilds that prayed for the repose of the departed parishioners.

In this way the women manage death, while the men turn it into a game through these wild sorties in the form of shooting parties and *embuscades*. In this quiet village where all seems calm, a tragic game is enacted whose outcome is death. The two sexes complement each other in this relationship with death – the masculine side inclines to-wards the wildness and excess of nature, while the feminine concerns itself with culture, ritual and the social arrangements surrounding death.[62]

But, for both, death is a familiar, almost a friend: 'Death is natural and real, so one can talk about it. It's a waste of time to try and con-ceal the fact that we're going to go.' In the village there is a language of death, which is spoken without embarrassment or inhibition. Silence has not buried, as elsewhere, this final stage of life. Further-more death is at every stage intimately associated with the daily and ceremonial life of the group through the old cemetery[63] that lies next to the church. Grandmothers take their grandchildren for walks there on fine summer evenings. . . . Married couples perpetuate their union by the photograph taken in front of the gate of the cemetery. Every funeral ends up in the cemetery, and there the community as-semble for a last tribute to one of their number. Old people still come every day to meditate at the grave of a relative or child. On occasions such as the saint's day celebration or 14 July, a dance floor is put in position under the walls of the cemetery.

In this village, as no doubt in others, relations between the living and the dead are close and their links are loyally maintained. One should bear this in mind when one hears the *curé* of a neighbouring parish complaining, 'In my view this whole region has never been Christianised. Look at catholicism; it's a religion of life, yet here there's only the cult of the dead. . . . Even Palm Sunday has become a feast of the dead. They pile it up on the tombs! The church is only full on that day, and for All Saints, and for funerals. On those occasions even the men come. Apart from that they never set foot in church.'

One of the only carved stones to defy time at Minot, while all around the old walls are being destroyed and the old houses transformed, is a slab let into the wall of a farm in the village. On it are incised these words – *mors omnia resolvet* – and the date – 1582.

3

The link of time

In this society where everything seems to have changed and shifted over the last few decades, the past survives through certain basic activities – exchange of services, solidarity and the cult of the dead. The past also lives in ways of thought that have never changed. This common behaviour, springing from the 'memory of man', gives coherence to the group and in addition links the present to the past.

Beyond the breaks in time which occur in every conversation, 'today' is constantly joined to 'yesterday', for certain behaviour and social practices continue unchanged, and there is also the phenomenon of things that 'return'. Under a new guise or quite unchanged they 'come back'. 'Since the arrival of motor cars, marriages between cousins are happening again. ... '; 'People these last few years are attending Mass again'; 'Ladybirds have returned to the gardens!' Even Nature conforms to this circular movement of return to itself.

So, in spite of breaks and apparent change, men always live within the same time. It is a time impelled by cyclical movements with more or less long rhythms. The return of the seasons, the periodic appearance of lay and religious festivals and the succeeding stages of life articulate the group in the short run. The return of practices considered obsolete and the revival of animals and flowers thought to have disappeared punctuate time in the long run. Beyond these cycles there is the memory of men, which initiates exchanges, gives rise to mutual aid, forges links between the living and the dead, and helps to keep this time of the community alive. Time is circular, marked by a perpetual renewal and an endless return to the 'same', and so to a static time, endless and unchanged.

The collective memory functions in accordance with a cyclical movement which constantly tends to seek permanence, to re-create what is indestructible and so ensure its own survival. It is as if the community needed to lean on its own unchanged past, where the ups and downs of History and the vagaries of modern life disappear, so that it may continue to exist in its present identity. The present, which is confused, incoherent and disturbing, is reconstituted by reference to the past – a stable, lasting and well-ordered period, a time outside the reach of Time.

Part II

The time of the family

All discussion of a person is first of all made up of proper names and indications of relationship. One is above all a father, son, spouse or brother of such and such an individual mentioned by name. Absence of such guide marks indicates 'the stranger', an individual of nebulous identity, without relations and sometimes without patronymic. These details convey and fix a group of facts, which allow the local community to decipher the status and origins of each of its members. Family names, the real tools of memory, place an individual in his descent and situate him in a known time and space. Parental details reflect his position in a social galaxy; matrimonial connections determine the subject's family and individual behaviour. Genealogy situates, terminology defines the destiny of each person.

So every person is fixed in a genealogical network in space and time, where past and present, kindred and community are intermingled. Each individual is set first and foremost in a time determined through the family. It is a time that is both precise and vague according to whether the near generations are recalled, i.e. three above *ego* or two below – or whether there is a plunge into the almost mythical depths, where the name itself is the only reference point. It is a time that is also situated in space and is bound by the matrimonial area. Finally it is time that has remained outside History and the circumstantial, and draws its rhythm from the succeeding generations, known or imagined.

There is no need for an absolute chronological reference point to consider this kind of time. Computation is provided by descent; memory is supported by biographical axis.

1

A lifetime

This family time gradually revealed itself as we listened to Albertine Chevenoz, the former draper of Minot.

Like other old people she always wears a grey dress, cotton in summer and woollen in winter, covered in an overall and protected by a cotton apron printed with tiny violet flowers or Paisley pattern designs. On her feet she wears comfortable thick felt slippers, which she slides quickly into clogs that are always handy in the yard next to the front door. A mottled cardigan knitted from bits of multi-coloured wool, a crocheted shawl of purple wool or a straw hat add a note of colour according to the season. Her husband Victor usually wears a shabby, threadbare beige suit, a bit too large for him. On days of strong sunshine he exchanges his grey cap for a topee-style straw hat.

Albertine and Victor have always lived in the village. They were born there in the first years of the century, were married there in 1927 and ran the village drapery shop for thirty years. When they decided to retire in 1957, they could not find a buyer for their business, so they remained in the house. The shop was part of their house, a square building made up of a first floor of bedrooms and a ground floor consisting of a parlour with an alcove kitchen and the shop. Nowadays all their living goes on in the two rooms downstairs. The former shop acts as bedroom. Albertine has screened off the back of the room with an ample cretonne curtain, behind which are still stacked cartons of underclothes and boxes of thread: 'I still come to a neighbour's rescue occasionally!' Blue and red cinerarias and bronze-coloured calceolarias bloom in the shop window in the summer protected by a lace curtain. The curtains and the plants give the room a spring look which is emphasised by the flower pattern and pinky-mauve colour of the wallpaper put up in the nineteen-thirties. Indeed the whole furnishing of the room recalls this period – the brass bedstead covered in a pink satinette quilt, the rustic wardrobe, the polished round table and the wood stove of red enamel. Only the refrigerator – 'it was the only place to put it' – strikes a discordant note. Time here seems to stand still in a season of perpetual flowers.

The parlour, which communicates directly with the bedroom, conveys a very different impression. There past and present exist side by side. From earlier days date the paved floor, the large wood range, the high chimney and the layout of the space – the master's armchair placed as near as possible to the hearth and his wife's near the window looking out on the street. The light-coloured wallpaper, decorated with rustic scenes, and the disposal of the chairs against the walls are evidence of recent changes, while the two nineteen-thirties-style cupboards and the hanging lamp over the centre table recall the period between the wars.

Here the strata accumulated by time enable one to detect traces of life styles dating from the distant past, the recent past and the present. The miscellaneous furniture bears witness to the origins of the couple. The rustic cupboard and the brass bedstead relegated to the bedroom show the country origins of the wife, while the furniture in the parlour has a more urban look and gives evidence of the commercial activities and recent arrival of the husband's family.

'Talking family'

When one reads family relationships or genealogies like a text, i.e. when one listens to someone unravelling them and putting them into order, one very quickly sees that there is a difference between the maternal and the paternal side. One is better known, is described with more care and consists of a larger number of relations than the other. This difference cannot simply be judged by demographic or geographical criteria. Personal choice – but which is always linked to a general tendency – plays its part and brings about a situation where one side is described in detail and the other is played down. It is true that in our society there is no sex difference in descent. Social status and possessions are handed down as much on the mother's as on the father's side. It is however still a fact that the two sides are not treated in the same way.

Every individual chooses the side to which he is attached and through which his social identity is handed down. He belongs to this side and always remembers its history. In other words genealogical memory depends on the value that one gives to one or the other side. Each individual in his family relationships weeds out and prunes according to his own criteria. Each individual uses his genealogy in his own way and manipulates his identity. Albertine does just that when she 'talks family', showing herself almost unstoppable when talking of her mother's relations and almost mute about her father's. The maternal side she describes in detail and adds to it, by complex processes, several individuals whose connection she cannot describe, but with whom 'she is still cousin', 'she is slightly related' or 'she is still friendly as a relation ... '. For it is her mother's ancestry that has given Albertine her membership of the village ('I am from Minot') and her family status ('I am a Grivot'). Hence the necessity of developing a vast lateral family record that far exceeds the bounds of the community, and links up all these 'distant cousins', these wide 'connections' and gives these relations their recognisable existence.

On the other hand, genealogical memory, stretching far back, aims to legitimate these different descents. Detailed memory of them is short – two generations, sometimes three, for the subject – and it fades out quickly, losing itself in a kind of mythical account of origins: 'The Grivots, they were very numerous; they were called the great Grivot family, and there was no end to them. There were seven or eight brothers and they all put down roots. There were many branches and they filled the village. I've even heard it said that there was a "Jean-Jean le Démocrate" who was a Grivot. He went out robbing cellars at night and took the loot to others. He was like that ... he wanted everyone to be at the same level, so he took from some and gave to others. Of course he kept something for himself from his robberies, but he stole from those who had too much, to give to those who had nothing. He had ideas of justice, poor fellow.' This legend gives the Grivots their political colour and, above all, their distance in time. Albertine is recounting in a way the mythical origin of her lineage. For it is in terms of lineage that she is talking when she adds, 'There was always talk of the famous Grivots. It was said that the region was run by Grivots, and that if there was a good atmosphere at Minot it was because we were all Grivots and all related. The Grivots kept together as a clan.

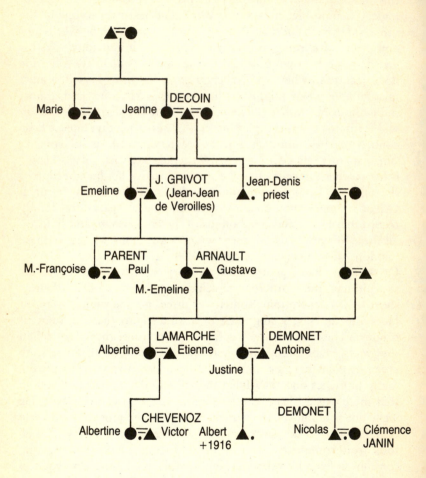

Fig. 6.   The Grivot genealogy

The triangle indicates a man, the circle a woman. The full stop indicates a bachelor or childless couple.

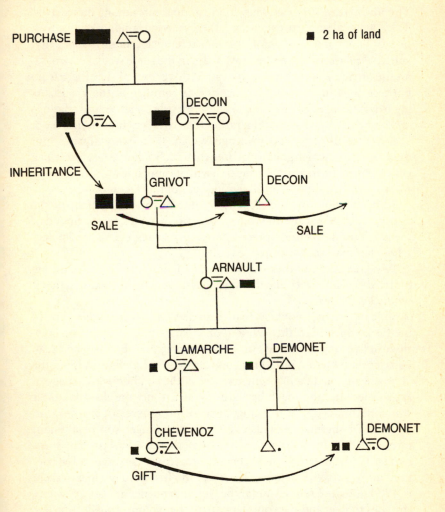

PURCHASE ■ 2 ha of land

Fig. 7. The transmission of land among the Grivot family

They were families who all had the same Christian names, such as Théodore, Jean, Nicolas. They found godparents among themselves. They were always in touch and they married among themselves, Grivot marrying Grivot.' Common references, family solidarity, spiritual relationship, endogamy, share in the same stock of names – all the attributes of a lineage are found there, except that there is no harking back to a common ancestor as founder of the group. As regards the origins of this group, Albertine evokes a nucleus of relations and a series of brothers so that, rather than to talk of lineage, it is more accurate to talk of a group of lineages which, as she expressly says, 'put down roots . . . which gave forth branches. . . . 'In short, she traces out a genealogy in the form of a noble tree with its appropriate terminology – root, branch, shoot – all so reminiscent of this forest country.

Starting from this, the scene is set; the historic legitimacy of the family is placed in time and space. Albertine can pick up the thread of the generations, mention precise dates, properties, events, and places where her maternal ancestors lived.

'My great-grandfather was known as Jean-Jean de Veroilles. He married Emeline Decoin, who lived at Minot in the farm down there, where I was born. . . . '

So Jean Grivot, known as Jean-Jean de Veroilles from the name of the farm which his father worked on village territory, came on marriage to live 'as son-in-law'[1] on his wife's property. Emeline and Jean had two daughters, Marie-Françoise and Marie-Emeline. In 1875, the elder one married Paul Parent, a dealer at the neighbouring village of Aignay-le-Duc, and so left her father's farm. Once the elder daughter was gone, it was up to the younger one to find a successor for the farm. So in 1879 she marries Gustave Arnault, younger son of a tenant farmer at Poiseul-la-Grange, who comes in as son-in-law. The same pattern is repeated in the next generation because Gustave and Marie-Emeline have two daughters, Albertine and Justine. The elder of them in 1903 marries Etienne Lamarche, yeoman farmer at Maisey, where she goes to live, and the younger marries her second cousin, Antoine Demonet, younger son of a family of tenant farmers in the region, who once again 'comes as son-in-law' to live on his parents-in-law's farm. Antoine and Justine had two sons, Albert and Nicolas. The first died early at the age of eight; the second was married to Clémence Janin in 1935, but the couple were childless. Also Nicolas decided in 1958 to quit farming after handing over his property to a nephew of his wife. But what property are we talking about?

The grandfather of Emeline Decoin had acquired, bit by bit, twenty hectares of land and some buildings in the village. Emeline, whose mother and maternal aunt died young, inherited the whole of the property, and it was on this that her husband Jean Grivot came to live. About 1860 Jean wanted to enlarge his estate and so bought several fields. But he had to borrow money and mortgage the property. When the recession and economic crisis came at the end of the last century, Jean was unable to repay his debts and meet his commitments. So he decided to sell his wife's estate to her half-brother, Jean-Denis Decoin, who was *curé* at la Ferté-Gaucher, reckoning that the latter, having no issue, would make his two nieces his heirs. But the future managed to thwart Jean's calculations. The *curé* kept on his brother-in-law as tenant, and then his nephew by marriage; but on his own death in 1900 he left his fortune to his religious institution situated in the Haute-Marne. The Minot land was then put up for sale. Gustave Arnault, who was the tenant at the time (Jean having died in 1890), had enough money to acquire the farm, but he obstinately refused to buy it on the grounds that the property ought to have come to him and that he did not want to pay for it twice. So the land and buildings were bought by Charles Villerey, a big landowner in the village. The latter kept Gustave on as tenant and even added twenty hectares that he had just acquired, and twenty others that he owned as well. So Gustave Arnault worked a farm of forty hectares, but never owned it. He was followed by his son-in-law Antoine Demonet, and finally by his grandson Nicolas.

By about 1950, the property was obviously too small to support the purchase of the modern agricultural machinery that was indispensable by now. Also Nicolas, being childless, retired early, handed over the farm and went to live in rue Haute in the 'little house' which his parents bought years before for their retirement.

So, for more than a century, the same family, generation after generation, remained on land which it had once owned. Three times the daughters, as sole heirs, kept a farm going which did not belong to them and, in order to stay there, married younger sons without land, who 'came in as sons-in-law' – a difficult situation in a society where life was generally spent on the husband's property. 'Justine used to chuck her husband out and say that the farm belonged to her, and that he could be off!' Nothing was too much to keep or recover 'family land'. Both men and women shared the same ideal and accepted all kinds of constraints and pressures. This concern to continue living on ground that ancestors had worked and owned explains these 'son-in-law' marriages and the calculations of a Jean Grivot. When the latter, out of economic necessity, had to sell the property, he approached a near relative so that the land should remain in the family group. He also hoped that it would be recovered by this expedient, for an uncle would not fail to favour his nieces.

Jean hoped to safeguard his land in this way and prevent it falling into strange hands. It is true that his son-in-law and daughter could have bought it back, as they had the chance. But in all honour they would not do so in the circumstances. According to them, 'the uncle' had not acted as a man of honour should. If keeping family land is a matter of honour, recovering it can only be achieved between men of honour. Even the buying back of ancestral lands can only be transacted if certain standards are observed.

It was now incumbent on the family to stay on this land which was once theirs and had always been cultivated and worked by them: 'You've got to stay. You've got to do the right thing.' This necessity, this powerful and restrictive link with the soil permeates individual destinies, dictates matrimonial strategies and gives marriages their real meaning. Furthermore, this story of a family line is not unusual. You could find, among the farming families, many other almost identical stories of 'land marriages' and conduct whose aim was to keep or increase the family estate. When Théodore Contot married his first cousin in 1909, he brought together by this move the few hectares that each of them had inherited. 'You loved this land above all, so you said to yourself, you're going to marry your cousin. She's got ten hectares, you've got ten, so look at the fine block of land you'll have. It will enlarge your estate. ... 'The marriage history of Albertine's maternal descent ran entirely along normal lines.

You must bear all this in mind – submission to the rules, respect for custom and tradition – as you listen to the rest of the tale.

The role of the maternal side

Albertine was born on 16 August 1905 on the Arnault farm. Although her mother Albertine Lamarche was living with her husband at Maisey-le-Duc, she had returned to her mother's home for the event, as was the custom then. The childbirth went badly; it was twins, and one of them was slow in delivery. The young mother was attended by an incompetent midwife – drunk, according to later reports – who could not or would not do anything to relieve her pain. The doctors were summoned too late and refused to stir themselves. The mother and one of the babies died.

All her life Albertine would carry the burden of this dramatic birth. Christened on the day of her mother's funeral, she was given the same name in her memory. This transfer of name bore witness to the replacement of the dead by the living within the immediate family. During her childhood and adolescence Albertine would fill her mother's place. When she was five, she was godmother to her aunt Justine's first child, a role which would normally have devolved on her mother. At the end of primary school her father called her home to look after the house, work in the fields and care for him, just as her mother would have done: 'Your mother's dead, you must stay with me', he constantly repeated to the young girl. Right up to her marriage Albertine knotted a black velvet ribbon in her hair every morning in memory of her dead mother. It was only after having placed her marriage bouquet on the grave of the mother who died before her time that she was able to give up mourning. But there was a last manifestation of this tragic destiny – Albertine would be childless. She herself issued from a twin birth, and they say here that twins are unable to procreate children.[2]

So Albertine was left an orphan and was taken in charge at birth by her mother's family, i.e. by her grandmother Marie-Emeline Arnault and by Justine Demonet, her mother's sister, who had married young. For one of them, of course, it was a question of looking after the child of a dead daughter – 'it was terrible for my grandmother to lose her daughter, so with me she was able to forget her grief a little' – and for the other it was a question of carrying out a solemn promise made to her sister on her deathbed: 'You'll look after my little girl, she'd asked her, you'll bring her up, so it was her duty.' But it was also an obligation that usually devolved on the mother's side. In cases of misfortune, or simply to help a young couple, it is to the mother's side that small children are entrusted as far as possible. In that same period in Minot mother Paul brought up the children of her daughter, who was a dressmaker in Paris. A hundred years before, Emeline Decoin, Albertine's great-grandmother, had also lived with her maternal grandparents after her mother's premature death. Even today, every morning between 8.15 and 8.30, before the bus arrives to pick up the few young women who work at the Valduc atomic factory, the village is alive with prams and the pattering feet

of children leaving their parents' houses and going off to their grandmothers'. And, if in the old days the young wife came back to her
mother's for her first baby, wasn't it a sign, amongst others, of the
role that was allotted to the maternal side of the clan?

Albertine's maternal relations played their part in a way that was
beyond reproach. For her father, embittered and taciturn after his
wife's death, took no interest in the child's fate. Up to the age of fourteen Albertine would stay at Minot and during that time her father
paid her only short visits. He showed no concern either for her health
or her needs. He provided no financial help to those who brought the
child up, and he showed them no gratitude. So Albertine would be
completely taken over by her mother's family, both materially and
emotionally. Her grandmother of course welcomed her and looked
after her lovingly; Justine and Nicolas, her aunt and uncle, considered
her as their own child. She lived with them and worked on the farm
just like her young cousins. They treated her with the same mixture
of tenderness and roughness. 'They always brought me up well and
sent me to school. They never took me away from school to work on
the farm. They might have said: "As we keep her, let her earn her
bread! . . ." No, I always went to school from 1 October right to the
end. It was they who dressed me. Even when I was at my father's, it
was my aunt who dressed me. My father never gave me a sou. It was
my grandmother who gave me pocket money.'

Up to the end of primary school, the uncle and aunt catered for the
needs of their niece. It was even they, on her marriage, who provided
her wedding dress and paid for the ceremony. Her father was not
even there. Albertine was always conscious from her earliest childhood of the role played by her mother's sister and her husband, and
she at once called them *papa* and *maman*. 'I called my uncle *papa* and
my aunt *maman*. I did this right up to their deaths. They would not
have been pleased if I'd called them anything else, even after my marriage. After all they had had the trouble of bringing me up; it would
have been ungrateful to address them otherwise. One can't be
strangers after all that.'

Even so there was great subtlety shown in the use of these terms of
relationship. Albertine never addressed her uncle or aunt by the
words *papa* and *maman* preceded by the possessive pronouns *mon*
or *ma*. *Mon père* or *ma mère, mon papa / ma maman* only signify
biological parents, and no other individuals may be designated thus.
On the other hand these terms accompanied by the definite articles *le*

or *la* can be used to address or name people who in practice have the same role as that of biological parents. The similar relationship does not involve exact substitution of terms. When in the course of her stories Albertine talks of *la maman*, we know that it means Justine her aunt; but if she evokes *ma maman*, we understand that her biological mother is involved. Albertine pushes the subtlety even further to designate her father. For this real father exists, but his behaviour and attitude do not make him a *real* father. Albertine finds in her kind and affectionate uncle Nicolas Demonet the equivalent of a father, but she cannot describe him as *mon père* and the same goes for her father as he does not play the role properly. So she avoids the issue and multiplies the number of fathers so as not to be the daughter of this father whom she detests. During her entire childhood she calls all the men in the neighbourhood *papa*. 'All the men, the farmer Brissot, the saddler Jodelet, I called them *papa*, and during the war when I was asked; "How's your father?", I replied; "Which father? *Papa* Demonet, *papa* Jodelet. . . ." Oh, I had a mass of fathers!"

In this way, by using different prefixes, terms of affinity, which are not abundant in French, offer the chance of pinpointing the reality of a social relationship. By using the terms *papa* and *maman* to address their uncle and aunt, Albertine shows that they play the part of real parents for her, but she qualifies these terms by using the definite article[3] and thus intimates that they are not her biological parents. So each recognises his own and is well satisfied.

Albertine, by addressing her foster-parents in this way, certainly thanked them for their good offices, but she still remained in their debt. If custom requires that the maternal side should *look after* and so *give* to their daughters' children, it is up to the latter to *return*. But as in all important exchanges of services, there is no question of forcing the pace or imagining that every kind and generous act can amount to a return that is sufficient to wipe out such a debt. Albertine had on many occasions had the chance of expressing her gratitude to her foster-parents. Thus, on the death of her maternal grandmother, she wanted to take only a modest part of the tiny inheritance. 'Oh, there was no difficulty. Justine gave me what she wanted to give me – two or three dusters. I said, "You brought me up. You don't owe me anything. . . ." She took the fine old wardrobe, and I had the other one, the little one. . . .' The stake was not very valuable.

Similarly, once she was married, Albertine, who lived just near her

aunt's farm, contrived to render various services: 'I went every day; I
helped to take calves out to the fields, to discharge a cartload of hay.
... I shut my door and went off. It was quickly done. And then again,
when we had a horse, it was they who helped us for the hay. They cut
it and tossed it. We could not have managed it on our own. So I used
to go and help them with the hay, and they would do ours. Then I
went to assist them with the milk and eggs, and they used to give me
some. "That's as it should be; you've worked", they said. I used to go
and help them dig up beetroot. I saw them finding it hard work, so I
said to myself, "I'll go shortly or this evening. ..." So they said to
me," Take away some bacon and some eggs." They were not close-
fisted; we arranged things.' These daily, domestic services rendered
by Albertine between adjacent households were at once returned and
could never serve to expunge the debt contracted. Furthermore,
thanks to the drapery business Albertine had all sorts of garments in
stock and so tried to help the family. 'They bought all their clothes
from us and we gave them special prices. We didn't charge them
normal prices.' But once again this was only usual.

If Albertine was to cease being beholden to her aunt, an important
gesture was needed, solemn enough to be different from the continual services that the two households exchanged with each other.
The opportunity presented itself in 1945, the day that Justine
decided to hand over her land to her son *inter vivos*. She remarked
then that she owned some land in common with Albertine. The two
Demonet sisters had each received half of several hectares acquired
by their parents.[4] Since the death of the elder sister the lots had remained included in the younger one's farm. 'When *maman* died, I inherited some of her land here in Minot. It was always Justine who
worked this land. I never asked them any rent for it. They brought me
up, and I had permission to plant some vegetables. So when they
talked of handing over to Nicolas, my aunt said, "Well, there is still
some land belonging to both of us." So my husband said, "You
might as well give it all to your aunt. You don't need it. She brought
you up. Just give it to her." So I handed over the land to her in front of
the lawyer. Nicolas got all the fields. But we've always got on all
right. When I want some vegetable rows, they give them to me. When
I need something, we come to an arrangement.'

A long enough interval had elapsed between the time that Justine
had rescued her niece and the time that the land was handed over for
Albertine not to feel obliged to do it. The gift of the land, which had

much gained in value, was substantial. Finally the act was passed in front of a lawyer with all due solemnity.

In this way Albertine settled her account with her aunt. The latter had brought up Albertine and treated her as her own daughter. Now Albertine was repaying the debt. But although matters between the aunt and niece were settled, a new account now opened between the cousins. Nicolas Demonet became Albertine's debtor, and a new cycle of exchanges (which still goes on) was set up between the households of the two cousins.

At the Maison-Dieu

Albertine says very little about her father's family, as opposed to her mother's side, which was so extensive and rich, and on which she never ceases to expatiate. Every time that we tried to set up her father's genealogy, she could only hark back endlessly to those two beings with whom she had to spend her adolescence – her father and her father's mother. Other relatives appeared, but only as part of an anecdote. One was her father's father, whom Albertine remembers as saying, '"I killed my mother." He had gone away to the 1870 war. There was no news, and his mother thought he was dead. He came back one evening without warning, dressed in his great white coat. His mother took him for a ghost and dropped down dead.' First accidental death, first tragedy among close relations.... Others were to follow in that family! She also spoke of a cousin – daughter of her father's father's sister, or mother's mother's, she wasn't sure – who was going to marry her father.... But from that side of the family Albertine has never expected any official recognition or claimed any identity. She can also pass over them in silence without difficulty. In fact, for Albertine, her father's family amounts to those pitiless beings who sought to bend her, as an adolescent, to their wills.

Her father, Etienne Lamarche, was tyrannical and sombre: 'What a nature he had! He was dictatorial, hard and quarrelsome. For instance, he was on the council for a year.... Well, they chucked him out, he was always picking quarrels. He was only happy annoying people. He was very intelligent, but quite impossible, and he was above all fond of himself. But what a character! Sometimes he went for a week without speaking even to his mother. I didn't even know where he went to work. I had to look out in which direction he went so as to be able to go and help him. I was so frightened of him that I didn't dare say anything.' But if we bear in mind the relations between parents and children that were usual in Albertine's childhood, we are not surprised that she finds excuses for her father's behaviour and does not allow herself the right to criticise. 'He certainly had a violent shock at my mother's death. He became embittered. He had to live with his parents, which wasn't funny. One can't say what he would have been like if my mother had not died. One mustn't judge ... one can't know. ...' His severity, his uncompromising attitude in work matters, his exacting ways, find justification in his family circumstances. He was a widower and had to live with his mother.

On the other hand Albertine's grandmother, Etiennette Cortot, was sour-tempered and a bully, and she had no excuse. She refused to play the part of protector and mediator which her situation demanded, and Albertine could see no reason to condone her. 'She wasn't a grandmother at all. She never gave me anything, she never helped me. For example, the day that I had to announce my impending marriage to my father, I asked her to do it. Her reply was, "You're old enough to carry out your duties on your own." She certainly wasn't a grandmother and she never eased my path in life. Oh she was wicked and malicious. ... She wasn't very large, but she was malicious! ...'

In the presence of those anti-social, malevolent beings Albertine never showed any interest in a family which in any case rejected her. They no doubt were never disposed to 'talk family' with her. But gradually, amidst the desperate cries and painful recollections which brought tears to her eyes, we came to understand the reasons for this abnormal behaviour and we got to the heart of the family drama.

In 1904, when he decides to marry Albertine Arnault, Etienne Lamarche is the sole heir to a farm of twenty-five hectares. At this time and for the region of Maisey-le-Duc, which is more fertile than Minot, this ranked as a comfortable holding. So Etienne Lamarche is a good match. Now he chooses to marry a girl who certainly comes from the same farming world, but is not well endowed with land and cash. Albertine Arnault brings her 'trousseau' as her entire dowry – a bedroom suite consisting of an oak wardrobe veneered with ash, a bedstead of ash complete with straw mattress, feather mattress, eiderdown, bolster and quilted bedspread, a bedside table of ash with marble top, and a savings bank book with 967,62 francs in it. ...'[5] So there was nothing there to satisfy the inheritance ambitions entertained by Etiennette Lamarche for her son. 'My grandmother never accepted *papa*'s marriage with *maman*. She wanted him to marry his first cousin so that the estate should not be divided, of course! But *papa* didn't care for this cousin. He had met *maman* at the village *fête*. . . . So all the time Grandmother kept on saying, because *maman* was dead . . . oh dear. . . . What a misfortune it was to have gone to the *fête*, where he found his misfotune. . . . So she bore me a grudge for it and often reproached me. . . . She would have preferred her niece as daughter-in-law. Now that niece was going to marry another first cousin who was killed in the 1914 war. So she remained an old maid and never married; but they wanted to marry her off to her *two* first cousins – it really was the limit! Oh, parents were terrible where land was concerned!' It was all a question of good matrimonial strategy, and it was usual practice, as we know, among the landown-ing and farming families. A projected marriage that combined a family connection and proximity in space, i.e. relationship and land, was the mother's dream. By acquiring a niece as daughter-in-law, she would know with whom she had to deal, and at the same time would join up stretches of land that were once shared out.

However, the son disregards the mother's wishes and prefers a love match to a marriage for money. He chooses heart rather than fortune. 'People often said to me; "You know they were very happy because your father loved your mother. . . ."' Etienne made the marriage of his choice. So Mother Lamarche could not impose hers, which at the time seemed absurd but was more understandable when one knew about the son's behaviour.

In this family there was another anomaly: the son was in charge during his parents' lifetime: 'He had been idolised as a child by his mother. He was a little god for her. Above all, he was an only son and it was he who gave the orders. . . .'

But destiny is lying in wait. After two years of marriage the young woman dies giving birth to little Albertine. So the death of the wife looks like a sanction for this double disloyalty towards a mother and an inheritance.

There still remained the little girl, born *in extremis* and expected to die like her twin. The father started busying himself trying to find a nurse, but the doctor's reaction was,' By the time you've got one, the baby will be dead!' Yet despite this gloomy forecast the baby thrived. If she had not lived, the chain of destiny might have been broken and the son's disobedience repaired. As a widower he could have married again, but the existence of an heiress prevented him. As Albertine survived, nothing would be erased.

This explains the grandmother's abnormal attitude towards her granddaughter. She was foiled the first time by her son. 'Ah, if only he had listened to me, his wife would not be dead. . . . I wanted him to marry Jeanne. . . .' Then she found herself foiled a second time by her granddaughter whose existence prevented her son from remarrying. Hence the rancour and resentment that she felt and openly showed for the child. 'Oh, she didn't love me. How many times did she say to me, "Your father can't stand you because it's your fault that your mother's dead." How often she repeated it!' The grandmother rejected her granddaughter because her presence prevented the realisation of her matrimonial plans.

For the father, Albertine alive is the incarnation of his disobedience, and his daughter must redeem his own transgression. So the little girl's future is logically all mapped out. An only child, she must spend her whole life with her widowed father and replace her mother, who went before her time. Let us call to mind those arranged marriages or those unmarried only sons or daughters, whose *duty* was to remain with their parents. Albertine's situation was along these same lines. The only heiress of a landed estate, she was in duty bound to work the family farm and to marry an heir in the village, or at least a younger son who would agree to 'live as son-in-law' on the farm. The inescapable obligation imposed by the possession of a landed estate is restrictive, as we know: 'When one has land, one must stay and work it.' In fact Albertine must get married 'for the land' and wipe out her father's romantic behaviour. But Albertine refuses this destiny.

When she had finished primary school at fourteen, Albertine left Minot and her grandmother's cosy home to rejoin her father at Maisey-le-Duc. There at la Maison-Dieu (the name of her father's farm) she worked hard, a prey to the hostility of her father and grandmother: 'My father used to send me to thin out sugar beet. It's tiring work and hurts your backside, I can tell you! One is bent over all the time. Well, he counted how many times I straightened up. He watched me from the garden and said, "You had guts this morning; you were getting up all the time!" Look here, when you can't go on and your back hurts you too much. . . . I used to say to myself sometimes, what must I do, I've never done enough.' She only came back to Minot for short stays. 'I went back for Easter, for the village *fête* in June, then for All Saints to visit my mother's grave, and then again at at Christmas.' She had only one thought – to return for ever. 'I'd have done anything not to stay at Maisey. I wasn't happy there and I wanted to leave.' Also when in 1926 her childhood friend Victor Chevenoz, the son of the draper at Minot next to her aunt's farm, proposed marriage, Albertine accepted at once, for it meant a return to her mother's village. 'I had already had proposals and had always refused. They came from young men over there at Maisey. I used to meet them at dances and they said to me, "If you like we could get married." I always said no because I didn't want to stay there. But I said yes to Victor.'

Albertine was now twenty, and the drama started again. 'When I had to announce my marriage to my father . . . oh dear, oh dear! . . . I still get the shakes when I think about it. . . . I said to myself that I must tell him, I must warn him. . . . And then the days passed and I didn't dare. . . . One morning I said it. I then had something coming to me, I can tell you!' For her father would have nothing to do with this marriage, which involved his daughter's departure and the end of the farm. He refused his consent: 'You won't be working for me, so I don't want it.' Etienne Lamarche voiced this refusal both in front of his daughter and of the fiancé's father, who came to ask for Alber-tine's hand, hoping by this solemn and official move[6] to change the mind of the pitiless father. . . . 'What a scene my father made that day when my father-in-law came to ask for me! Oh he received him all right and even gave him a meal. But as for marriage, he said no. "I shall never say yes as long as I live. Of course it's unfortunate she's going to be twenty-one in two months, so I can't stop her. But as far as I can, I shall hinder her and she will not marry. She works well, she's making a fine match, and I've got nothing against the family or the boy, but it just doesn't suit me. Her mother's dead and she ought to stay with me!"'

The drama gathers momentum and the father will not accept the marriage even though he has no objection to the fiancé – 'I say noth-ing against the boy or his family. You're making a fine match.' This is all because Albertine is deserting this land which will come to her, and she is leaving it for good. '"Her mother's dead, so she ought to stay with me", that's what he repeated all the time. This was the grievance – I ought to stay with him because he was a widower. There it was, simply that.' In fact the grievance expressed much more than an insistence on Albertine working, and was more than a desire to safeguard the inheritance. It was a question of morality. Albertine, the incarnation of her father's error, had according to the rules to *expiate* and *redeem* by her exemplary behaviour the sins that he had committed – disobedience to his mother, refusal of a landed fortune, the death of a young wife .... Instead of that, Albertine acted like her father, refused to accept her destiny and chose to let her sentiments and her heart have their say rather than follow the moral course laid down by her father's side. 'Oh, I've been very happy. I regret nothing. . . .'

Albertine repeats her father's action, and these two marriages, father's and daughter's, are real victories for freedom of feeling. But the father cannot bear his daughter doing what he himself did. Albertine, of course, describes the conflict with her father in a language which belongs to the code of society: 'For what was it that divided *papa* and myself? It was the fields. We quarrelled on a question of land. He wanted me to marry a farmer to work our property and then later to enlarge it.' 'Remain on the land', 'increase the heritage', it was in these terms that marriage negotiations were conducted at the beginning of the century. So it is normal that Albertine should state this reason as crucial and at the heart of the drama.

However, in our view, this reason does not entirely explain the father's violent reaction to his daughter's marriage. He had assigned her a role which she refused to play – to atone for the marriage that he had contracted and wipe out the punishment which followed. If his daughter acted as he did, no expiation would be possible, and hence his strong feelings. He would never be able to accept such a marriage, whatever Albertine might think: 'A few days before leaving, I said, "Well, *papa*, don't you want to come to my wedding?" "Never. I swore to your grandmother that I wouldn't go to it." I might possibly have changed his mind, but her. . . . It was my grandmother who was adamant.' As for the grandmother, she insisted on her revenge and perhaps thought that, twenty years later, she might at last be able to be rid of this awkward child.

In spite of her father's opposition and her grandmother's hostility, Albertine did not give in. 'My goodness, I made some requests for parental consent. Even at twenty-one you had to have them. They were papers that the *notaire* brought. Every time my father replied 'no', and every time we had an argument. My aunt at Minot wanted me to come and stay with her, but I didn't want to leave them with all the work.' If she could not satisfy all her father's demands, at least she would see that she would have nothing with which to reproach herself. So Albertine finished off all her jobs before leaving la Maison-Dieu: 'I stayed till November, when we finished all the tasks and got in all the sugar beet. ... I didn't want them to say "Look, she's left us in the middle of all this work."' Apart from her marriage, which she refused to compromise, Albertine respected the normal rules of conduct between parents and children.

Three months before the day of the wedding Albertine left la Maison-Dieu for good. The day of her departure her father handed over her mother's trousseau intact and her savings bank book; and bid her come back to collect her few pieces of furniture as soon as possible. So all trace of the mother's and daughter's existence was removed from the house.

On the doorstep at the moment of leaving, Albertine tried again to make her father change his mind: '"So you'll come and see us. We'll invite you to our house." He replied, "I'll come and see you if you are in trouble." He would have come for my funeral, but not before.' The break with her father's family had been completed.

The marriage took place at Minot. Etienne Lamarche was not present and it was a great-uncle, the oldest male relative on the mother's side, who gave Albertine away. 'It was a brother of my grandfather who said, "Well, that's not right. I would never have expected that of your father, not to come and give you away." He was old and he said to me, "Somehow or other I'll come and then I'll give you away. As your mother's not there it's up to me to do the job."' The situation in which Albertine found herself, reduced as it were to the status of an illegitimate child, demanded a rallying of her maternal relations round her. At every solemn occasion, every time her father failed to support her, her mother's family came to the rescue, masking by their presence the tragic aspect of the situation and showing at the same time their disapproval. 'For instance, at the time of my first communion the war was on. My father was on leave, but he didn't come, whereas my aunt Mélie Arnault came on foot from the Grandes-Fosses farm so that I should not be alone.'

Despite the harsh and unequivocal words uttered by her father, Albertine did not want to believe in a final break; and after her marriage she tried to make it up. She wrote to her father for festivals and New Year's Day, but in return got 'only nonsense; letters without meaning.' On the first of every month she went back to the Maison-Dieu to do the washing and look after the linen; 'but they did not say a word to me. I sat in a corner.' So her husband Victor

Chevenoz protested and forbade Albertine to go back. 'As they don't talk to you, you'd better stay with us.' Soon all relations between father and daughter ceased.

A few years later Albertine heard indirectly of the death of her grandmother Etiennette. 'Bleeding would not have hurt me more.' The pain came from the fact that she was not told personally. Her father thus treated her as a stranger and showed that he had struck her off the family list. In the same way she learnt a little later of her father's remarriage.

Many years later, Albertine met her father on a road. She moved towards him without rancour, and for the first time in his life her father kissed her: 'You know what I've done? I've married again.' 'You did right' was Albertine's only reply. She got to know her stepmother who was an officer's widow and mother of a grown-up son. Soon afterwards this woman wrote to her: 'I like things to be clear. After your father's death you will get nothing!' Her aim was simple: she wanted Etienne Lamarche to sell his property so that Albertine could more easily be excluded from inheriting. Etienne refused obstinately. The 1940 war broke out and all communication between the two families ceased. In 1944 the stepmother died a violent death in the troubled period that followed the Liberation. 'Tormenting my father did not bring her happiness' commented Albertine drily.

A few months later the father fell ill and summoned his daughter, who went at once to look after him. ' "I've caused you a lot of misery. I oughtn't to have done as I did." "Oh it's all over now", I replied. "I never blamed you, but I must say we would have been happier if things had been different." ' Etienne Lamarche died in 1945. Albertine took care of the funeral without even thinking of going to the *notaire*. She thought that she had been disinherited. She was pressed to go and see, and she found that her father had left her all his property. She let it for ten years to a neighbour, then sold it. From that moment she would never go back to la Maison-Dieu. So all links with her father's family 'country' of origin were severed.

Rules and practices

The stories of the two sides of the family told by Albertine are quite different from one another. On the mother's side it was life according to the social rules. Marriages were contracted so as to maintain the landed estate and continue the farming of soil on which their fore-bears had laboured. In every case the customary rules had been respected – the grandmother rescued the daughter's child, the aunt brought up her niece, the senior male in the line replaced the missing father, the senior woman supported the orphan during her rites of passage.... In everyday life, as on ceremonial occasions, the mother's family held the role and the place assigned to them by society. On the father's side the rules had been flouted. By giving free rein to their sentiments, the father and then the daughter had neglected their inheritance and abandoned their interests. Hence the tragedies that ensued – the death of the young wife, the flight of the young girl.... Destiny is implacable when you fail to act according to the rules laid down by the group.

As one listens to these two stories, one understands why Albertine chose to remember her mother's side and forget her father's. But one should notice that the personal criteria which Albertine adduces to repudiate her father's side do in fact result from the existence of these rules. The story of these two groups only makes sense in relation to these rules. The mother's side illustrates them positively, and the father's side negatively, but even more vividly. It is significant how little Albertine says about the marriages contracted in her mother's family. She confines herself to recalling the main characters but she does not enlarge either on the circumstances or the consequences. These marriages, being neither brilliant nor imprudent, are never out of the ordinary, and there is nothing to say about them. They exist in their own right within the context of the times and they obey the social rules. On the other hand, Albertine never stops talking about her father's marriage or her own, which aroused massive opposition. This is because these two marriages were extraordinary, in the sense that they broke the established rules. One knows that a bold personality is required to attempt such a match. These exceptions allow us to appreciate the full weight of social sanctions, and they are living proof of what happens when men or women try to bend the rules to satisfy their deepest feelings.

One can talk at length about these marginal, unusual marriages – in fact one must. Indeed for Albertine every marriage *tells a story*. The most unorthodox ones as well as the most normal can all be explained. First of all Albertine places them in a time continuum, a series where one follows another and one explains another. If a father and a mother have made a match, the son or daughter must do the same or else make up for any errors committed. If an elder brother leaves the family farm, the younger must stay on the property. In every line of descent each marriage can only be understood in relation to all those others that have preceded it, and every marriage is determined by the others.

Then Albertine clearly lays down the rules and the social context in which these marriages have taken place. She endlessly describes this context when she condemns 'marriage for the land', as do all the woman of that generation. 'How they loved this soil! Admittedly it was hard to acquire; one bought it piece by piece, stinting oneself of everything. So they were above all the owners of their little property. They would never want to leave it.' It is not surprising that Albertine, who broke the rules by her own marriage, has revolted against this excessive love of the soil. 'It was really something terrible, this feeling of my family for their land. Sometimes I said to my grandmother, "Oh! They'll chuck some soil on you when you're dead, much more than you'll want!" My God, how she loved her land. Unbelievable! I was disgusted to see them love this land more than anything else. It counted more than anything!' In justifying her own behaviour Albertine denounces this exaggerated attitude and emphasises the necessity of keeping a fair balance both as regards land and personal sentiments. Exploiting parents ('My father wanted me to marry for his own comfort, not for myself') are as guilty as ungrateful children ('It would have shown ingratitude not to call them *papa* and *maman*'). She disowns and condemns all these excessive positions.

Albertine describes in detail the services that relations ought to exchange with one another[7] and the duties incumbent upon each ('I'm not going to leave them in the middle of a job . . .'). In the same way she lays emphasis on *speech* as a link in communication and intercourse.[8] Everything can be and is said among relations: every action, the best and the worst, is put into words. The father openly desires his daughter's death ('I'd go if a misfortune befell you'). The grandmother calls down infidelity in love on her granddaughter ('Oh, you're marrying a commercial traveller. He'll soon have had enough of you. . . .'). Yet so long as this verbal exchange continues, even at the height of the drama, the rift is not final and everything can start again. The break becomes irreversible when silence finally descends. Victor Chevenoz forbids Albertine to go back and work at la Maison-Dieu: 'As they won't talk to you, you mustn't go. . . .' Albertine understands that she has become a stranger for her father, who never told her of her grandmother's death. Yet again Albertine shows up the negative, excessive side of her father's family — the cruel, uncompromising words uttered by her father and grand-mother are not normal talk.

All the rich mixture of conventions that control family relation-ships are to be found in this story. You could not find a better example of a single case illuminating the general rule.

The trip to Lourdes

Albertine and Victor were married on 21 January 1927. As one might have expected, the wedding was gloomy. The ceremony was bound to be difficult, being the outcome of a troubled courtship and an irregular engagement. 'Oh, it wasn't cheerful. I had no mother to support me, and then there was *papa* with whom I was not on speak-ing terms. I think I didn't eat anything, and Victor's grandmother had died not long before, so we said there would be no dancing, and we hadn't invited many young people.'

Tragedy had dogged Albertine ever since her mother's death. Drama followed drama, marking every ceremony of passage. 'I was christened the day of *maman*'s funeral. . . .' 'At my first communion Albert (her cousin) was on his death-bed and there was a war on. . . .' The marriage followed on this dismal series of events. Furthermore her mother-in-law, assuming the spiteful role of her father, was more or less opposed to any change in her way of life. First of all she for-bade the 'pursuit' of the married couple, which usually finished off a wedding in a friendly outburst of laughter. 'We had no pursuit with the chamber-pot. . . . No, my mother-in-law didn't want it. She said, "I think these customs are not suitable for the young. . . . I don't want them to go and wake up the married couple. . . ." So they didn't come.' Also, on the night of the wedding, the mother-in-law chose to make her requirements known. 'On the day of the wedding there's Victor's father who calls him, "Come and see, your mother's crying." So we go and see what's happening, and I say to her, "You're not pleased with the marriage." "It's not that", she replied, "but now that Albertine's there we shall have to go away. . . ." Really, fancy crying on the evening of your son's wedding, that was really not nice.' Albertine's views were clearly expressed, followed at once by an assertion of her independence: 'If you want to stay in Minot, we shall go and open a business elsewhere.'

Albertine's parents-in-law decide to stay for a year with the young couple, the pretext being to initiate her into the drapery business. During all this time they treat their daughter-in-law like a servant, as often happens in such circumstances. 'It was they who ran everything here'. My father-in-law said, "Why, now Tine will get up first, feed the horses, prepare coffee, then call us. In this way we should be able to sleep an hour extra." No really, it was taking me for a maid! I did this for Victor of course, but I wasn't going to do it for them.'

A few months after the marriage Louis Chevenoz, Victor's father, decided to give the young couple a trip. He chose to send them to Lourdes and informed them that her mother-in-law would be coming too. Indeed it was she who took everything in hand. 'She dressed me in a special way. Dresses with short sleeves were already worn at the time. She told me that one shouldn't wear that sort of thing at Lourdes. . . . She had been to Lourdes when she got married, but you can imagine things had changed since then! But in the end she got me to make a navy blue, woollen dress with thick stockings – Gosh, was I warm!' Even outside the village the mother-in-law supervises her daughter-in-law's clothes, just as she assumes the right to dictate her conduct. 'I thought that during the day I would be going off with Victor for walks in the neighbourhood. *Maman* said, "You'll be coming with me to the grotto every day." Victor came the first day, after that he left, and I stayed praying with my mother-in-law. He came back in the evening and said, "Look, Tine, it's really beautiful. I've seen this and I've seen that ...". One evening he said to me, "We'll go in the funicular" and his mother replied, "No, it's the hour of prayer, you mustn't go." She liked visiting the Palais du Rosaire, and she bought lots of medals and statuettes. . . . So one day she went shopping and Victor said, "Come, Tine, we're off!"

And we fled. What a wonderful day we had, and we had a good laugh. . . . When we returned in the evening she said nothing, but right up to arriving home she didn't utter a word to us. What a ticking-off we got from my father-in-law on our return. Victor didn't answer back, and nor did I.' Neither the son nor the daughter-in-law dared stand up to his mother, and only cunning enabled them to escape her grip. This influence was so strong that again it prevented Albertine from escaping the drama that dogged her life. 'When we arrived in Lourdes, we were offered rooms with two or three beds. . . . *Maman* said, "Why don't we take one room for all three of us?" Victor said nothing in reply, nor did I. But the day they reproached me for not having a baby, "It's not my fault', I said, "for the one day that a miracle might have occurred, *she* was there. " Oh yes, I was insolent, but I said it. I couldn't keep it back. . . .'

In this heavily religious atmosphere and this holy place, Albertine thought that her destiny might change and that her father's curse might be removed; but another baleful presence, this time a stock character, barred the way. Under this double influence it became clear that Albertine would never have a child. Fate pursued Albertine, not through her father whom she had left in a painful manner, but under the eye of her wilful, unbending mother-in-law, who hoped to control the young woman's life. Albertine would get rid of her without too much distress.

At the end of a year, the Chevenoz parents no longer felt inclined to return to their native Savoie. However Albertine, who could no longer bear the communal life in which she had no liberty, decided to go away: 'As for me, I'm off, and you, Victor, you do as you like, but I'm not staying. Choose between me and your parents! To which Victor replied, "I'm going with you."' Once again Albertine rebelled against outrageous conduct: 'If I've got to spend the rest of my life like a lap-dog, no, I refuse. . . .' She had not escaped the heavy paternal yoke in order to submit to her parents-in-law. Albertine is a woman of character and was not on her own as her husband made common cause with her. In 1930 Victor's parents returned to Savoie and left the business in the young couple's hands. 'We valued the house and the shop with its stock, and we paid so much a month to his parents. But in addition, as Victor had worked a long time without pay, his father gave him a van full of goods and the horse to go with it.'

The golden wedding

Although they have no children, the Chevenoz couple are not isolated or lonely. Relatives and neighbours live around them and they all have a life rich in contacts and exchanges, as is usual in Minot. Their cousins the Demonets gravitate towards Albertine and her husband, and so do the Fleurots and the Moulaines and their children, who are related to Clémence Demonet. All these households live together in the high part of the village.

Albertine, Clémence and the other women of the group assemble nearly every afternoon in one of their houses. They carry out certain domestic tasks together or they do charitable visiting: 'Every time we go and fetch the milk, we go a bit early and call on the "ladies of the château".[9] Oh they're very pleased to see us: "We're delighted when you come", they say.' On long summer evenings they like to walk about: they go along the old paths and roam the outskirts of the village. Seated behind their windows, the other village women look at them passing with astonishment. It is so unusual to see folk strolling in the streets: 'Well, you don't run anyone over. You can see there's no one in the streets. Here people only go out in their cars.' These gregarious habits, the animation of these laughing, talkative women, have earned them the name of 'the joyful band'. 'Hello, here comes "the joyful band" out for a walk!' The description is half-envious, half-critical. So let's talk about the members of the 'band'.

A year after the Chevenoz retired, Nicolas Demonet left his farm and went to live in la rue Haute, almost in front of his cousin's old drapery shop. The two households are neighbours just as in the old days and the close cohabitation of those days has been resumed between the cousins. 'Formerly we never went to bed without going down to see them; now it's the same, we never turn in without going up to Nicolas's house. We visit them every evening. When they don't see us, they wonder what's going on.' As they have always lived near one another and worked side by side, the cycle of mutual services has never been broken, mutual aid has never ceased, and the generous exchanges go beyond the normal conventions. Any goods and any objects may be given or shared between the two households of cousins. Signs of this are those unmatched objects on Albertine's mantelpiece, whose counterparts are to be found in the same places at Nicolas's house. 'That's the Grivot soup tureen. Nicolas had the large one and I had the small one. We had one brass candlestick each and one fly trap.' Debts between them are never liquidated and the series of exchanges never ends: 'Honey we get from Clémence because it was I who brought papa's hives for Nicolas. That was how he started his hives. So they give me some when I want it, as it was I that was at the start of those hives. They always give it to us. But we don't eat it. . . . The other day I took two kilos to give to friends, and she made me a present of it. I said to her, "You could well sell it to me." "Oh no', she replied, "I give it to you, I don't sell it." ' In fact everything happens as if each of the main characters concerned does not want to risk breaking the circuit, and each piles on presents so that the relationship should never cease and so that money should never come to upset the accounts.

Another feature that brings the two couples together is that they have no children. They both find substitute offspring in the many nephews and nieces of Clémence.

Nicolas surrendered his farm to the son of Clémence's sister, who was himself a farmer at Minot. This arrangement 'between relations' allowed the traditional links of mutual aid to be set up between the new and the old farmer, who became a builder's hand. This aid concerns mainly 'the land and the cows'. Nicolas's vast *chènevière* is ploughed once a year by the farming nephew in exchange for 'a hand with the hay and the harvest'. In the same way Nicolas puts the two cows, which he has kept, with his nephew's cattle and Clémence sees to the milking of the whole herd.

It is the children and grandchildren of her sister's daughter that Clémence has looked after and brought up, and indeed still looks after while their mother works. Albertine takes a large part in this child-minding, to such an extent that she and her husband are looked upon by the whole group of children as real grandparents and are known as 'Grandpa Victor' and 'Grandma Tine' A quasi-parent-hood has thus been created, built on the same lines as real parent-hood – same names, same type of kind and tender family relationship – 'I like playing with children, hugging them, coaxing them, kissing them. The other day we were playing blind man's buff with Pascal. He caught me and said "Hi, this is Tine because she's got old skin." We had a good laugh.' Their behaviour is also the same: 'As Perrine is setting up house, we're going to lend her a bed complete with eiderdown. If she doesn't give it back to us it doesn't matter. She can keep it. We'll always have enough for ourselves. When you have no children, you can't do otherwise. It's like the silver bracelet I had from *maman*. Lucille liked it. I said to her, "I have no child of my own. Take it and keep it. I give it to you."'

Nicolas and Clémence also gave up a plot in their *chènevière* to a great-niece so that she could 'build herself a chalet'. Moreover all the members of 'the joyful band' are next to each other on this *chènevière* that slopes down in front of the Demonet house. They all have plots generously allotted by Nicolas.[10] Also Albertine could say, 'When Perrine is settled in her house, she can help herself to vegetables from anyone in the *chènevière*, either Fleuriot or Demonet or me, it's of no importance. "You can just take what you please", she was told.' The exchanges between members of the group are so close that there is almost common pooling of production, without of course going so far as contravening the social rule 'to each his own', and thus putting them on the margin of society.

Finally it was the members of this group who decided to celebrate the Chevenoz golden wedding in January 1977. 'At the start I wanted to do something simple with us two, Victor . . . and then my godson. But the Moulaine girls said that we were not going to do it all on our own. They would have to be invited of course, so they talked it over with their mother and said to us, "You will be our guests. We'll pay for your dinner and you'll have no expense." "No", I said, "that's not possible; for one thing we've got some guests." So we decided that we would pay for our side, and they would each pay their share.' Once this question was resolved, the party took a quite different turn. Albertine, full of enthusiasm, took her 'wedding' in hand and organised the ceremony. She decided on the place: 'We shall have it at Minot, at the café. "We must let the village have their profit", I said.' She had lively discussions about the menu. 'We thought of starting with fish, but not everyone likes fish, so we put on *hors d'oeuvres variés* (cold sausage and radishes), then *bouchées financières* (vols-en-vent), then *filet mignon* and mixed vegetables. We wanted leg of lamb but the Moulaines don't like lamb. For dessert, *gâteau maison*. I wanted tartlets, but I learnt indirectly that the Cochois had put them on their first communion menu, so I didn't want to copy them. Then coffee and liqueurs and champagne provided by Monsieur Chevenoz . . . .' A menu out of the ordinary, with grand-sounding dishes, exactly like a wedding feast. It only remained for Victor to write it out in his fine round hand.

Quite apart from those invited to the party, Albertine wanted everyone, both neighbours and relations, to know about the happy event and take part in it. 'On Sunday after Mass I asked Lise and then Julia to come and have coffee, then Clémence and Nicolas and the Moulaines came too. We uncorked a bottle of good wine and laughed a lot! Then afterwards I brought them dragées and also to others in the village, to lots of people. . . . I gave some to my doctor and to the lady doctor who works for him.'

From one circle to another, from 'a good wine' to dragées, relations, friends and acquaintances are told of the good news, not forgetting the departed. 'On the Sunday we had Mass for the families'. Once the necessary publicity was done, the party could start. 'Oh, it lasted all day. They began to toast the bride in the morning! We sang the old songs *La Valse bleue, Frou-Frou, Le P'tit vin blanc.* I also sang *Femme que vous êtes jolie, Elle est toujours derrière*, and so on. My godson sang some too, and even Monsieur le Maire. How we laughed, and we made a merry din, I can tell you! And then we told funny stories. Oh, at weddings in the old days one heard some stories, even some pretty crude ones! For instance, the morning of my wedding, Nicolas killed three magpies, so they said in the evening they would have a reception with magpie *pot-au-feu.* So all day we said, "Those magpies, they're plucked and ready." It kept us amused all day.' Albertine's 'wedding' was gay, noisy, long-lasting, with funny stories and broad jokes. It was a great success.

Albertine was keen to describe these celebrations to us in detail, telling us exactly how it was all worked out. It was certainly a recognition of her social standing and her position within the group, even though she was never isolated or marginal, despite having no child or brother. A large number of people gathered round her ('We were forty-one; ten on our side and and thirty-one from the Moulaines') and the distribution of *dragées* went on endlessly ('I must buy some more as I haven't finished yet'). But this wedding at the end of her life was above all intended to wipe out the memory of the first one – that gloomy marriage saddened by the tragic figures of her father and mother-in-law. So the protocol and ritual had to be scrupulously organised, and Albertine concentrated on this. 'Oh, I really had my wedding. Everything that was not done at the first one was done this time. . . . Oh, it gave me great pleasure. . . . I was happy. . . .'

So Albertine's big moment, the climax of her life, was no longer her marriage but her golden wedding. She even nearly went on her 'honeymoon' to Lourdes – the illusion would then have been complete. Her cousin had won a free trip to Lourdes on the parish tombola, and he offered to give it to her. But she refused, giving some bogus pretext. 'Nicolas said, "Here, I give you this ticket and you can go for your fifty years" and Monsieur le Curé also said, 'It'll be perfect for your golden wedding", but I was tired and my husband would get difficult and irritable and would not stay still. I said to Clémence, "I shall be cross with him for eight days on end, and I'll be running after him all the time. . . . The idea of this trip frightens me." So I gave the ticket back. I'd really like to go on my own so as to have more peace. . . .' The place and the time at which she made the first journey had been so full of hope, and the disappointment caused by her mother-in-law so cruel, that one can understand why Albertine would not embark on a second pilgrimage. You can repeat a wedding, but it is impossible to find one's youth again; and Albertine knows that there is no such thing as a miracle.

This was, then, time of rich living, individual and full of savour, whose comings and goings conjure up the vision of a world that has largely passed away, of ways of living that have mostly disappeared and of customs often now obsolete. But these outward signs are not the most important revelations of this biography. Behind appearances there emerges a village society such as one does not usually glimpse. In spite of the family strait-jacket and the weight of social rules, Albertine has known how to live her own life as she wanted, even if she paid a heavy price for this liberty. She has also shown that, even if rules exist, there are also ways of getting round them. Rigid conventions may regulate the life of the community, but these need not prevent the flowering of personality. The village is made up of a profusion of types: it is a world of persons.

2

Breaks and continuities

We come across other rhythms and other scansions of family time when we look at the Chevenoz, Albertine's husband's family. Immigrants to Minot from Savoie, they have kept lively links with their province of origin for nearly a century. Neither time nor distance has led to breaks with their relatives living far away. Dealers in drapery, they adapt their lives to the programme of their journeys, where regularity is a condition of profitability. This time, which revolves entirely round commercial activity, is organised (and this is significant) round the two great periods of family reunion, which also bring together the living and the dead: the patron saint's festival and All Saints' Day. The time of the trader and the time of the family coincide in the village.

A line of small drapers

Louis Chevenoz, Victor's father, arrived at Minot around 1890 as a packman. He came from Savoie, 'from a family of seven children. As his father and mother died young, it was the eldest sister who brought them up. There's nothing to do up there in winter, so an effort had to be made to find a bit of money. Many people left during the winter and went on the road. They returned to Savoie when the birds began singing.'

Louis Chevenoz was born in 1871 at Fessoz in Maurienne (Haute-Savoie). At seventeen he left his native village in the bad season to 'carry a pack' of drapery goods, the traditional form of peddling or *colportage* practised in the valley.[1] He followed in the steps of his elder brother, François, who had preceded him along the roads of the Côte-d'Or. François prospected the north-west of the department and suggested to Louis that he visit the north-east.

My father-in-law started to carry his pack around 1890. It was a chest with drawers and two straps nailed to one side enabling it to be carried on the back. He arrived by train at Dijon, making his first purchases there and having them sent to the station at Poinçon. He probably left his pack in store with someone for the summer. He filled his chest with goods, for example, tape, cotton, shoelaces, socks, stockings, needles, thimbles, etc. The chest weighed about a hundred kilos. Then he went off on foot with the chest on his back, carrying a large umbrella, a real family one. The first time that he came to Minot, it was Albertine's grandmother who took him in, gave him some soup and allowed him to sleep in the barn on the straw. He was always grateful to her, and when he came to Minot every year he went straight to her place. He hung his chest up for the night at the end of the grandmother's bed, so he must have trusted her. Of course he never paid anything. What is an extra bowl of soup in a family? He may have given her a reel of cotton or a thimble from time to time, but certainly not money. He stayed one or two days in Minot, working through the village and the farms outside. Then he went on further. The grandmother always said that he left the house at about two in the morning and, when he reached the last houses of the village, he began to sing *Manon, voici le soleil, c'est le printemps*. He sang all along his route and so he walked carrying his pack as far as Til-Châtel, then he returned the length of the valley: Dienay, Avelanges, Luxerois ...

Itinerant business at Minot, as in all the other villages, has an ancient and varied history. In 1735 you read in the parish register of the death in village territory of 'Barthélemy or Bernard Maviore, tinker from Colandre in Auvergne'. The old people remember having seen him pass through the village:

Carnaval, the pedlar of small seeds, who appeared in the first days of March and announced the spring. He carried a box on his back with scales and he weighed the seeds, always adding a pinch for the hen. There was *la Mère aux Chiens* who sold contraband matches. There was *Charlotte* who unpacked a whole bazaar in the square. There was also a packman with rings, necklaces and toys for children. I've forgotten his name: he unpacked his chest and it was so beautiful. There were also grinders who came from Auvergne. They sharpened knives and scissors and plated saucepans. Others sold articles of tin such as funnels and buckets....

Dispensers of dreams and picturesque passers-by, the packmen heralded the seasons of the year: 'We would never think of spring until we had seen Carnaval pass....'

For ten years Louis carried his pack along the roads every winter through villages and hamlets, sheltered under his large blue umbrella, to show his wares. He managed to amass a little capital and decided to 'set up shop', substituting a horse and cart for his

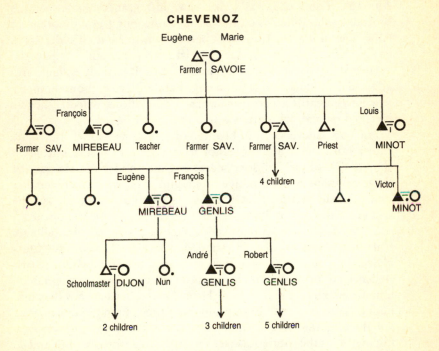

Fig. 8. The Chevenoz family of drapers

pack. He chose Minot, which was in the middle of his clientele. Meanwhile Louis had married in Savoie and brought his wife from there to Minot when he was settled. This business, which combines mobile and sedentary activities, requires the presence of a man and wife. The wife looks after the shop while the husband does his rounds. The Chevenoz had two boys. The elder one, Marcel, took on the rounds when the 1914 war broke out and his father was mobilised. But he had no taste for the job and returned to Savoie to end his days there as a bachelor. The younger brother Victor worked with his father from the age of sixteen onwards. Soon he made his own rounds and up to his marriage 'there was never any question of a wage. I worked for my father; I was fed, lodged, dressed and I got pocket money.' For the sons of farmers and tradesmen the arrangement was always the same. The child worked for his parents without pay until he in turn started a family. In 1927 Victor married

Albertine Lamarche, his neighbour and granddaughter of his brother's godmother. For it was the welcoming grandmother of Albertine whom the Chevenoz had chosen to be their elder son's godmother. This pseudo-parent relationship certainly helped the Savoyard draper to insert himself in this Burgundy village and allowed the young people's marriage to take place without difficulty (except as regards Albertine's father). It is relations, whether they be invented or real, who often watch over marriages.[2]

François Chevenoz, the brother of Louis, had much the same career, both family and professional – marriage in Savoie, setting up shop in Côte-d'Or with sons succeeding him, and the final return of the old parents to their native mountains. You will remember that François had preceded his brother on the road. He travelled the region north-west of Dijon. After marrying in Savoie, he opened a shop at Mirebeau and worked through the neighbouring villages from there. François Chevenoz had four children. The two daughters Hélène and Eugénie, helped their mother in the shop, while the two sons helped their father on his rounds. The two daughters remained unmarried. Eugène married a girl from Savoie, 'a Chevenoz like him, but everyone is called Chevenoz in that valley.' François married the daughter of the butcher in Genlis, a large village about twenty kilometres to the south of Mirebeau. She came from the Jura and so was an immigrant like him. The two brothers followed their father's trade after marriage. Eugène, the elder, looked after the shop and the Mirebeau round while François, the younger, settled in his wife's village where he built up his own drapery business. Neither of Eugène's two sons took up the same line and on his death the shop was sold. On the other hand the two sons of François did stay in the trade. One kept on his father's shop while the other opened another one in the same town where the population was rising fast. The shops of the two brothers were under the same sign: 'Chevenoz. Drapery and Clothing.'. 'The elder brother, Dédé, specialised in baby linen and fancy clothes. Robert had more classic things, clothes for both men and women. Both are married and their wives help in the shop. They still do rounds, but by car, twice a week, not more.'

So in the Chevenoz family they have been drapers from father to son for three generations. The stay in Burgundy was temporary for the first generation, the one born and married in Savoie, to which Louis and François belonged. On reaching retiring age the two brothers returned to Savoie after handing over their shops to their married children. In this generation family connections were still constantly being duplicated in both provinces. The godparents of the children were selected, one on the spot among the new acquaintances made in the receiving community, the other among the relatives who stayed in Savoie. Contact between the relatives living in Burgundy and those who stayed in Savoie was kept up by a copious correspondence and frequent stays in one another's home.

A different fate awaited the second generation, the one born in Burgundy, to which the children of François and Louis belonged. The unmarried ones returned to their relatives in Savoie; there they had family ties and there they found a welcoming circle in which it would be agreeable to end their days. The married children stayed put in Burgundy, even the one who had, like his parents before him, found a wife in the mountain valley. In this generation the large number of bachelors (three out of six) can no doubt be explained by migration. Far removed from Savoie and not yet integrated in Burgundy, the members of this generation found themselves fish out of water both in the province of origin and in their adopted community. In these conditions the choice of a spouse is a difficult matter. Links between brothers and sisters dispersed between Savoie and Burgundy remained in good repair. Between cousins relations, although constantly maintained, gradually took on a more formal aspect. 'We write to each other between cousins for saint's days and anniversaries. We send each other family news. If we went there, they would invite us to a meal. ... '

In the third generation, the one to which the descendants of Eugène and François living in Genlis and Mirebeau belong, no member thinks of returning to live in the valley, but contact between Savoie and the Côte-d'Or remains active: 'The ones at Genlis still return to Savoie. For one thing they have aunts who live there and entertain their great-nephews in the holidays. ... ' In the fourth generation one always takes the road to the valley.

Up to now, going to live permanently at a distance has not meant a break with the province or origin. For more than a century the distant family links have been kept fresh and continuous, and identification with the surrounding everyday life has not been complete.

The contacts between the two branches settled in the Côte-d'Or have never been very close. There are no regular meetings and no repeated invitations. In fact they are seeking to integrate themselves into new communities while still taking care to keep up links with their Savoie family. So connections with their close relatives living in the neighbourhood have been more or less sacrificed. Only official ceremonies such as weddings and funerals provide occasions for the members of the two families to meet. No godparents are exchanged, there are no chance visits or any of those encounters that keep family links fresh. Also the relationship between the families has gradually faded and then disappeared, probably because of the absence of descendants in the Chevenoz family of Minot and the prosperous commercial standing won by the Genlis family. 'They've become gentry', Albertine says of them. The break between the families is now complete. At the golden wedding of the Minot Chevenoz, there was no Chevenoz from Genlis or Mirebeau present.

Craftsmen and shopkeepers

Around the nineteen-thirties when Albertine and Victor took over the drapery business, Minot still had four craftsmen – two saddlers, one wheelwright and one sabot-maker – and four shopkeepers, three café-owners and one baker-grocer. These few shops were all that remained of a once bustling trade and commercial activity. Up to the First World War, Minot boasted of many craftsmen connected with agriculture, either in building or woodwork. One still found coopers and harness-makers who worked for the vine growers on the Côte, sabot-makers, cobblers and weavers. The women were linen-maids, dressmakers, milliners and laundrywomen.

The craftsmen and shopkeepers were divided between the 'upper' and the 'lower' village. Each of the two quarters was autonomous with its own businesses, cafés, drinking fountains and washhouses. On the central axis were grouped the public buildings, for example, the church, the cemetery, the *mairie*, the schools and the post office – places where members of the community met from time to time. In the two quarters, the 'upper' and the 'lower', the daily life of the inhabitants took place and there the families found their real living-space and identity. Now depopulation and economic changes have upset the old organisation of the village, which in the nineteen-thirties was already disintegrating. As the years went by, the last of the craftsmen and most of the shopkeepers were to disappear. In

1976 there remained only the baker-grocer and the café-owner, who also ran a hotel and restaurant.

In 1930 the oldest of the two saddlers was called Adrien Jodelet, a native of Léry, a village in the Côte-d'Or, who came as an apprentice to Minot at the end of the last century. In 1899 Adrien married a village girl, succeeded his master and set up in the rue Haute. He was an excellent craftsman and soon won an enormous reputation: 'His speciality was horse-collars. He made superb ones, and it was to him that they sent horses who had been injured by harness. He looked at them carefully, took out a bit of padding, extended or cut the collar a little, and the horse suffered no more. A collar made by him never injured a horse.' He trained many apprentices, among them Marcel Autisset, who came from the nearby Haute-Marne. The latter found a wife in the village and in 1920 took over the saddlery shop in the rue Basse.

For another ten years the two saddlers existed together, sharing the local clientele, one having his shop in the 'upper' village, and the other his shop in the 'lower'. But on Jodelet's death no saddler replaced him. The clientele and job applications diminished. Marcel Autisset took over all the clients and pursued his trade alone. He trained his two sons in the craft, but only Louis, the second one, persevered and took over the shop on his father's death. It was Louis whom we met. His workshop is on the ground floor of his house and opens straight into a little yard surrounded by high walls. Every spring Louis carefully polishes a magnificent black leather horse-collar with brass studs, which he hangs over the entrance door of the workshop; so everyone knows that a saddler lives and works there. In spite of his sign and his good reputation, his activity is now much reduced. The technical changes that have occurred in agriculture have brought an end to much of his business. No work awaits him on his bench, and the collar frames hang dusty on the beams. He occasionally cuts a calf's halter or makes a belt. The repair of mattresses remains from his former business, but that is not enough to give him a living; so he must work as an assistant postman as well. He is not training an apprentice and his son is working for the entrance examination for the postal services.

Sometimes he recalls the days when he worked with his father and there were 'four hundred horses to maintain in the whole region. During the war we were three of us in the workshop, and we were still short-handed. We did all the leather work, the repair of tarpaulins, hoods for traps, and mattresses. We worked in the shop all year except when we went on a greasing tour.[3] These tours ran from 1 April to 15 May, and then from 15 August to 15 September. We stopped at haymaking and went away again after the harvest. On the first trip we left Minot for Chemin d'Aisey, the de la Borde farm; they are cousins. They had twelve horses and we stayed at least four days. Then we went to the Dartois farm, again relations, staying there for at least a week. . . . We ate and slept at the farms.'

It was varied work and the clientele was large, based to a great extent on family links. It was a sedentary activity interspersed with trips into the near neighbourhood, a familiar world. It was, in short, a way of life regulated by custom. The saddler, like the other craftsmen connected with agriculture, found his true centre at the heart of the group. Take, for example, the modes of payment between craftsman and farmer, which was partly based on mutual exchange of goods and services. 'In the case of my brother-in-law, my father borrowed his horses to go on greasing rounds, and we looked after his harness in exchange. We were often paid in kind – a piece of pork, five kilos of butter for melting, some potatoes.' When there was question of a payment, this was never made immediately after the work was done. By tradition all monetary payment was deferred. 'People always paid at the end of the year, usually at the January fair. Everything was written down in a notebook as you went along, then it was transferred into a large ledger.'

On these trips and visits to 'settle accounts' there was exchange of hospitality and conviviality between craftsmen and farmers. Special social links were forged between them. Work done and payment due became parts of a series of exchanges where each party always remained in the other's debt. Every service came to look like a favour. The notions of profit and viability faded away and lost their importance, hidden behind this mask of social relations, personal links and continual exchange. Between the craftsman and his client, the farmer, the economic gave way to the social.

It is with nostalgia that Louis recalls his work in the old days. 'The job of saddler was rewarding. Of course it involved being continually on the move. You were never at home, and the work was dirty too. But it was freedom. You did your round and you were well received everywhere. It was as if you were going to a wedding.' Work was a treat for the craftsman. These rounds twice a year took him from farm to farm, from relations to friends, and they turned into cheerful events and reunions. At each stop the craftsman stayed a good while, shared in the life of the household, and took time to renew friendships and make exchanges. You will see that the difference from the sombre reminiscences of the salesman is striking.

The sabot-maker and the wheelwright express the same appreciation of their jobs and describe the same network of contacts and exchanges with friends and family among their clientele. 'Nouël' – he was born on Christmas Day – was a sabot-maker during the week and acted as hairdresser on Sundays. On that day all the men in the village assembled at his little shop. 'On Sunday, Mother went off to Mass. She put the stew on the range and, donning her long black dress that trailed on the ground, she went to church. Mass in those days was a real ceremony and it lasted a long time. Meanwhile Father became the barber. All the men came to him to be shaved. They chatted and told shooting stories, huddled round the cast-iron stove. I can see the wicker chair, the shaving bowl and Father sharpening the razor on a leather strop and pinching the client's nose to raise his head. All the men were there. Some smoked cigarettes, others took snuff, while we children looked and listened.' The company, the movements and the discussions all gave the place a special atmosphere. Only the men of the village entered the sabot-maker's shop: the stranger and the passer-by never came in. Social differences disappeared among the men gathered there, all teased in turn and equally held up to ridicule. The young boys, hidden in a corner, watched and listened in silence. As they quietly observed, they became familiar with the talk of the group and learnt of the realities of power within the village.

The shopkeeper occupied a different position and played another role, no doubt because of his specialised work that was not connected with farming. He also had different habits where sociability was concerned, for ancestral custom and tradition had very little place in his world. Yet, like the craftsman, the shopkeeper worked in his own premises and did his rounds.

However, the journeys of the shopkeeper, unlike those of the craftsman, continue throughout the year and for this reason his wife runs the shop. So the shop is woman's territory, though nowadays the husband is less taken up with his rounds and manages the shop between times. The customers are invariably women, so it has certain special characteristics and holds a definite place in

the life of the village. This explains a number of differences between
the craftsman and the shopkeeper.

As we have already said, the husband, be he shopkeeper or
craftsman, is responsible for relations with the outside world. It is his
job to leave home and face the dangers and fatigue of the road. He
maintains contact with the exterior, the other villages and their
inhabitants. All the activities of the husband are directed towards the
outside. He is the element that moves and communicates, while his
wife constitutes the stable and permanent element.

So for more than thirty years Victor the draper did his rounds,
while Albertine ran the shop at Minot. His travelling consisted of
three distinct journeys. One was to the north-east of the village
towards the Haute-Marne, where in the course of three weeks Victor
covered about a hundred and fifty kilometres. The second round
extended in the opposite direction, towards the south-west in the
direction of Saint-Seine, and covered about a hundred kilometres.
The third was shorter in time because it was centred in Minot and
consisted of many short trips to visit nearby villages in one day or
two (see fig. 9). The rounds followed one another without a break.
Every six weeks Victor revisited the same places. Rain or shine,
winter or summer, he returned to display his wares and show off his
novelties. These repeated runs and unchanged itineraries were inevitable in this kind of business where the dealer left his place of
origin, passed the limits of his familiar world and so tackled a
'foreign' clientele. So regularity became a token of familiarity and, as
we shall see, people in these regions only buy freely from people they
know.

Walking beside a two-wheeled cart and holding the horse's bridle
(after 1936 he had a motor van) the draper tramped the scattered
roads of the region, avoiding the important centres with their shops
and preferring remote farms and level crossings, villages and hamlets. He always came to rest at the same places where bed and board
were deducted from the goods sold. Victor does not have happy
memories of these rounds which kept him constantly on the move,
far from home. The road was tiring and the solitude oppressive: 'I
was more often out travelling than at home and I was separated from
my wife most of the time.' The work was hard as there was severe
competition and the clientele was not rich. 'There were some districts
where I only did well when the hops prospered.' Yet by taking over
his father's territory, covering it month after month and always

visiting the same houses, Victor ended up by being well known and sometimes welcomed. He remained nevertheless the passer-by, the seeker after business, the one who offered goods in return for money, and who refused credit, let alone barter. 'People always paid cash. What would we have done with foodstuffs? One tried not to give credit because it led to trouble. People said all your goods were rotten, and it was an endless business getting paid. Everyone tried to bargain, but I didn't let myself be had.' The craftsman allowed barter and exchange of goods and services, and if payment in cash was involved, it was never at once. The trader-shopkeeper, on the other hand, claimed his due immediately and did not enter into a cycle of exchanges such as was usual among farmers and craftsmen. One gets an impression of ill temper and melancholy from Victor's reminiscences of 'the road', which contrasts with craftsman's memories of their trips. They talk of freedom and celebrations: Victor talks of business. It was furthermore a business full of craftiness and pitfalls.

A village shopkeeper must always be available, which means among other things that she must never close her doors. This condition is essential to a successful operation. Albertine's drapery shop was never closed: 'As soon as I got up, I opened the shutters and I didn't close them until I went to bed in the evening. One often had customers at mealtimes, and it sometimes happened that we were woken up at eleven o'clock at night. We stayed open all day Sunday, which was our best day for sales. All the farm hands came to buy clothes – trousers, shirts, ties, etc. Market days were good too. On the day of the *fête* we only stayed open up to the time of Mass.' Marguerite Colleret, who ran a grocery store in the village from 1910 to 1927 remembers that: 'the shop was open all the time, even on Sundays. There was no question of closing, never. There were even people who came before I'd got up. I remember one woman who always forgot her coffee. She used to come before I'd got up to buy a quarter of a pound of coffee.' In recent years one of the Minot grocers, wanting more modern conditions of work, thought he would change these habits, but retribution was not long in coming: 'Chartier, he never opened before three o'clock and he refused to work on Sunday. He had to go.'

The new habits of family life based on domestic intimacy, and the separation of time spent on work and time spent at home, make such practices seem out of date and intolerable for young shopkeepers, who refuse to remain at their clientele's disposal in this way.

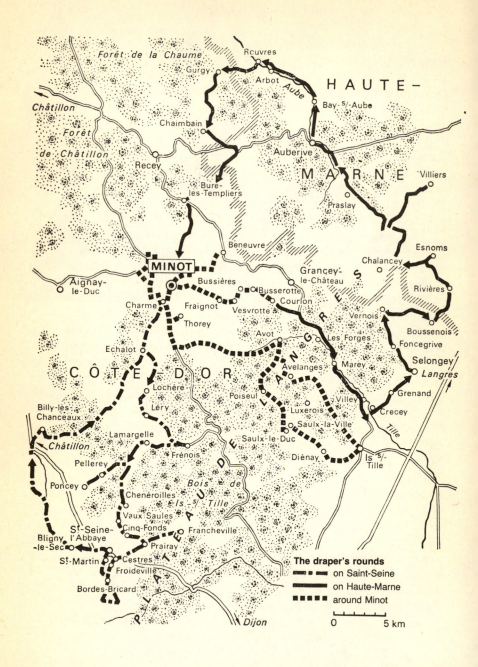

Forêt de la Chaume

Rouvres

Gurgy

Arbot   *Aube*

HAUTE-

Châtillon

Chaimbain

Bay-s/-Aube

Forêt
de Châtillon

Recey

Auberive

MARNE

Villiers

Bure-
les-Templiers

Praslay

Esnoms

Beneuvre

Chalancey

Aignay-
le-Duc

MINOT

Bussières

Busserotte

Grancey-
le-Château

Rivières

Charme   Fraignot

Vesvrotte
Courlon

Vernois

Boussenois

Thorey

Avot

Les Forges

Foncegrive

Echalot

CÔTE   D'OR

Avelanges

Marey

Selongey
Langres

Lochère

Poiseul

Grenand

Billy-lès-
Chanceaux

Léry

Villey

Crecey

Châtillon

Lamargelle

Luxerois

Saulx-la-Ville

Tille

Saulx-le-Duc

Pellerey

Frénois

Diénay

Is-s/-
Tille

Poncey

Bois   de

Chenéroilles

Is-s/-Tille

Vaux Saules

Bligny-
-le-Sec

St-Seine-
l'Abbaye

Cinq-Fonds

Francheville

St-Martin

Prairay

Cestres

Froideville

Bordes-Bricard

Dijon

The draper's rounds

— · — · — on Saint-Seine
———— on Haute-Marne
▪ ▪ ▪ ▪ around Minot

0   5 km

Fig. 9 (Opposite). The draper's rounds

Until I bought the van, I always went on foot. With the 'two-wheeler' I did from twenty to twenty-five kilometres a day. The winter season started in October. I left about the 15th for the Saint-Seine round: Echalot, Lochère farm, Léry, Frénois, and I spent the night at Frénois at the café Gautherot. The second day I did Pellerey, Poncey, a few farms round Lamargelle; and the third day I visited the farms around Vaux Saules, Chenéroilles and Cinq Fonts. The other days I was around Saint-Seine and Saint Martin-du-Mont; there were a lot of isolated farms there. . . . I lodged at Mathilde Brion's café or with Widow Duthu. . . . Then I returned towards Minot passing by Bligny-le-Sec, Billy-les-Chancraux and working the hamlets of Blessey, Chanceaux and Jugny farm. . . . I was always back home for All Saints' Day and stayed for two or three days, using the time for checking stock and sorting out the articles on board. On 3 or 4 November departure for the Haute-Marne round: Courlon, the home farm and then La Forge farm, and I spent my first night at Marey-sur-Tille at Salomon's, where one ate a delicious trout or wild rabbit. It was one and a half francs a night with meal, but I paid no money, giving merchandise instead. I pushed on towards Villey and stopped at the tollgate. . . . At Crecey I stayed two days and did Selongey, Grenand farm and a few houses towards Foncegrive. . . . Then two days at Vernois staying with Follot. . . . On towards Boussenois I climbed the track which leads to the Montagne farm; you had to pull the horse up. . . . I went on towards Rivière, it was infernal country, all hills and corners, and there was ice in winter; the horse slipped and stumbled. . . . You had to be careful not to overturn, and the tracks up to the farms were full of ruts in which you could get stuck. I arrived at Vaillant, left the horse and load with Lallemand and took the train to Poiçon-Beneuvre. Then I walked to Minot, spent the night there and left next morning with the mail. I took the opportunity to buy provisions, take orders and see if merchandise had arrived safely. I was very pleased to come back for a bit, it broke up the journey. . . . Return to Vaillant, on to Chaloncey and La Thuilière farm. I stopped at Auberive where I paid for my meal, Gurgy-la-Ville, Chambain, Colmier-le-Haut, le Bas, La Girarde farm, then Minot. This trip lasted three weeks. I got back at the end of November and stayed a few days at Minot. I took the opportunity of doing the villages in the neighbourhood. There was Saint-Broing where I had the horse shod; I left in the morning and came back at night. Same for Moitron, Fraignot, Vesvrotte, Bussière, Beneuvre, they took a day. Two days for Salives, Poiseul, Saulx, Luxerois. I visited all areas about every six weeks.

Listen to Jean Delombes, who now runs the bakery-cum-grocer's shop. Jean and his wife took it over in 1958, but a bare ten years later they talk of leaving. 'Conditions of life are too hard here', he says. Yet Jean likes his job. he kneads the dough himself and then bakes it in a wood-burning oven. The grocery store, run by his wife, is well stocked. 'I've gradually tried to widen the range. I've added confectionery, dried vegetables, pasta, chocolate, then tinned goods. We also do a bit of dairy produce, butter, cheese, fresh vegetables and fruit. Finally we sell cleaning materials and we have a small perfumery selection. We've gradually added things in response to demand; everything that goes with bread and fits in. ... ' The business runs smoothly. Despite this the conditions of work and the difficult relations with the farmers mean that Jean Delombes views his future with pessimism.

Relations with the clientele are indeed difficult. The shopkeeper handles money. Purchase of goods supposes a price that is paid at once,[4] and every sale involves a payment. The obligation to pay cannot be postponed very long. 'We tried not to give credit', said Victor the draper. And the value of the goods required can only be paid for in cash: 'What would we have done with foodstuffs?' wondered Albertine. Yet the baker knows that the farmers 'prefer barter. It's an old system. Above all they hate having to produce cash.' The impossibility of exchanging one product against another or against a service, and the obligation to pay in cash at once, weigh heavily on relations between shopkeepers and their clientele.

All the complex web of services given and received between craftsman and farmer – the payments from far back in time, the convivial contacts, the endless cycle of reciprocity – all these fade away and disappear in relations with the shopkeeper and are replaced by a 'pay, pay' attitude that is unsatisfying. 'Above all, they (i.e. the farmers) think that you make money every time they pay you something.' Business relations with farmers are sometimes strained, often abusive, and always difficult. 'Our clients are mostly farm labourers. If there were only farmers, we'd die of hunger. They buy cheese off us, when they don't make it themselves, oranges and bananas for their children, sugar for jam-making, some dried vegetables .... And you never get any compliments from them, only criticism. I don't make brioches any more, because this is what happened. The farmers used to buy eggs, butter (which they get in exchange for milk) and flour. They just wanted to pay forty centimes for the making of the brioche. That cost them only eight hundred or a thousand old francs for several laundry baskets of brioches – and I'd worked all night. Then, to show you how things are with the farmers, Wiltz – and yet he's a good fellow – he brings me eggs for which he charges me full price, three hundred francs a dozen, and on his side he orders potatoes from my wholesaler, which are already taxed so there's nothing in it for him. . . . The labourers buy off me; they're not like the farmers about money.'

Money did not circulate easily or openly in the village as this society was by tradition inclined towards the exchange of goods and services. So the shop and the pedlar's van, which were places where money passed, were reserved areas where only one person entered at a time. In the baker's yard you often saw a woman waiting for the shop to empty for her to go in and make her purchases. The same manoeuvring went on in front of the post office where 'one goes in as the other comes out'. The transactions put through and the prices paid, if they were known, became the subject of calculation and comments by other clients; so all these operations had to be carried out in the privacy of the shop. 'Women can't bear others seeing what they buy. If a woman client comes in to buy an expensive bottle of aperitif, she'll go away without buying it if someone comes in.'

These conventions involved a special layout for the premises, which had to have two waiting-rooms. In addition to the room in which the goods were presented, there had to be a yard, a street-corner, back premises or the shopkeeper's living-room. The draper's shop, a large rectangular room, gave on to the street in front and on to the living-room of the house at the back, so there was no real separation between the public space of the shop and the private space of the home. Albertine passed constantly from one to the other and sometimes, while a customer was choosing something, she put another customer into the living-room. This layout of the living quarters enabled her to satisfy the two major imperatives of all good commercial practice – to be always available and to give enough choice of space for customers to prevent them from spying on each other. 'A lot of women don't like others to see what they're buying. If there were a lot of people in the shop and others arrived, I took them into the living-room. "Come in and rest and get warm", I used to say. And I waited for everyone to go away before seeing them.'

To soothe susceptibilities, the travelling dealers had to go from door to door. Every lady of the house waited for the van to stop as near as possible to her house before going out to make her purchases. Sometimes, when the wares indicated it, for example drapery and shoes, the customer invited the dealer to come into the house. Then she would make her choice and discuss it away from the eyes of the neighbours. 'For instance, the shoe salesman', said the draper, 'he goes from house to house, it's what we did on our rounds: we went from farm to farm. We entered the houses and courtyards, so others couldn't see what the farmer's wife bought.' One day we met Julienne who was coming back from the grocer's and in a temper she explained: 'I spent a long time today. . . . I let everyone pass in front of me. . . . I don't like people to see what I buy and how much I pay. Lise always asks me; "How much did you pay for your butter?" She gets on my nerves and makes me angry. She's not paying the bill. We are both Blaises for butter and we don't eat much, so I take the best quality. She said, "You paid a lot." What's it got to do with her? When the travelling salesmen stop in the village, she arranges to arrive when they start serving you, and she always waits to be the last.'

A tacit rule of discretion governs relations between members of a community. One should never know or seek to know what has been bought and what has been paid. These are secret matters that are kept concealed. The salesman is the only one to know and he is bound to hold his tongue. It is necessary to preserve these corners of discretion and secrecy in a village society where each person's life is lived under the scrutiny of others, and where attitudes and behaviour are at the mercy of the group's censure. . . . So one can understand the virulence with which Julienne castigated Lise's attitude. In a village, business is transacted far from the eyes and ears of neighbours.

In this society which claimed equality for all, no one was free to buy more than another in quality or quantity. This being so, the relations between buyer and seller were crucial for the smooth running of operations. Confidence had to be the rule. Most of the shopkeepers in the region were known from father to son. 'Take Descombes de Lamargelle, for instance, who sells fish and a few groceries. I've been going to him for fifty years. I knew his grandfather and I remember his father coming in a vehicle drawn by a horse. Oh, we know each other, so he looks after me. I know what that job's like, so I don't pass comments on his merchandise, and he's very good to me. It's the same with Corviset de Salives. He is baker, grocer, and even florist. He always chooses good things for me and charges me reduced prices. He married an Antoine girl whose mother is a Boitevin de Salives. She was rich. He took over the bakery and now has two or three vans that travel the roads.' These familiar shopkeepers, whose place of origin one knew and whose genealogy one could reel off, were allowed to penetrate the living-room, the private part of the house. The gipsies, who offered wicker baskets, and their women, who unpacked lace at the gate or in the courtyard, never crossed the threshold of the house.

Exchanges between customer and tradesman always proceeded according to the same ritual. A dialogue ensued between the pair doing business. 'It's always been like that with bakers. People come to talk. One came and stayed for twenty-five minutes and only spent one and a half francs. Women come to talk about children, illnesses, the weather. I get in a word as I can. ... They sometimes give us an order. It often happens that they push off when they see someone else coming.' Everything happened as if the customer were trying to gain time and wanted to forget that she was there to make a purchase, as if she were seeking in this time spent in gossip the necessary distance to carry out the transaction. It was also true that such a dialogue formed part of the social intercourse that required every encounter to be accompanied by a short verbal exchange. One could not, without being considered impolite, run across people in the street and simply hail them with an ordinary 'good morning'. One was required to stop to ask after their health and linger with them for a while. In the village you had to be free with time if you wanted to establish good relations.

The shopkeeper and the customer were in the same case. It would show impoliteness and a certain lack of *savoir-vivre* to display excessive keenness in suggesting or buying articles. A certain formality was necessary: 'One always had to be at their disposal, to be there and to listen to them, but saying nothing', Albertine recalls. After this delay and interval that was necessary for establishing good trade relations, the client would at last announce the object of her visit and the shopkeeper could pursue her strategy: 'Then you had to avoid giving all the women of the village blouses of the same colour or similar fancy slippers. You had to dissuade them from taking such-and-such a colour or such-and-such design, without saying who had bought them. That was a secret.' Everything is a matter of form and tact between

shopkeeper and customer. You have to talk without saying anything and say things without seeming to know. The rituals of
selling are strewn with traps.

As for the shop, it looked like a crossroads for the women of
the village. They passed by one another but did not forgather:
they kept an eye on one another but did not mix. It was at the
washhouses, those 'hotels for chatterboxes', that women used to
meet in the old days. There the talk flowed merrily; they aired
their dirty linen and their grievances without inhibitions, and they
worked off their feuds. The washhouses had the same function of
socialisation and sociability for women as Nouël's shop had for
men. Since the arrival of running water and washing machines, the
washhouses have been deserted. They say that the women never
met each other now in Minot.

The tradesman's shop, which is neither meeting-place nor social
centre, does fill another role. It is the inevitable port of call for
commercial travellers coming from every corner of France, and so
acts as a point of contact between two worlds. Victor and Albertine saw them arriving regularly in their shop: 'The firm Dumas of
Thiers in the Puy-de-Dôme used to sell us knives. A representative
passed by every year with his catalogue and we gave him an order.
We had a firm in Orléans for men's and women's working clothes,
one in Cholet for handkerchiefs. In Neufchâteau (Vosges) there
was a house that supplied pillow-lace and sheeting, and one in
Auxerre for velvet by the metre. All the representatives called
twice a year.' As the orders were passed, information and topical
news were exchanged. Through this trading the village took part
in the life of the nation and the wide world, whereas through its
craftsmen it was turned in on itself and its limited region, where
people only knew each other because spouses or services were
exchanged.

Craftsmen and shopkeepers make up, or rather used to make
up, two balancing poles in the life of the village. The former
assured communication between members of the group, whereas
the latter were middlemen between the village community and the
world outside. Complementary in their roles and quite different in
their practices, the two groups were condemned to the same fate.
One by one the craftsmen have closed their workshops and the
shopkeepers have ceased to trade. Minot is now no longer
enlivened by salesmen passing by and by colourful pedlars. The

busy noise of craftsmen no longer punctuates the days and the seasons. The village seems to have gone to sleep.

But what are the stages, the key moments that stand out in this gradual vanishing act? The detailed stocklist of goods put on sale in her shop by Albertine give us a means of examining and understanding this train of events.

The articles that one found in the Chevenoz shop for half a century (1901–1954) were traditional and hard-wearing. They catered for the needs of a clientele consisting essentially of farmers, craftsmen, farm hands and woodcutters. Men, women and children found there every article of clothing they needed, from shoes to hats.

For women we sold cotton knickers, slit or unslit, and knee-length embroidered chemises, either cotton or flannel. One slept in this chemise, adding only a camisole, which was a short, wide-sleeved jacket of cotton or wool. Night-dresses did not come in until the 1940 war, or not long before. The men also slept in their daytime shirts, which had long tails. My husband still insists on the full length and, as shirts sold nowadays are shorter, I have to sew tails on them, and I find it a bore. We used to sell lots of these long-tailed shirts, slit at the sides; and they came down to the knees. In the morning the men had to tuck all this stuff into their trousers. There was an old man in the old days who, when he had had a drop to much to drink, made his wife dance 'the dance of the tails' with him, twirling his tails as he went round and round. For the women again we supplied stockings in grey or black cotton, and lisle for Sundays. For winter wear they were of black or fawn wool, ribbed or plain. We sold socks for men and stockings (knee-length) for children, in cotton or wool but invariably fawn or grey. For women we also had strong blue aprons to be worn on top of their working overalls. For Sundays there were fancy aprons and flowered satinette overalls. For children the overalls were of black satinette, and sometimes the girls wore dark gingham, which did not dirty so easily. We did not stock ready-made dresses or blouses for women. There was a dressmaker in the village for those. But we did supply all sorts of materials sold by the metre: shirting, white cretonne for pillowcases, satinette for overalls and aprons, corduroy for men's trousers, imitation leather for patching, flannel, ticking for mattresses of feathers or horsehair, lace for curtains, chintz for quilted blankets and eiderdowns, different materials for kitchen towels and napkins, striped or plain flannel for shirts or women's knickers. For men we supplied all varieties of underwear and ready-made work clothes, for example, corduroy shooting jackets, with matching trousers and waistcoats that were blue, black or grey. In summer the men wore suits made of 'devil's skin' or drill. They wound a sash of flannel round their waists, either red, blue, grey or black in colour. It took three and a half metres to make one, but it did keep them warm round the middle. No one wore the old blue smocks any more except the cattle-dealers, who still wear them. We also sold all types of hats. I remember they hung on a string from the ceiling of the shop: black or white straw hats for summer, both for men and women. In winter men wore smallish hats of stitched felt, the brims giving good protection against sun or rain. Everybody wore their old hats during the week, and kept the best one for church. The women sported little boaters. For smarter hats they went to the village milliner or to a shop in Dijon. I almost forgot to say that for nightwear we stocked nightcaps for men and *cales*[5] for women. We also sold white linen or cotton handkerchiefs for women, check ones for men, and yellow ones for those who took snuff. We also had all sorts of neckerchiefs, of cotton or wool, polka-dotted navy or grey with flowers, for both sexes. On the right-hand wall of the shop were shelves with all sorts of footwear for men and women: smart slippers for Sundays and the so-called herringbone slippers with soles of tough leather; soft hide slippers to wear inside clogs. Working boots with studded soles for the men, *galoches* for the children, and gaiters, the full-length ones called leggings, the short ones anklets. Rubber boots did not exist in those days. I also had the whole range of haberdashery items – sewing cottons, needles, knitting needles, mending wools, lace thread, embroidery cottons and canvas. We also stocked some perfumery lines such as eau-de-Cologne, face powder, shaving soap; also some small items of stationery like exercise-books, pencils, rubbers, and then lots of knives; a great variety for men and women, and little pocket knives for the children. We also had the agency for the *Almanach Vermot* ... '

This medley of stock evokes a whole range of rural life styles and habits. Everyone seemed to conform to a fixed fashion in clothes – uniform, classic, in dark tones so as not to show dirt, economical and without a trace of allure. The only exceptions were the men who, by sporting a cummerbund or a neckerchief, added a note of colour to their clothes. It was only the men who adorned themselves at work. The women and girls reserved style and colour for their party clothes. In the old days clothes signified different work and different seasons. They changed from summer to winter, from weekdays to Sundays, from Sundays to festivals. These differences are gradually disappearing. These two ranges of clothes were formerly looked after with frugal care: 'Dresses and overalls lasted us five to six years. One bought them large so that they should have long wear. Mothers lengthened, altered, shortened .... And then one mended ... Lord, how one mended!' These habits of saving were carried into everyday life because underclothes were kept on at night, and all changes were in response to various tasks and various holidays. 'We didn't use much linen. We didn't take off our underclothes to go to bed, and we only changed them once a week on Sunday, and sheets once a month. ... ' Thus the habits of the group became settled and the body adapted itself to the ways of the time.

In addition to these practical, solid and sombre garments, Albertine offered her customers a generous choice of material by the metre and a selection of drapery that enabled them to make their own under-clothes and trimmings. 'One made blouses, knickers and petticoats at home. A lot of embroidery was done and lacework too. You know the knickers had a garter and then a flounce, so we made the flounce of lace. My aunt made fine lace and the young girls embroidered their trousseau. . . . One had a dress or a blouse made by a dressmaker, but not underwear.'

The material and clothes put on sale by Albertine in her shop recall a certain rural style from a definite period that ran from the old days, when clothes were entirely produced and made up on the spot, to nowadays when they are bought elsewhere, away from the village. It was a stretch of time that extended from the beginning of this century up to the Second World War.

The men and women of the generation of Albertine's parents, the ones who lived up to about 1914, wore the traditional peasant dress to the end of their days. This dress was almost entirely produced and made up in the village out of hemp grown in the *chènevière*, stripped at home and woven by the local weaver. The women wore a loose jacket falling on an ample skirt of *droguet*,[6] with two or three black or brown petticoats underneath. Then on top they wore a *devantin*, a black or brown overall. Their hair was gathered in a black or white, finely embroidered bonnet of carefully goffered lace. The only articles that were bought in town were the cashmere marriage shawl that was given by the parents-in-law, and the black mourning shawl of fine wool, which the mother gave her daughter on her wedding day. The men wore a long shirt made of hemp, and trousers of linen or wool. To go out they donned an ample blue smock.

At the turn of the century factory-made clothes and manufactured materials appeared on the market, brought to the village by travell-ing salesmen and the representatives of firms selling by catalogue. This quickly led to the end of hemp-growing and so of the weavers. The last weaver at Minot hanged himself in 1913. The generation of Albertine's aunt abandoned traditional dress to follow the city styles rather late in the day. Underclothes and working clothes were bought at the draper's; the 'fine stuff' and formal wear were made for women by skilful dressmakers and for men by the visiting tailor – 'at the March and November fairs he tried on the suit ordered at the previous fair, or he took an order for the next fair.'

The second upset of country fashions happened in the nineteen-fifties. It coincided with the technological changes in agriculture during this period. Almost at once, within a very few years, men abandoned jackets and shooting coats in favour of ample wind-cheaters and pullovers. Women started wearing trousers to be more comfortable at work. For half a century the Chevenoz, father and son, had sold the same merchandise. Every decade did indeed bring its share of changes, but fashions and markets developed slowly without shocks. 'We took over all the merchandise that my parents used to sell. We went on selling it as it was, and we added very little. There was no real change between the time of our parents and our time. It is between us and the people in business today that the real break has come in the clothing world. Women have become smarter and they seem younger. A woman of seventy wears flowered aprons like a youngster, and the men, too, dress quite differently. The tractor and other forms of machinery require looser clothes; nailed boots slip on pedals, and gumboots are required. When agriculture was modernised, all clothes changed too.

The Chevenoz were confronted with this dramatic development of the local market which, for survival, required an almost complete renewal of their stock. At the same time they were sum-monsed by the tax authorities to pay a heavy fine and to keep complicated accounts. They preferred to shut up shop. They were old and had no child for whom to carry on. In 1957 the stock was sold off, but as there was no purchaser for the business, they stayed on there in retirement.

There has constantly recurred in this account mention of the clean break that came about 1950, when an economic upheaval brought about a radical transformation of village life within a few years. As we have seen, this break in continuity, caused by techno-logical change, manifested itself at every level – in housing arrange-ments, in the life of the community and in family relationships. In short, the agricultural revolution gradually took with it the whole of society, breaking up a balance that had been achieved after earlier mutations.

For it is certain, and Albertine's story confirms it, that this village society had for decades been subject to change. At the end of the last century, the economic crises experienced in the region gave rise to the first break in the subsistence economy and, among other things, there was an end to growing hemp and weaving at home. In the same period the weavers disappeared and the shopkeepers set themselves up. The draper opened his shop in 1904. Later on, other material innovations arrived – electrification, piped water, the motor car – each bringing adjustments and adaptations of a social kind.

Yet, in the eyes of the people today, this past seems static when compared to the violent changes of the fifties. In fact this recent upheaval arose out of a series of transformations that had succeeded one another since the begining of the century, and even earlier. But during this time the innovations occurred against a background of permanence. Old things crumbled slowly, new things established themselves quietly; so people had the impression of controlling time. Around the fifties the rhythm of change speeded up. So these gradual adjustments and long movements of adaptation broke up, and a new era really began. This is what has created the tone of the present day and has marked it as a time of discontinuity and revolution.

3

Time remembered

In listening to these accounts of a life full of proper names and people affected by family destiny, and hearing how one generation succeeded another, one was struck by the absence of all reference to the historic events of the period. The wars of 1914 or 1940 do not crop up spontaneously to mark the stages of Albertine's life or affect its development. We already knew that the collective memory had not retained these historic moments to mark the time of the community. It was more surprising to learn that the same held good for individuals. Albertine did indeed mention the two World Wars and even the war of 1870, but as part of an anecdote or to pin down a recollection – like that of the paternal grandfather who appeared like a ghost and made his mother die of fright! – or again to re-establish a truth:

My grandmother talked about the Prussians and didn't complain. According to her they didn't cause us much distress when they came in 1870. . . . They were in the barn and took their coffee and stayed quiet. . . . Oh, we got into a real panic about them. People said that they stole children and attacked women, but it wasn't true. My grandmother said they let us get on with our work, and relations were good. . . .

Sometimes Albertine, when plied with questions, described the long journey that took her in 1941 from Minot to the Landes to try unsuccessfully to join her husband, who was mobilised to work in the *préfecture* at Dijon and was withdrawn to Toulouse:

I went off and got stuck in the Landes for three months while he was in Toulouse, and we couldn't correspond. He returned to Minot before me. . . . I was over there staying with some very nice people. . . . Oh, the banks of the Adour were beautiful, but I was sorry that there were no potatoes. As for tomatoes, I never stopped eating them, but I would rather have had potatoes! I then asked to be taken back home and I was held up in the station at Tours. I took three days to arrive at Dijon and I was as thin as a rake! On arrival at the station in Dijon I met Robert Perron's brother, and we fell on each other's necks. As we were both from Minot, we were pleased to find one another. So I went home with him. We took the train as far as Is-sur-Tille, and then on to Poinçon, and then we walked to Minot. We had been told not to leave for Minot as there was a curfew and the Boches would pick us up. We left just the same. My husband came along the road to Poinçon every evening to see if I had arrived. As we got near Minot, we saw someone on the road, so we said 'Let's hide, it's a Boche.' In fact (howls of laughter) it was Victor! We often retell the story when we find ourselves with Robert's brother: 'Do you remember the Boche who came to meet you!' I'd written to my husband that I was coming, so every night he came along the road. Oh it makes a good yarn now. What a laugh!

These joyous and comic memories are all that she now evokes about those troubled times of the war. We had just the same experience with other people, both men and women, whom we questioned. Replies were evasive or neutral, in the sense that they did not expose the real conflicts and exact events that occurred in the village during the last war. For a long time it was all that we could get out of them. Later on, in other interviews and other circumstances, we would learn what happened during this period. We would then find out that memories of these events were not effaced, but were protected by a collective secrecy which was still sensitive thirty years after. The 1940–45 war and perhaps other historic events belong to another layer of the group memory, and access to it is not necessarily open to the inquisitive strangers that we still are. This memory only comes to the surface in certain circumstances – at election time, for instance, when politics mobilise all public opinion. We shall come back to this later. In fact we can see that this history of events never appears as a prop for individual time nor does it act as a framework for community time. To organise personal time and commit it to memory, one leans on the key moments of the individual life cycle. Birth, first communion, marriage and death make up the points of reference around which the individual constructs his time.

These stages are always very precisely dated and remembered. 'My father-in-law came to ask for my hand on 24 July 1926. I came back to Minot on 1 November 1926 and I was married on 21 January 1927.' A recital without a slip, which comes out unasked for in the course of conversation with Albertine and others. 'I was married on 23 May 1924.' 'I arrived at Minot for my wedding on 3 June 1922.' 'My husband and I got acquainted on 5 April and were married on

15 June 1931.' 'My first communion was on 18 April 1910 and my husband's was on 10 May 1905, and we got married on 12 July 1920.'

There is exact recall of the stages of life, of the dates that structure the past and set remembrance in motion. This is time lived and the cycle of life, where points of transition and critical events mark for ever the unfolding of the individual memory. The facts of family and home life are referred to these key dates – 'Grandmother died the year of Lise's birth' – and of History too: 'When I made my first communion, it was wartime.'

So History is dated in the village through family events. Family time organises historical time. Events, whether national or local, for example, wars, the Popular Front, May 1968, the arrival of mains water or the connection to the electricity grid, are recalled in relation to dates that mark family life and make up the tissue of the family tree.

Biography structures the sequence of events, selects what is remembered and puts recollection in order. Each family of course works out its own record and organises History with its own points of reference; but in the closed universe of the community, where everyone knows everyone else, it is always clear what time is in question.

This family time is concrete, with special rhythms and ordered around a few reference points in nature. So the morning is the most favoured part of the day, and the man who tunes his existence to the natural play of day and night keeps in good health, says the proverb: 'Bed with the hen and rise with the crow; you'll stay longer here below.' Other signs affect life on the farm. When thistles abound in the *chènevière*, it is time to let it lie fallow again. When meadow saffron multiplies in a field, you should plough it up and resow it. In the same way the agricultural work that goes with the cycle of nature determines the rhythm of the year. So one distinguishes two seasons – 'winter', which starts in November when work on the cultivated plain ceases and work in the forest begins, and 'summer', which starts in March when the centre of activity moves again towards the plain. The two seasons start with two funerary festivals – Palm Sunday and All Saints's Day – for at Minot death is always closely linked with life. These seasons are used to situate a memory that goes back a short way in time: 'last winter' and 'we shall see each other next summer'. In the same way recent or recurring events are indicated through farm activities: 'it was just before haymaking' or 'it happens between haymaking and harvest . . . . ' Beyond these brief periods which mark all activities, one uses a biographical axis to organise the unfolding of time.

This concrete, practical time, made up of small stretches of varying duration, is made up of certain fixed moments which exert great influence. Friday is a day of ill omen when one should undertake nothing that engages the future. A flight of magpies which crosses the sky in the early morning bodes no good, and it is better not to go out that day. An owl hooting on a house means an early death. These signs of prophecy or revelation give Time its singular quality. One sees that in the village everyone is subject to Time and must take account of Time.

It is not so much a question of describing man's dependence on the weather, which of course exists, but more particularly of showing the way in which everyone plays with Time. In the course of these pages we have remarked those occasions on which Time has been used to forward certain designs and to transform personal frictions into fruitful relationships. Let us call to mind that matrimonial planning which renews alliances and introduces them into the family continuum; the fixed duration of rituals, observation of which is an earnest of good results; the leisurely prolongation of business negotiations, which gives them the appearance of a gracious exchange. This Time, which we manipulate and which sometimes manipulates us, does not have to be exactly measured or carefully counted. Time here belongs to everybody and is shaped according to what people make of it. These people are those whose life stories make up the web of memory, who are part of a family line, a series of generations and a group of relations. In other words, the individual in a village lives first of all in family time, and his kinship structures his memory of this time.

Memories and identity

Communal time and family time are experienced entirely outside all linear and continuous development, for they are subjective. They are reversible times, and the permanence of certain reactions, the recourse to the same thought-processes, and the recurrence of the same names stress and punctuate their progress. They are cyclical times, which are lived on the reliable basis of the returning seasons and the continuum of generations, and so they harmonise with nature and life. This return of the same, this repetition of events that are simultaneously different and identical, colour these times in a strange fashion. They are seen as immovable and are apprehended outside History.

Yet in the village History is not ignored, but one only has recourse to it out of necessity. In this way History is considered responsible for the social changes which have affected the community down the centuries. As we have seen, technical changes and economic upheavals are made scapegoats at Minot: it is they who are held responsible for all the evils that poison the life of the group. They are said to be at the origin of families' confinement to the home and the disappearance of communal life. In the same way national History has been called into service to give reality to the structural confrontation of the 'upper' and the 'lower' village, which divided the village politically up to the 1914 war. For decades the two clans, topographically opposed, would take contrary positions in the face of historic events. When one was republican, the other was royalist: when one was radical, the other was clerical. History was exploited to explain and support an antagonism that was really age-old, and in fact structural. Now that this bipolar division of political power has gone and a new power centre has emerged in the middle of the village, it is historical events that form the background for candidates at election time. The last World War, the Resistance and collaboration, with the settling of old scores that ensued, are supported and denounced during each campaign.[1]

In the present this History intrudes on the closed world of the village, which cannot escape it, but always lives it in the immediate, and as a break and interruption in the smooth progress of local life. It is History which is called in to explain the results of present-day upheavals. It is also true that historical events, duly dated and written down, turn out to be the most effective and adaptable weapon at the service of present-day political debate.

So the village also lives in historic and objective time that has been chronologically mapped out, with each event having its own duration. For some people this duration is short – just a generation – but for others it lasts several decades; there is even one that lasts for ever, i.e. that prehistoric period of the village's origins, which is at the basis of communal time. Let us leave it at that and take up with the historians that typology of events which they have tried to grasp.

Ever since Lucien Febvre[2] and Marc Bloch, historians have analysed those moments of disruption and fission which give rise to events, breaking the course of History and speeding the arrival of a new era. Taking up the questions raised by Halbwachs on the various types of social time,[3] they have tried, as Le Goff says, 'to introduce a scientific chronology which dates historic phenomena according to their influence on History rather than the moment of their occurrence.'[4] Long time, medium time, short time[5] – these are three types of duration which characterise the historic event, and historians think they have been able to isolate one from the other. However they must now link, cross-reference and blend them so as to avoid giving rise to misleading orders of importance and to restore continuity to history.[6]

But human time is not only made up of History. It can be seen in different ways in different societies, springing from a wide variety of categories. Evans-Pritchard[7] demonstrated this when he investigated the categories of time among the Nuer and found that they accorded with the rhythm of the seasons, the cycle of age-groups and the stories of mythology. Later ethnologists, looking at other societies near or far,[8] have discovered these successive memories which operate according to the moment, the circumstances and the person being addressed. Each of these memories has its own function.

So this family time, for ever re-created by the recounting of family history, relayed by successive generations and committed to memory through a stock of Christian names, introduces man to his social position. It is a position made up of constraints that are accepted, of rules imposed by his membership of a group of blood relations, by a network of extended family and departed forbears. Indeed this time gives rise to the idea of social man, a man who is first and foremost a member of a kin group. It is this kinship that is at the base of society, for in the village the old inhabitants are designated by a term that belongs to the vocabulary of the family: '*Our grand-fathers*, the men of old who came before us, they knew. . . . ' As if it were necessary to identify the village with a family and with a group of relatives, and as if living there implied an ideology of blood relationship and family feeling: 'In the old days Minot was one large family' is how all descriptions of former life begin. 'In those times we got on well, we exchanged things. . . . ' and so it still goes on: kinship gives rise to solidarity. So family time joins up with community time, which is also permanent, endless. In this community time, History is concealed and its duration reduced and controlled.

The collective time, so stable and immobile, does not however enslave the group to its past, nor does it stifle it under the weight of tradition to a point where it cannot integrate change or follow the progress of technology. Quite the contrary. These small societies, having for decades had to face the problems of the moment, have found in themselves latent powers of adaptation and survival. Furthermore, as we have seen, the village has changed in appearance in the course of this century, the houses have been altered and behaviour has changed. The group has not remained static and a prisoner to its past, but has yielded to the pressures of History without radically changing, as we have also shown.

In the same way one has thought of these societies as being incapable of projecting themselves into the future. It is true that the future in a village seems non-existent. Yet it is far from being absent, even if it is not mentioned. The fact is that in these cultures where the spoken work is influential, in these societies where speech[9] is respected and every word carries weight in terms of action, talking of the future means laying hands on it and possibly harming its healthy development. Furthermore in these parts one does not make a display of wealth, one does not boast of one's unusual good fortune, and one does not utter the name of a child before his christening. The future belongs to nobody, so it is dangerous to talk about it and risky to trust in it. So in the village the future has no fixed shape or real definition, yet people think of it all the time, and they work and prepare for it.

Crops sprouting in the fields, trees growing tall in the forest, the child assuming the role of heir from his earliest years – all these are signs and modes of behaviour that presage a future, but cannot be expressed in so many words. This voluntary silence, in which everyone buries his dreams of the future, has helped to spread the notion that these small rural communites are incapable of thinking of the future, so taken up are they with their past and their traditions, and so busy coping with an agitated present. In fact it does seem that these societies have a planned and organised future, but there is no talk about it. For this future is situated in a territory that has been owned and managed communally in a way that has not changed for a thousand years. Here space helps to shape time. It is a space that is rich in promise for the future, and out of it there still springs a form of social life.

This time of the community does not have to explain the present or foretell the future, nor does it vegetate under the weight of the past. Its function is to create a time-span in which the group can work out its own life. There is a stability that is essential, an exceptional individuality in which each group invents its own history and has a memory that is entirely personal and differs fundamentally from the memory of the next social group. In fact, in these societies where forms of sociability magnify differences, this form of Time helps to create the Other. The collective memory conceives the notion of otherness, where possession of a history that is not shared gives the group its identity.

Notes

Preface

1   See map, p. 184.
2   This study of the village of Minot, which was linked to a co-operative
    research project of the CNRS (for an account, see M. C. Pingaud's
    book), was carried out with the resources of the social anthropology
    laboratory of the *Collège de France*, the *Ecole des hautes Etudes en
    Sciences sociales* and the *Centre national de la Recherche scientifique*,
    by Tina Jolas, Marie-Claude Pingaud, Yvonne Verdier and myself. The
    research was carried out during stays of varying length, spread out over
    several seasons.
3   It seemed important to us to publish the results of our work as it was
    completed, even if it proved necessary to revise and readjust them at a
    later stage. This is the origin of those articles which enabled the
    physical, social, historical and economic picture of the community to be
    laid down. Then there were other, later articles which round off the first
    ones or touch on particular aspects of the group's life. In any case, these
    publications are fragmentary as regards subject, and slight compared to
    the conclusions reached by each of us in our studies of a special theme.
    In our individual works we have all dipped into the common pool of
    interviews with the inhabitants and the village archives. It will be
    evident in the reading of these texts that our interests were comple-
    mentary and that our accounts differ. Sometimes they confirm, often
    they illuminate and complete one another. The policy of publishing as
    we went along, the teamwork and the overlapping of our various
    interests explain the abundance, not to mention excess, of our writings
    on Minot (cf. Bibliography, p. 216).
4   The Minot dialect was recorded at the beginning of this century by
    G. Potey, in *Le patois de Minot*, Paris, Droz, 1921 (posthumous).
5   A criticism often made about ethnologists, cf. in J. Goody, *La raison
    graphique*, Paris, Editions de Minuit, 1979, the foreword by the trans-
    lators, Jean Bazin and Alban Bensa.
6   We have merely followed the research methodology proposed in *Textes
    de et sur Claude Lévi-Strauss*, collected by R. Bellour and C. Clément,
    Paris, Gallimard, 1979.
7   The *tableau du temps* made up every day by the pupils of the school was
    a sort of illustrated journal of village life. It consisted of seven headings

– temperature, atmospheric pressure, state of the sky, human life, animal life, plant life, and events of the day (cf. 'The world of childhood', I.2).

The enduring memory

1 First period of the Iron Age (1000–500 BC).
2 According to G. Potey, *Histoire de Minot*, MS lodged in the departmental archives (AD, 1, F. 169–1.6).
3 These conclusions owe much to the article by Tina Jolas, 'Parcours cérémoniels d'un terroir villageois', *Ethnologie française*, VII, 1, 1977.
4 Georges Potey, in particular, has deciphered the seigneurial records found in the castle of the last seigneur of Minot and bought by his father. He wrote a work in six manuscript volumes on the history of the village, which is lodged in the departmental archives. Cf. G. Potey, 'Les mines gallo-romaines ou gauloises de Minot', *Mémoires de l'Académie de Dijon*, 1954; 'L'église Saint-Pierre de Minot', *Bulletin d'Histoire de Littérature et d'Art religieux du Diocèse de Dijon*, 1906. Louis-Philippe Chaume, former village schoolmaster, left a manuscript written about 1910 and entitled *Monographie de la commune de Minot*, one copy of which is lodged with the cantonal archives, and another is to be found with a family in the village.
5 A team led by Professor Peyre of *l'Ecole normale supérieure de Paris* has carried out archaeological excavations around Minot. One can read a first account of them in *Gallia*, XXII, fasc. 2, 1974.
6 Refusal made to M. Cécille, dealer at Minot, to enclose 'his inheritance with a wall, seeing that it crosses a common path which the public has used from *time immemorial*'. Community deliberation of 16 January 1791 (Municipal Archives).

The village: yesterday and today

1 On the economy of the Châtillonnais at the end of the nineteenth century, cf. P. Mathal and P. Evrard, *L'Evolution en longue période de l'agriculture d'une petite région: le Châtillonnais*, Paris, INRA, 1967, duplicated, particularly Chapter 2, where the causes and consequences of the economic crisis are analysed – poor sales of wool and wheat, and the closing of markets for iron and wood.
2 Up till after the end of the Second World War there were six fairs a year at Minot: 14 January, 1 March, 4 May, 28 June, 28 September and 6 November.
3 Here we leave aside the *Messieurs*, a group composed in the main of two leading families who opposed one another for nearly a century, but disappeared at the end of the 1914 war. On the social groups, cf. T. Jolas and F. Zonabend, 'Gens du finage, gens du bois', *Annales*, I, 1973.
4 The outlying farms are the single agricultural units situated all round the village, on the edge of the central plain and the forest.

5   This was the *affouage*, the right granted for a very small fee to inhabitants of the village to take their wood for heating from the communal woods.

6   The houses of the village run along the two thoroughfares which cross each other. On the north-south axis, which cuts through two neighbourhoods, *le Mont* and *le Vaux*, are to be found the public buildings: the church, the cemetery next to it, the market, the presbytery, the post office, the *mairie*, the school and the war memorial. The south-east axis is bordered by crosses which mark the limits of the village: the cross of the *Monchiers au Mont*, near the old seigneurial castle, and the cross of the *Levée au Vaux*, near the meadow where once was the Carnival bonfire and now the rubbish is burnt.

7   To these transformations should be added the connection of the village to the national electric grid in 1927, and the arrival of piped water in 1958.

8   Since 1967 there has been no *curé* at Minot church. The parish is served by a *curé* living at the main village of the canton, who looks after twelve parishes.

9   On the situation of the farms, see the work of Marie-Claude Pingaud, *Paysans en Bourgogne. Les gens de Minot*, Paris, Flammarion, 1978.

10 There are a few small businesses – a dairy and cheese factory, two builders, a general engineering firm and a carpentry business. They employ from two to ten workers each.

Daily living

1   As the principal person we interviewed belonged to the *gens du finage*, we have chosen a dwelling of this group to describe and analyse. In any case, the homes of the *gens du bois*, though smaller, darker and more spartan, do not differ basically from those of the craftsmen or farmers.

2   The arrival of the boiler at the beginning of the century changed the twice-yearly routine of the 'great wash' into the weekly wash.

3   The *hébergeages* – buildings used to shelter animals on a farm.

4   See 'The world of childhood', I.2.

5   The preposition 'chez' attached to a surname designates the group of buildings inhabited by the father, mother and unmarried children (on this parental terminology, cf. T. Jolas, Y. Verdier and F. Zonabend, 'Parler famille', *L'Homme*, X (3), 1970). At Minot the houses in the village have no names of their own, so they are designated by the generic term 'chez' followed by the surname of the occupant. When he changes, the name changes too.

6   Bottled gas appeared in the village in 1931.

7   These pierced stones are limestone nodules which are found lying in wooded areas. The fashion for these stones is recent, but is so popular that some people go in for a regular trade to get hold of them; for it is illegal nowadays to remove them from their natural setting. The decorative effects achieved with these stones remind one of the rockery gardens so admired in the eighteenth and nineteenth centuries, which the villagers saw and still see in the neighbouring country houses.

8   Claude Lévi-Strauss, lecture at the Collège de France, 28 February 1978.

9   *Meix* includes the house where a family lives, with its farm buildings, yard, orchard and garden. As P. de Saint-Jacob stresses, it is the *aera domus*, the house and its attachments.

10 P. de Saint-Jacob, 'Le village: les conditions juridiques de l'habitat', *Annales de Bourgogne*, XII (51), 1941.

11 On exploitation rights in local land, cf. T. Jolas, Y. Verdier and F. Zonabend, 'Les verts anneaux acides … ' *L'Homme*, XIII (3), 1973.

12 As always where innate gifts are concerned, it is only men who possess them. As for women, they simply fill roles and acquire skills.

13 The 'ginger moon' has a bad reputation at Minot. It is said to be cold and to bring frost that 'burns' the vegetation.

14 On this subject, cf. the first chapter of E. Le Roy Ladurie, *Paysans du Languedoc*, Paris, Mouton, 1966.

15 Hemp was cultivated up to the last years of the nineteenth century. It served to clothe the members of the household. Stripped by the men, it was then turned into material by the local weaver, and the women made garments out of it (cf. 'Craftsmen and shopkeepers' II.2). Hops replaced hemp in the *chènevière*: it was a commercial crop that was ruined after the 1914 war by competition from the hops of northern France and Germany.

16 In addition to a sum of money paid annually by the heir, the latter undertakes to supply his parents with their daily milk, their weekly butter, and two or three cartloads of wood every year.

17 Cf. T. Jolas, Y. Verdier and F. Zonabend, 'Les verts anneaux acides …', *L'Homme*, XIII (3), 1973.

18 For identical practices, cf. Marshall Sahlins, *Stone Age Economics*, London, Tavistock, 1974.

19 On nicknames, cf. F. Zonabend, 'Pourquoi nommer' in *L'identité*, a seminar directed by C. Lévi-Strauss, Paris, Grasset, 1977.

20 Work on the hives – capture of the swarms, collection of the honey crop, maintenance – is not always undertaken by their owner. 'Bees love those who love them', and loving them is a 'gift' possessed only by men. So in each generation two or three men in the village have charge of all the local hives. The learned old *curé*, an archaeologist and herbalist, was an adept: 'he loved bees and they loved him'. This same *curé* one day inflicted a cruel punishment on a magpie who was pillaging his hives. He trapped the bird and nailed it up on his door with its wings spreadeagled and a notice: 'The punishment of a magpie who eats our bees'. This gesture illustrates the almost magical relationship that this man had with the animal world. At the moment Nicolas Demonet, a former farmer, knows how to look after bees. He has learnt by watching and consorting with other men so gifted. The bee man receives for his work either a part of the honey crop or the right to keep his hives on the land of the man whose bees he maintains. He is never paid in money.

21 Cf. Marcel Mauss, 'Essai sur le don. Forme et raison de l'échange dans les sociétés archaïques' in *Sociologie et anthropologie*, Paris, 1968.
22 Remo Guidieri, 'L'abondance des pauvres', *Critique*, 371, 1978.

Time of life

1 On the choice and giving of Christian names, cf. F.Zonabend, 'Pourquoi nommer?' in *L'identité*, a seminar directed by C.Lévi-Strauss, Paris, Grasset, 1977.
2 A woman in the village who, as we have said above, is present at all human moments of passage. She helps at childbirth, gives the baby its first bath, cooks for weddings, assists the dying and washes the dead.
3 'On 7 February 1771, a female child of Claude ..., farmworker, and Marie ..., having been given an emergency christening at home by Anne ..., her maternal grandmother, and having died the day before, was buried in the cemetery of the said parish. ... On 8 April 1789 a female child of Jean ..., gardener, having died the day before after being given an emergency christening by Hugues Rouhier, surgeon at Minot, was buried in the cemetery. ...' Extracts from parish records (Municipal Archives).
4 'One does not christen or bury on a Friday. One does not change one's vest or one's sheets on a Friday. There was a girl who had to go and see the doctor at Dijon. She didn't change her vest because it was Friday.' Friday is a negative day.
5 On the choice of spiritual parents and the social repercussions, cf. F. Zonabend, 'La parenté baptismale à Minot', *Annales*, 3, 1978.
6 'Tricöts: bonbons et fruits secs que les parrains jettent aux enfants après un baptême.' (G. Potey, *Le patois de Minot*, Paris, Droz, 1930, p. 52.) A. Van Gennep, following F. Marion, reports that the *tricöt* in Côte-d'Or is the 'small christening meal consisting of four or five people'. A. Van Gennep, *Le folklore de la Bourgogne*, Gap, Louis Jean, 1934, p. 28.
7 It is difficult to find an explanation for this phrase. A Cévennes proverb says, 'Who makes you pick you up', i.e. who gives you birth brings you up (cf. J.-N. Pelen, 'La vallée longue en Cévenne', *Causse et Cévennes*, special number, n. d., 184 pp., duplicated). Does that mean that each person in the village will help bring up the child who is left on its own?
8 Menu for Aurélie and Florent, 30 March 1969: *Lunch*: galantine with truffles, rolled ham Lucullus, chicken *chasseur*, French beans, pork fillet, salad of the season, iced cake Florent and Aurélie, champagne, coffee, liqueurs. *Dinner*: cream soup, canapés, *bouchées financières*, *foies gras Périgord*, lettuce hearts, almond tart, fruit salad, Dijon brioche, wines, champagne, liqueurs, coffee.
   Menu for Sylvanie, 9 March 1969. *Lunch*: galantine with truffles, Burgundy ham, hake with Nantua sauce, chicken *chasseur*, dwarf kidney beans, Châtillon lamb, lettuce hearts, ices, Sylvanie's cake, *millefeuilles*, wines, champagne, coffee, liqueurs. *Dinner*: Windsor

soup, chicken *sauce ivoire*, roast beef, kirsch cake, brioche *mousse-line*, fresh fruit, coffee.

9   Cf. the article by N. Belmont, 'Comment on fait peur aux enfants', *Topiques*, 30, 1974.

10   At Minot, cats are the only animals allowed to enter the parlour, but they are given no name, or rather they are all called 'Minette'. This is unlike the dogs, horses, cows and other domestic animals who receive personal names of every sort – humorous, pompous or affectionate – which distinguish one from the other: 'Horses had names like "Fanfan", "Garibaldi", "Casimir", "Marceau" ... and dogs "Boby", "Black", "Barbet" or "Rustic". We had "Follette", a little Brie dog, and "Guillaume" (in the 1914 war, to make fun of the Kaiser); we had "Rita" and "Diane". Cows were like horses, you had to follow a letter of the alphabet, but each one had a name. There was "Querelleuse", "Quëteuse", "Têtue" or else "Brunette", "Franchette", "Rosette". They knew their own names and never made a mistake. Cats were always "Minette" or "Moumoune", sometimes "Zézette".' The names always ended in 'ette'. When they were old, it was simply 'old Tom' or 'the old girl'.

     Are they named in this baby language because they belong to the children? One must add that, even if cats are given to children, they are also often brought up by old people to keep them warm in winter, sitting on their knees. The cat is neutered young so that it should become large and fat. It is these cats that are called 'toms' or 'the old girl'. They are destined for the two age-groups who have not yet got power or have lost it, so no trouble is taken to identify their favourite animals. Even in death dogs and cats are not treated in the same way. The dog is hung from a tree in an orchard and its body is thrown into a hole in the Buge, where the carcases of all domestic animals are thrown. Cats are put in a sack and knocked senseless against a wall. They are then thrown on a heap of manure on the farm. Dogs are treated like men, for hanging is the commonest form of male suicide. As for cats, to borrow a popular expression, they are 'treated like dogs'.

11   A. Van Gennep in his *Manuel de folklore français* had already noted these two forms of teaching.

12   On similar forms of education, cf. C. Suaud, 'Splendeur et misère d'un petit séminaire', *Actes de la Recherche en Sciences sociales*, 1976, 4.

13   Further on, in ch. 2, you will read of a grandmother who refused to intercede and fix up the marriage of her granddaughter. The latter still remembered it fifty years later.

14   Cf., for example, M. Moscovici, 'La personnalité de l'enfant en milieu rural', *Etudes rurales*, I, 1961. Only L. Wylie in his book *A Village in Vaucluse*, Paris, Gallimard, 1968, deals with certain aspects of the child's socialisation.

15   On death, cf. F. Zonabend, 'Les morts et les vivants. Le cimetière de Minot en Châtillonnais', *Etudes rurales*, 52, Paris, 1973.

16   It is the mayor who receives the parents' complaints.

17 *Les capitaines*: these are the mothers who supervise their daughters' outings.

18 On the definition of the matrimonial area, cf. T. Jolas and F. Zonabend 'Gens du finage, gens du bois', *Annales*, I, 1973.

19 *Parentèle*: combination of blood relations and connections.

20 On these marriages between more or less distant cousins, cf. T. Jolas, Y. Verdier and F. Zonabend, 'Parler famille', *L'Homme*, X (3), 1970.

21 *Les loups*: nickname of the neighbouring village of Saint-Broing.

22 This conventional language of the age-group was intended to codify relations between the sexes.

23 This is a way of saying that the latest union renews a link which had already bound the families together.

24 The wood folk, being less well endowed with property, have a less integrated matrimonial world.

25 Until recently and since the Council of Trent (1545–63) the only marriages forbidden because of 'spiritual affinity' were between godfathers and godmothers and godchildren, between baptisers and the baptised, between spiritual and biological parents. But although the Church no longer forbids marriage between godfather and godmother, society rejects it.

26 Public rumour and malevolent gossips are sometimes enough to break up marriage plans.

27 'Nowadays parents have to face the *fait accompli*. Then, most of the time, the children don't even marry; they live together and all is well.'

28 It is noteworthy that in two cases, including the one that brought on the infanticide, the parents' refusal of their child's marriage was caused by an earlier marriage between a member of the clan and the brother of the rejected suitor. If the parents had accepted this second union, there would have been double marriages in these families. Given their number, one would have thought that such marriages were well esteemed. However, these refusals should encourage us to have a closer look at this type of matrimonial exchange, so as to see the circumstances in which it is sometimes approved and sometimes vehemently rejected. These double marriages, which unite two brothers and two sisters, are superfluous. In effect they restrict the number of new relations and thus hinder an attempt to develop a vast network of connections. In these societies the study of marriage ought not to deal only with unions that occurred; it should also take account of broken engagements.

29 We borrow this notion from Pierre Bourdieu; cf. the definition of 'symbolic capital', *Esquisse d'une théorie de la pratique*, Genève, Droz, 1972, p. 237.

30 The use of the term *maison* here is to be noted. According to Diderot's *Encyclopédie*, this term is only used by aristocrats to describe their families. Ordinary people never use it. In fact the Burgundy peasantry of the twentieth century seems to use it in the aristocratic sense.

31 On the origin of the term *croque-avoine*, cf. A. Van Gennep, *Le folklore de la Bourgogne*, Gap, Louis Jean, 1934, p. 31.

32   We will see an example in the next chapter, 'A la Maison-Dieu'.

33   Cf. F. Zonabend, 'La parenté baptismale à Minot', *Annales*, 3, 1978.

34   Between 1770 and 1969 in Minot there were 8 illegitimate births from mothers who were farmers' daughters, 15 from seamstresses and 33 from day labourers.

35   Marriage contracts are becoming rarer and rarer. Between 1859 and 1889 there were 47 contracts for 84 marriages, i.e. 1 in 2. Between 1890 and 1909 there were 12 contracts for 34 marriages, or 1 in 3. Between 1919 and 1949, there were 10 contracts for 52 marriages, i.e. 1 in 5. Between 1950 and 1969, there were 2 contracts for 32 marriages, i.e. 1 in 16.

36   'When I got married in 1965, I had in my trousseau: twenty-two pairs of sheets all marked with my initials, three dozen Turkish towels, two dozen honeycomb towels, two dozen hand towels, two dozen dish-cloths, two dozen pillowcases, two sets of table linen for twelve, one set for six, handkerchiefs and two or three spare petticoats.'

37   Marriage for girls nowadays seems to be the fulfilment of their destiny. Encouraged by their upbringing and way of life to think of themselves as married, they are bound to give much thought to the quest for a mate: 'One is an old maid from 23 onwards. If one is not married at 25, everyone wonders what has happened. Girls marry very young, at 18. If they're not married at 20, they'll take on anyone, so as to say they're married. To be married is a girl's pride. At 18 one is in love with anyone; at 20 one is so keen to get married that one does not even seek to be in love. Marriages are none the worse for it; love comes after-wards.' These views of a modern girl tell us a lot about romantic love!

38   It is important to know that the rope of the hanged man brings luck. Besides this symbolism of the rope, death is always closely linked to life and its joys in these societies; so the wedding was not unduly disturbed by this discovery.

39   C. Lévi-Strauss, *Le cru et le cuit*, Paris, Plon, p. 334.

40   *La jarretière*: a long white ribbon which the bridesmaid cuts up and distributes among the guests while the best man auctions it. Van Gennep emphasises in his *Manuel* that 'the distribution of the garter is not an act of magic, but simply a symbol of brotherly feeling shown by attendance at the wedding meal of the two families. The married couple accounts carefully for the sales, and the proceeds are usually divided among the school funds or the good works of the married couple's parishes. These acts of charity are reported next day in the local press so that everyone knows about the generosity of those assembled.'

41   'In the old days the bride was not supposed to sing on her wedding day. It was forbidden, it brought bad luck. ... The same applied to her mother; and of course her mother was sad.'

42   Cf. N. Belmont, 'La fonction symbolique du cortège dans les rituels populaires de mariage', *Annales*, III, Paris, 1978.

43   Cf. *ibid.*

44   Cf. C. Lévi-Strauss, *Le cru et le cuit*, Paris, Plon, p. 307.

45   For several years now every wedding gives rise to a full photographic

record made by an official photographer. Each stage of the ceremony is amply photographed: appearance of the bride at the door of the father's house, signing at the *mairie*, exchange of rings in church, kisses on leaving church. However this mass of photographs has not put an end to the group picture.

46 We must recall here, though we have already pointed it out in the make-up of the household (cf. ch. 1) that among the people of the *finage*, whether farmer or craftsman, the marriage of children is not the moment when inheritance is decided or other rights, powers and possessions are transferred between members of the domestic group. It is only at the moment when the parents give up the management and leave the house that there is transfer of power: authority passes from the old to the new owner, from father to son or from father-in-law to son-in-law. Then symbolic possessions are handed over, for example, the mother hands over the black mourning shawl and the family candle – and there is division and settlement of property. Marriage and death are two moments of transfer, but they are not the only ones. The moments when the domestic group breaks up and the old owners retire to give way to the heir are other important points in the transmission of inheritance. These moments of rupture are no less important than marriage or death, though they are less formal and ritualised.

47 *Fannöt*: a man who involves himself in woman's work; see G. Potey, *Le patois de Minot*, Paris, Droz, 1930.

48 The breath of a woman having her period 'turns' the bacon in the salting tub.

49 The cow figures in marriage contracts, just like land. It is a cow and its calf that the young man or girl bring to the new home: 'On my marriage I had a trousseau, a bedroom suite with wardrobe, bed, bedside table, dressing table, three cows, kitchen equipment and an ancient brooch.'

50 M. Sahlins, *Stone Age Economics*, London, Tavistock, 1974.

51 If by chance a second son is born, he becomes a priest or remains unmarried. 'I had a brother and I arrived 15 years after him; I wasn't expected', said the *curé* of a neighbouring parish.

52 Average ages on marriage of sons and daughters of farmers between 1859 and 1969 (figures supplied by M. Laurière, LAS):

Period	Men	Women	Gap
1859–89	29·05	23·25	5·80
1890–1909	27·58	22	5·58
1910–19	31·1	24	7·1
1920–49	25·96	21·84	4·12
1950–69	25·03	22·40	2·63

In the course of a century the average age of girls at marriage has shown great stability. This is understandable in a society where an older female has less value on the marriage market. In the old days, as now, 25 was considered the age at which one was considered an 'old maid' (cf. n.37). On the other hand, the marriage of a man was put off as long as possible.

53 We do not know much about abortion practices in days gone by, except for the use of artemisia 'to bring on periods'.

54 Hence this woodcutter's wife who left her husband and children to follow her lover. Later abandoned and left on her own, she committed suicide.

55 Before the 1914 war, Minot had its theatrical troupe, made up at first only of men. The troupe performed at *fêtes* in the village and surrounding villages. About 1940, women started to take part. Activities came to an end about 1955.

56 The *Confréries du Rosaire et de Notre-Dame de la Bonne-Mort* had a lot of women as members.

57 Young marrieds keep away, and so do those who for any reason, for example, death of a parent, or illness of a child, cannot go out or celebrate without incurring public disapproval.

58 The hunts in the woods ended with a meal of *gruotte* (heart and liver of boar mixed with its blood in a stew). The meal took place at the village hotel, and women were not allowed to attend.

59 At Minot there is no recourse in case of illness to a 'sorcerer'. On the other hand, people often consult 'bonesetters' for fractures or sprains.

60 It was the 'home-help'.

61 Each death calls for different behaviour. An old person, whose death is inevitable, is not mourned like a child. 'For old man Camuset it wasn't a sad funeral; no one wept.' Adult deaths are particularly felt if they leave families in difficulties. 'Léonie is now quite alone. She had bad luck. Her husband was killed in the 1914 war without having made over his property. So when her daughter died of measles, she didn't get the farm. Her brothers-in-law got everything. You can see what happens if you don't make arrangements early.' The premature death of adults upsets inheritances, disperses land and deprives natural heirs of their rights. To avoid disaster you must prepare for death and 'put your affairs in order'. If you fail to do so, shame and retribution are the painful result: 'One is sold off on one's own doorstep.' The death of a child at an early age or an adolescent is never accepted philosophically or forgotten: 'When you've looked after him as a baby, it's too much' said a weeping mother about her child, who had died fifty years before. Child deaths, now rare, were still frequent in the first decades of the century, and they were always felt with emotion and sadness. 'There were many deaths of very small children, through lack of care and other reasons. ... They were much missed, the little angels. ... Inevitably there were many that died. ...' Death has its own language and its own code of behaviour.

62 In this European rural society, women are quite different from their counterparts in so-called exotic societies, where they are more associated with Nature.

63 The history of this cemetery is told in F. Zonabend, 'Les morts et les vivants. Le cimetière de Minot en Châtillonais', *Etudes rurales*, 52, Paris, 1973.

A lifetime

1 *Mariage en gendre*: a marriage in which the husband comes to live with his wife's parents.

2 On beliefs about twins, cf. George Sand, *La petite Fadette*. Anyway, at Minot, the last-born is considered the eldest, i.e. the opposite of what George Sand reported.

3 On the role and use of the definite article, cf. F. Zonabend, 'Pourquoi nommer?', in *L'identité*, a seminar directed by C. Lévi-Strauss, Paris, Grasset, 1977.

4 Even though they did not buy back their farm, the Demonets later acquired some hectares of land that could be cultivated.

5 The inventory drawn up after Albertine Lamarche's death gives an exact list of the property she had brought with her. Her trousseau consisted of one dozen pairs of linen sheets, one dozen linen cloths, one dozen hand cloths, one tablecloth, eighteen hand towels, six summer and winter vests, and six kitchen aprons.

6 It was so rare to meet with a refusal at this stage of the discussions that Albertine probably hoped that her father would not say 'no' to her future father-in-law.

7 So Albertine, who had to go back and get her official papers at the *mairie*, said, 'I shall not go over there (to Maisey-le-Duc) and I shall not visit them.' It would have been odd for a daughter to go to her parents' village and not call on them. When Albertine did visit them, they gave her dinner, but never spoke a word to her.

8 At Minot relationships are expressed in exchange of words: 'They go and talk to one another' is often said of two people who visit each other.

9 The château at Minot is now used as an old people's home. 'The ladies of the château' are the inmates.

10 Cf. fig. 4, the plan of Nicolas Demonet's *chènevière*, p. 00.

Breaks and continuities

1 On this subject cf. E. Besson, 'Les colporteurs de l'Oisans au XIXe siècle', *Le Monde alpin et rhodanien*, I–II, Grenoble, 1975.

2 On the role of invented relations in marriage, cf. F. Zonabend, 'La parenté baptismale à Minot', *Annales*, 3, 1978.

3 The greasing tours were regularly undertaken by the saddler to keep greased the leather of the harnesses and saddles on the farms. One can read about a saddler's tour in H. Vincenot, *Le Billebaude*, Paris.

4 In former times the village tradesmen gave credit to the local people. Customers did not pay for their purchases at once, but only at the end of the month, or when their *taille* was full. 'The *taille* was a stick split down the middle. The tradesman kept one piece and hung it on the wall with the customer's name on it. The family kept the other half. Everyone used to buy bread on the *taille* system. One mark meant one kilo. You paid when the *taille* was full. Then you passed a plane over it and started again.'

5 *Cale*: a small cotton bonnet with a lace border, worn by married women.
6 *Droguet*: material made of wool woven on a warp of linen or cotton (Larousse).

Memories and identity

1 Many Maquis of all types took refuge during the last war in the forests of the Châtillonnais. They found food and protection among the villagers. Resistance activity in Minot was as great as elsewhere, but it was matched, again as elsewhere, by denunciations, and many old scores were paid off at the end of the war. It is these conflicts and these events that periodically turn up again during electoral campaigns.
2 L. Febvre, *Le problème de l'incroyance au XVIe siècle*, Paris, A. Michel, 1968, cf. especially ch. 3, para. 4, 'Temps flottant, temps dormant'.
3 M. Halbwachs, *Les cadres sociaux de la mémoire*, Paris, Alcan, 1925.
4 J. Le Goff, 'L'Histoire nouvelle' in *La nouvelle histoire*, ed. J. Le Goff, Paris, Retz, 1978, p. 239.
5 Cf. F. Braudel, 'La longue durée', *Annales*, Paris, 1958, pp. 725–53.
6 Cf. M. Vovelle, L'Histoire et la longue durée' in *La nouvelle histoire*, ed. J. Le Goff, Paris, Retz, 1978.
7 E. E. Evans-Pritchard, *The Nuer*, Oxford University Press, 1940.
8 See the chapter devoted to time and space in L. Bernot and R. Blancard, *Nouville, un village français*, Paris, Institut d'Ethnologie, 1953.
9 Let us remember the place taken by speech in the upbringing of children and the allocation of the right to speak among generations. Research remains to be done on the role and place of speech in these peasant societies.

Books and articles on Minot

Jolas, T., Parcours cérémoniels d'un terroir villageois, *Ethnologie française*, VII (1), 1977.

—, Verdier Y., Zonabend, F., Parler famille, *L'Homme*, X (3), 1970.

—, Verdier Y., Zonabend, F., Les verts anneaux acides, *L'Homme*, XIII (3), 1973.

—, Zonabend, F., Cousinage, voisinage, in *Echanges et communications, Mélanges offerts à Claude Lévi-Strauss*, La Haye, Mouton, 1970.

—, Zonabend, F., Gens du finage, gens du bois, *Annales*, I, 1973.

Pingaud, M.-C., Paysage, population et histoire foncière dans le Châtillonnais, L'exemple de Minot (Côte-d'Or), *Etudes rurales*, 32, 1968.

— Terres et familles dans un village du Châtillonnais, *Etudes rurales*, 42, 1971.

— Relation entre histoire foncière et parcellaire d'exploitation à Minot (Côte-d'Or), *Bulletin de l'Association des géographes français*, 397–98, 1972.

— Le langage de l'assolement, *L'Homme*, XIII (3), 1973.

— Chronologie et formes du pouvoir à Minot depuis 1789, *Etudes rurales*, 64–65, 1977.

— *Paysans de Bourgogne. Les gens de Minot*, Paris, Flammarion, 1978.

Verdier, Y., La Femme-qui-aide et la laveuse, *L'Homme*, XVI (2–3), 1976.

— Les femmes et le saloir, *Ethnologie française*, VI (3–4), 1976.

— Le langage du cochon, *Ethnologie française*, VII (2), 1977.

— *Façons de dire, façons de faire, la laveuse, la cuisinière, la couturière*, Paris, Gallimard, 1979.

Zonabend, F., Les morts et les vivants. Le cimetière de Minot en Châtillonnais, *Etudes rurales*, 52, 1973.

— Pourquoi nommer?, in *L'Identité, Séminaire dirigé par C. Lévi-Strauss*, Paris, Grasset, 1977.

— Jeux de noms, *Etudes rurales*, 74, 1979.

— La parenté baptismale, *Annales*, 3, 1978.

— Childhood in a French village, *International Social Sciences Journal*, No. 3, 1979.

Index

apprenticeship, 67, 83, 84
archaeolgy, 3
Arnault, Gustave, 146, 148, 149
Arnault, Marie-Emeline, 146, 151

bachelors, 100, 109
baptism, 58–60, 95
birth, 15, 57–8, 60, 115
birth-control, 124–5
Bloch, Marc, 201

carnival, 80, 92
Châtillon-sur-Seine, 81, 82, 124
Chènevières, 33–6, 47, 48, 49, 169, 198
Chevenoz, Albertine, 143–71, 176, 182, 189, 191, 194
Chevenoz, François, 176–7
Chevenoz, Louis, 173–6, 177
Chevenoz, Victor, 143, 159, 162, 164–70, 175, 182
Chevenoz, Nicolas, 48–9
children, 22, 57–80
church, 7, 52, 55, 58–9, 71, 72
clothes, 191–4
communion, first, 60
contracts, marriage, 107
courting, 87–93, 99
craftsmen, 14, 17, 67, 84, 178–81

dances, 87–9, 91–3
daughters-in-law, 115–18

death, 15, 132, 135–7, 198–9
Decoin, Emeline, 146, 148, 149, 151
Decoin, Jean-Denis, 146, 149
Demonet, Antoine, 146, 148, 149
Demonet, Justine, 146, 148, 149, 151, 152, 153, 154
Demonet, Nicolas, 146, 148, 149, 152, 153, 154, 155, 168–9
dialect, viii–ix
Dijon, 53, 176
drinking, 127–8

economy, habits of, 44–6
embuscades, 128–32
engagements, 102–9, 110
Evans-Pritchard, E. E., 201

family relationships, 15–16, 19, 22, 89, 119, 130, 142, 164, 177–8
fathers-in-law, 115
Febvre, Lucien, 201
festivals, 72, 80
finage, 5
flowers, 24–5, 27, 51–2, 143
food, 38–44, 46–9
forest, Minot, viii, 3, 6, 73–4
freezers, 42–4
fruit, 25, 35–6, 40

gardens, 20, 23–36
godparents, 58–60, 95
grandparents, 26, 62–5, 69, 75–6, 84, 119, 134, 136

Grivot, Jean, 145, 146, 148, 149, 150

Halbwachs, M., 201
history, 139, 196–8, 201–2
houses, 10–20
husbands, 120–5

illegitimacy, 104–5, 161

Lamarche, Etienne, 146, 148, 150, 155–62
Langres, viii, 29, 32
Le Goff, J., 201
Lévi-Strauss, Claude, 110
living arrangements, 10–21, 143–4
Lourdes, 166, 171

marriage, 60, 86, 87, 93, 95–102, 164
matchmaking, 100–2
meals, 38, 42, 60, 170
medicine, plant, 132–4
memory, viii, x, 138–9, 199
mines, 3
moon, influence of, 30–1
mothers-in-law, 115–18
motor cars, ownership of, 7

noise, 110–12

oral tradition, 4, 31, 197–9

population, 5, 8

parents, 66, 74–5, 85, 86, 115, 119
photograph, wedding, 112–14
population, 5, 8
proposal, marriage, 102, 105

reading habits, 15, 26, 64, 134
repas d'entrée, 105–6

saints, 31, 88
Savoie, 167, 172, 176–7
School, 70, 77–9, 90
sex education, 77, 82
shopkeepers, 181–95
'symbolic capital', 98

taste, domestic, 18, 21
television, 7, 132
time, x–xi, 2–3, 9, 57, 138–9, 197–9, 203
traders, 173–8
trousseau, marriage, 107–9

Valduc, 8, 151
vegetables, 25, 27–9, 32, 47
veillées, 4, 7, 74
virginity, 103–4

'walking-out', 93–5
wars, 196–7
weather, 29–30, 35, 199
weddings, 89, 92, 109–14, 170–2
wives, 196–7